A Bike Across the Sea

Steve Dyster

With a Foreword by Alan and Cheryl Gerrard

North
Staffordshire
Press

North Staffordshire Press

Newcastle-under-Lyme

Staffordshire

i

A Bike Across the Sea

All Rights Reserved

© *Copyright Steve Dyster*

No part of this book may be reproduced in any form by
photocopying or any electronic or mechanical means,
including information storage and retrieval systems, without
permission in writing from both the copyright owner and the
publisher of this book.

ISBN 978-1-9160152-0-3

Published in 2019
North Staffordshire Press
10 Queen Street
Newcastle-under-Lyme
ST5 1ED

With thanks to those who inspired a life-changing trip; Alan and Cheryl Gerrard.

To those who allowed it, Emma and Edward.

To Mark Dally for his company on it.

To all those friendly people we met on the way, Dutch, German, Polish, Turkish, Hungarian, Czech and Slovak.

To looking forward from our past.

Preface

There follows the story of a cycle trip from the north-west Midlands of England to the Czech Republic. It is not a long way; about the same as when I rode Land's End to John O'Groats. Same for Mark Dally, whom I rode with. In that sense it was an unusual trip for me – almost all my major trips have been solo.

Usually, I avoid cities and keep to the rural roads in the mountains. This time, I spent many miles on the great plain of northern Europe, gently pedalling along riverside cycle-paths. Rather than a route selected for scenery and remoteness, this one sought out towns and cities. It also intended to celebrate a renewed international friendship. The origin of that friendship, with its slaughter, tragedy, defiance and hope, is woven into the narrative. On an emotional journey one is bound to reflect occasionally on one's own experience, so there's a bit of autobiography too. But not too much.

When I showed the first two chapters to a friend, I was asked a simple question. He asked, "Who is your audience?" I could not answer it. So, I suppose I must have written this for myself as much as for anyone else. Travelling across Europe in the year of the Brexit referendum would have been interesting. Add to that a mission to deliver two works of art commemorating one of the Second World Wars darkest days, a first cycle trip to the former communist bloc, and a good deal of German and Czech beer to slake the thirst. Well, this is a book about a cycle trip from the north-west Midlands of England to the Czech Republic, and more.

I claim no great insight into international affairs, past or present. Observations are my own and I try to be fair. It is easy to judge, but harder to understand, when travelling. Even the most astute minds can get things wrong - and I do not count myself amongst that band.

Almost everything I knew about the Czech Republic before meeting Alan and Cheryl Gerrard and deciding to head for Lidice by bike derived from teaching about the Munich Agreement of 1938, and that great Czech novel, The Good Soldier Švejk and His Adventures in the Great War, plus vague memories of the Prague Spring and so on.

The Good Soldier Švejk, Jaroslav Hašek's wonderful creation, whom some say is the epitome of the Czech character, introduced me to Czech place names and pubs whilst I was at University in the late 1970s. I still find the whole book a treasure trove and often dip into its pages.

It has my favourite opening lines of any book.

"And so, they've killed our Ferdinand," says the charwoman, clearly referring to the assassination of the Archduke Franz Ferdinand at Sarajevo, the spark that lit the touch paper that led to the Great War. Švejk points out that he knows two Ferdinands and "neither are any loss." The charwoman sets him right.

Švejk states that the cause was Austria-Hungary's seizure of Bosnia from the Ottoman Turks, provoking the Turks to kill the Archduke. Of course, the assassin was the Serb, Gavrilo Princip. The outcome? Well, they'll be a blood bath asserts Švejk. "Russia and Serbia will help us." "It may be, if we have a war with the Turks that the Germans will attack us, because the Germans and Turks stick together."

Well, Švejk was wildly wrong - except for the blood-bath. Hašek excuses this; "If the situation subsequently developed otherwise than he had expounded it at The Chalice we must bear in mind that he had never had any preparatory training in diplomacy." He'd also been dismissed from the army as an "imbecile". Only an urgent need for more cannon-fodder saw him return to the colours of the Austro-Hungarian Empire, under which many Czechs, rather unwillingly, fought.

Well, nor have I had any special training in diplomacy, though I thought I knew something about history. I set out on a journey thinking I knew where I was going and what I would find. Geographically I reached the destination, but cycle touring is about much more than riding a bike. So, if things turned out differently to my expectations, then that is just travel by bicycle.

I have that much in common with Švejk. Whether I should be expelled from anything as an imbecile is a matter for others.

SD April 2018

Foreword

As I write this foreword on November 22nd 2018, at the kind invitation of Stephen, I must confess a sense of melancholy at Britain's impending withdrawal from the EU. The Lidice Shall Live campaign is associated with openness, internationalism, lack of prejudice and love for fellow human beings regardless of place.

Contrary to theories linking poverty to social immobility, isolationism and xenophobia, it was a time when working class people in Britain were drawn towards an open determination to assist victims of the SS in Czechoslovakia. If they didn't feel the iron hand of Nazi subjugation they certainly understood what the threat of it meant. In Stoke-on-Trent, the launch pad and heart of the campaign, they lent full support to Dr Barnett Stross, a Polish, Jewish immigrant, with all their might!

For many of us heavily involved in today's project to raise awareness of this truly international campaign, it feels our ancestors would have felt more reticence about flippantly disconnecting from a club drawn together for peace than today's residents - who now perhaps take peace for granted!

In 2011, at our first meetings with Mrs Ivona Kasalická and Mr Cervencl of the Lidice Memorial; the Mayor of the village, Mrs Veronika Kellerová; and staff at surrounding schools, there was a resounding consensus to combine efforts to restore the name of Sir Barnett Stross and his work in creating an international network which worked for peace. A classic example of this would be the tremendous Garden of Peace & Friendship which he conceived and opened in 1955. Henceforth, projects run from Stoke-on-Trent would highlight the celebratory, as well as the commemorative, aspects of Lidice, its relationship to Stoke-on-Trent and its ongoing international legacy, to emphasise the victory of love over hate...

To date, with partners in Stoke-on-Trent, Lidice, Prague and the United States, Lidice Lives have directly completed and facilitated: exhibitions, sculptures, commemorations, books, cultural exchanges, school exchanges, dance pieces, plaques, films, presentations in schools, resource packs, merchandise and social media campaigns to share knowledge of this inspirational account.

But the wider vision remains to fully celebrate Sir Barnett Stross and the gift of international fellowship - for Stoke-on-

Trent to provide an opportunity to present land for a sculpture garden for communities associated with the Lidice Shall Live campaign to express themselves. This could be from the experience of atrocity, such as Putten in The Netherlands, who now look upon Stoke-on-Trent as a city which stands up to tyranny; but also those towns and cities in the North, Latin and South America, and elsewhere with a direct empathetic bond with Stoke-on-Trent in terms of their commemorative relationship with Lidice.

Alan & Cheryl Gerrard
Lidice Lives
November 2018

Contents

Chapter One   1

Chapter Two   19

Chapter Three   33

Chapter Four   51

Chapter Five   75

Chapter Six   96

Chapter Seven   116

Chapter Eight   129

Chapter Nine   149

Chapter Ten   165

Chapter Eleven   175

Chapter Twelve   203

Chapter Thirteen   232

Chapter Fourteen   247

Chapter Fifteen   265

Chapter Sixteen   310

Chapter Seventeen   326

Chapter Eighteen   336

Chapter Nineteen   353

Chapter Twenty   361

Chapter Twenty-One   372

Postscript   393

Credits and Acknowledgement   396

About the Author   398

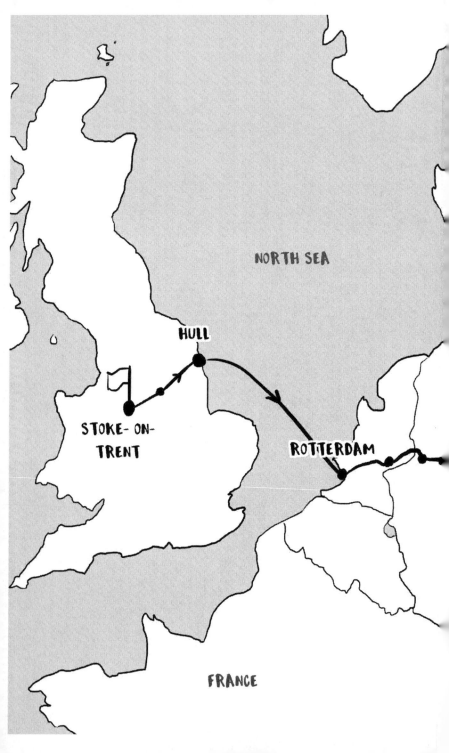

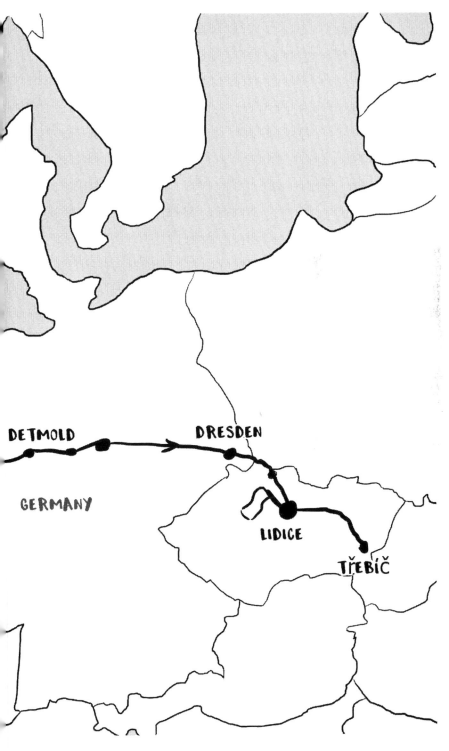

Chapter One

From a first floor window in the Haus vom Guten Hirten, on the leafily suburban Mauritz-Lindenweg, just a couple of kilometres from Münster city centre, a few early-bird commuters could be seen walking purposefully to the tram stop a couple of blocks away on the main road. June 10th 2016 dawned brightly in the Westphalian city. Two of the hotel staff sat in the garden awaiting the arrival of early-rising guests in the breakfast room in some fifteen minutes. The receptionist who had welcomed us the previous lunchtime, arrived for her days work and a few minutes later the night porter, who had seen us return from our brief exploration of the old town, left for home.

To set up the day's cycling - an eighty-six or so, miler - we took full advantage of the buffet. Sumptuous? Almost. Fruit salad, yoghurt, quark, bread, pastries, ham, slices of cheese, cereals, salami; typical German hotel breakfast buffet. Strong coffee and fruit juice. Mark, my cycling companion on this trip, tended towards the fruit; I tended towards the bread and meat. With whatever filled our bellies, we filled them.

Replete, rather than stuffed, with the prospect of a day's cycling in the sunshine; what could be better? Fill the bottles, collect the panniers and head out of town across the farmland of Münsterland. Well, after a while you might beg for a hill or two, but they come eventually and it doesn't really do to be that fussy.

As Mark finished packing his neatly organised rack-pack, I looked again onto the Mauritz-Lindenweg. By now, a few cars were on the move, but mostly there were children walking with parents or in little giggling groups, on the way to school. Bicycles propelled by adults with child seats or by children with rucksacks on their backs or school-bags in baskets, went more or less happily to their lessons. None of them seemed aware that they were doing, what many in the UK would regard as, something dangerous. That was the Münster school-run. All the mundane day-to-day life that we take for granted passed along into its hopeful, homely future.

The nearby cemetery, which Mark had stated was amongst the prettiest and kempt he'd seen, was silent as the sun poured down its warmth. It would be a hot day, but a good one.

Cycling to the edge of the city to turn onto a track passing a typically-Westphalian timber-framed farmhouse and mill, we paused by a river that fed the large millpond. On the far bank stood a multi-storey trailer loaded with kayaks and canoes. How much my family would like to be out there on the water or hiding in the willow boughs that touched the still surface. Waiting to surprise and splash each other. I could not help but think that they would love it and that they should be there. I'd be happy watching them from the decking with a glass of one of Munster's beers. Having sampled a couple the day before, one could only want to return to the Pinkus Muller brewery for another. A long detour to a bar is not what the first miles of a cycle-touring day requires. It would not be open at that hour, anyway.

Such were the concerns of daily cycling-life.

It was only a little way beyond this, amongst cornflower-fringed, golden fields of wheat, that I was suddenly struck by the significance of the day. Peculiar? Very, peculiar. This was, after all, the day that gave purpose to our ride. It was, so to speak, why we were heading across Europe.

****

Near our eventual destination, early on June 10th 1942, a group of men were leaving the night shift at a mine just outside Kladno, a few miles from Prague. Even before they had washed, their workmates on the in-coming day shift told them of the news from their home village. They took them to a window and showed them plumes of smoke rising into the morning sky.

Eduard Stehlík, author of "Memories of Lidice", quotes one miner from the nearby village of Drín;

> On Wednesday, June 10th 1942, I was going for a morning shift. Miners from Hřebeč and Buštěhrad caught up with me, got off their bikes and walked along with me. They started telling each other about some strange goings-on in Lidice. They said that the Nazis had been raging there from the evening as if it was a war front. They had seen many cars going to and fro. All the livestock was being driven to the Buštěhrad state farm. Some shooting was reported, and animals and poultry screaming. We reached the pit, but did not feel like work at all. Our mine is (sic) on a hill, so we saw smoke rolling into the sky from

Lidice. Everyone was talking about it, there were speculations that it was being destroyed because of the Horáks and Stříbrnýs, whose sons were abroad, and that the Gestapo had found something there.

Meanwhile, the shift had ended, so we went to change in the bathroom and searched for the men from Lidice who had worked the night shift. Four of them came up from the underground: Václav Kovařovský, Václav Kaiml, Václav Hanf and Bohuslav Straka, then twenty years old. They noticed the excitement and asked what it was about. The miners took them to a corridor and showed them the clouds of smoke coming from Lidice. We told them that the Nazis had been raging there from ten o'clock the previous night. We could all see the pain in their faces. We warned them against going there. They left the showers without a word. When they got dressed, Václav Kovařovský said: "It can't be helped boys, we must. We have our families, houses and belongings there. If they took our women and children and homes, let them take us, too. Let's

5

go!" Our eyes were all wet when they were leaving, but we still had hope that it would not be that bad. They took their bikes, didn't even mount them, and walked slowly towards the gatehouse.

Bikes were important; transport to work, excursions into the countryside for the youth, visits. Apparently boys tended to borrow father's bike, whilst girls were beginning to get their own as the twentieth century progressed. A popular and necessary machine in the 1930s. There were other ways for Lidice-lad to meet Lidice-lass, but not so many away from the parental eye - or that of the neighbours.

Lidice was not an isolated village, but it had a strong cultural and sporting life of its own, revolving largely around the Church, pubs, ice-hockey, football and, to our eyes more unusually, a fire-fighting brigade, with its own fire-engine. Václav Hanf was commander of the brigade, who not only rehearsed drills but performed plays, had parties and kept fit. In the 1930s he had encouraged more girls to get involved with the club. It was flourishing, even in the war years.

The wonderful fire-fighting machine would have been an antique by 1942. In fact, it would have been antiquated in most places by the time of the Great War. However, if, like me, you'd secretly love to have seen such a vehicle clattering down the street with the firemen holding on tight, uniforms glinting brassily in the moon-light, sparks flying from the horses shoes as they struck the cobbles, a crowd of the less-well-to-do chasing after to earn a few pennies by manning the pumps, then you'll get the picture.

The fire-engine was not in the village on June 10th 1942. On loan to another municipality on that day, it is now one of the largest of two artefacts that survived the Nazi assault. The other is the Church door. Unless one counts the numerous bullet-holed and blood-stained identification documents and a handful of name-plates from houses and a few miscellaneous odds and ends, there is little material evidence of old Lidice, apart from those.

On his way home, Hanf and his three friends, stopped at the cemetery in Buštěhrad to talk with some miners who were on their way to the afternoon shift and had been watching lorries full of butchered animals go by. Warning the Lidice men not to go home, they wept when Kovařovský said, "Here, friends, take our bicycles as keepsakes, we're going in whatever may happen!" A short way down the road, as they entered the fog of war they were approached by some German guards, who escorted them into the village. A few moments later, the men by the cemetery heard a volley of gunshots.

The corpses of the four miners lay alongside those of 168 other Lidice males over the age of fifteen who had been in the village on the evening of June 9th. There was also the body of Josef Hroník. Under fifteen, he should not have been amongst the men. When the families were split-up, his father had beckoned him to come with him as his mother had her hands full with the rest of their children. Yet, some might wonder if that did not turn out not to be such a bad thing.

One body, at least, has never been identified - amongst those of the miners, steel-workers, shop-keepers, farmers, aged veterans of the Great War. It is assumed to be that of a coach-driver who had not yet registered with the village Mayor. He had moved in on June 9th. Another body was believed to be a labourer, his name unknown.

****

And here was I pedalling along with barely a care in the world, other than where the next coffee and cake stop might be, or

8

whether to eschew a refreshing beer at lunchtime, or pondering why I bothered to stop to send my son a photo of a sign saying Fartmann. I apologise to Herr Fartmann. He may like to know that other languages rarely respect the good-name of decent folk like us. According to an on-line Swedish dictionary, "Dyster" means "gloomy, dreary, murky, black, dark, heavy, darksome, sombre, dismal, disconsolate, sad, glum, blue, doldrums: in the doldrums, beetle-browed, grave, cloudy, bleak, angry, lugubrious, morose, doleful, funereal, sepulchral, saturnine". I did not think I had Viking blood, but this is uncanny; you'll understand, should anyone ever bother to read this. I'd always thought it was from the same cloth-trade roots as "Dyer".

So, back to good old cycling and the start of our tour. Cycle-touring obsessions first; mid-weight tour (i.e. carrying more than very basic gear, but not loaded with camping kit). It would have been light-weight had it not been for;

1. Lots of electrical stuff to enable blogging, tweeting, phoning, SatNaving, photographing and, of course, re-charging everything that does those things. Never before had I carried so much of this gubbins, nor will I again.

2. Two cables and an immensely heavy U-lock, for securing Mark's sparkly new nick-able Shand Stoater to my very old in-need-of-another-respray less-nickable Dawes Supergalaxy, and both to any convenient piece of street architecture.

3. A crazily exuberant ceramic sculpture created by the crazily exuberant Mark Dally, of Mark Dally Ceramics (commissions welcome), who has not paid a penny for this mention. Artwork to celebrate our ride and the story we were exploring. Packed carefully in rubber, foam and box, we wondered if it would complete the journey in a more crazily exuberant multi-piece format or arrive safely. At times this provided a good deal of excitement.

4. A painting by Stoke-on-Trent artist, Harry Davies. A generous and appropriate contribution for the artistically untalented Dyster - either Swedish or English versions - to take as a gift, along with Mark's triumphantly exuberant sculpture. Crazy really. We could have posted both. However, we spotted a possible publicity stunt; tipping off the Dutch, German and Czech authorities that two international art-smugglers were using bikes to evade the forces of law and order. It would have been good publicity when we let ourselves be caught, had we gone ahead

with it and been charged with wasting police time. More of the artwork later.

5. All the basic tools: multi-tool; puncture repair stuff; spare tubes; chain-tool, magic links, oil; brake blocks and cables for my old banger. The new Stoater, hydraulically disc-braked and belt-driven, required none of these. In fact, other than replacing brake blocks on my bike half-way through, the bikes remained incident-free, mechanically. Mark did need the zip-ties for his shoes and the oil for a squeaky cleat, but that is another story for later, if at all.

Second... no, if you want to know details of bottom brackets, wheels, gear inches and other stuff some cyclists love to yarn about, you can apply in writing and await a reply at my leisure. As we were to see, our drop-barred tourers were very much in a tiny minority amongst tourers on the continent and no cyclist enquired after the make or model of our wheel bearings, though Mark was keen to tell - quite rightly, because it is fabulous - everyone about his Rohloff Speed Hub, were they unwary enough to get drawn in. Mind you, hub gears of all kinds are more common on the Continent, though Mark is an enthusiast and not one to be stymied so easily.

11

Third cycling obsession. It was a sunny day when we set off, and remained so for the next day and the next until we had some rain. When and if the weather gets really interesting the narrative will supply sufficient detail. Look at it like this, until we had completed our voyage we were going to cycle on, whatever the weather might do.

With all that and a few spare clothes on board, accompanied by my wife, Emma, and my son, Edward, and Larry the Lurcher - not an aged uncle, just our dog - we bimbled along the Trent and Mersey Canal towpath as far as Barlaston. Ed kept us company for a bit further, but it was there that I left my family behind for three weeks.

Remarkable really. Ed and Emma were generous enough to let me go. I was facing redundancy at work and they were happy for me to spend some of the imminent pay-off on a trip they would not be coming on. Before family came along - and getting to the age of forty-five before child was born - I'd many years of multi-day tours in my legs. Commuting to work, family rides and occasional weekends away on the bike had kept a good degree of cycle fitness - though any request to buy a lighter-weight bike would have been greeted by cries of, "Lighter bike? Start with your belly."

There is, in my opinion, nothing like moving on day after day by bicycle, relying on what one can carry - be it camping gear, a change of clothes or a just a credit card. Stress-relief, appetite-building, health-bringing, simplicity; perhaps it is an addiction with a rapid pathway through the brain. Having done it once, life without it is unthinkable. Truth is, I need to get out on the bike for a few days every now and again. Without the drug I become restless and even grumpier than the most literate Swedes could describe. Not surprising that the family were keen to see me go for a while... except Larry, who, loyal beast, did not eat properly for two weeks.

The plan for the first day; cross the Peak District and spend the night near Worksop, Nottinghamshire. Lots of climbs and descents, some pleasant traffic-free sections, mixed with lovely lanes and some busier bits. Quite a challenging first day, especially since we were both a bit short of miles. So, impractically, we had decided to start the day with a diversion to Burslem.

****

There was logic to this. Those four miners who walked to their deaths in Lidice would have fitted-in in Burslem. On June

10th 1942, miners in Stoke-on-Trent were working as per normal, doing their bit to power the nation's heroic efforts to defeat Nazism. Most famous for its ceramics, Stoke-on-Trent, the Potteries, was full of pot-banks, in the local parlance. World-famous names filled the city in a smoky agglomeration of towns and villages; Wedgwood, Minton, Spode and so many more names that graced the tables of rich and poor alike. It is commonly held that the pottery industry has disappeared. It hasn't. Stoke-on-Trent is still the largest city producer of ceramic products in the world. Even with the industry in decline around 8% of the population still worked in pot-banks in 1991, with a further 8% in associated industries. In 2016, ceramic businesses were growing again.

The importance of ceramics to economic and social life in the city during the mid-twentieth century is hard to overestimate. At one time there had been four thousand of the characteristic bottle kilns, though reduced to 2000 by the mid-twentieth century - new technologies and later Clean Air Acts saw their demise. Forty-six still exist, some standing in derelict factories, others preserved as feature conference rooms in refurbished eco-centres or, bizarrely, at first sight, built amongst terraces of houses. The latter brings home just how much life in the city was entwined with the fortunes of the ceramic manufacturers. It is not that the city has lost its ceramic industry, it is just that it was so colossal that its decline could only have a matching impact.

However, steel-making was also important in North Staffordshire and then there were the collieries of the North Staffordshire Coalfield - almost all within Stoke-on-Trent and Newcastle-under-Lyme, with outliers around Leek and Cheadle. Just like the pot-banks, those in the city had grown up higgledy-piggledy as the six towns and numerous villages poured into the gaps. A landscape of pits, potteries, mines and works with houses gathered around them; an un-planned mass of life and labour - much of it highly skilled labour, with strong community identities and spirit, living in a unique industrial landscape.

Amongst the collieries working during the Second World War was that of the Sneyd Collieries Company, Sneyd Pit No4. Tradition had it that, amongst colliers, working on New Year's Day was regarded as unlucky. Maybe, this feeling was not necessarily shared by all, not even a majority. Then there was the war. Coal was the fuel of industry and transport. Maintaining production was a patriotic duty. Turn-out was high on the morning shift at Sneyd Pit on New Year's Day, 1942.

A little before 07.30am an electrical cable became entangled with a truck's wheel. Wires were exposed and an explosion shattered the Banbury seam. By the time the rescue teams had finished, fifty-seven bodies of men and boys had been recovered. Others had made remarkable escapes, despite injuries and being blinded by a choking fog of coal-dust. Such was the life of many a coal-mining community, especially before nationalisation and stronger safety standards. Life or death, any miner anywhere in the world understood.

Major pit disasters grab the headlines, but a glance through the local newspapers give a litany of individuals injured or killed by isolated roof collapses that shattered their skulls, or broke their backs. A long, grim list of the perils of working underground, a list that grew longer week by week. Then there was miner's lung and respiratory diseases that curtailed lives of otherwise fit, strong men.

And there we were, cycling in the sunshine and fresh air of an almost chimney-less, smoke-free city. Our official starting point was the Sneyd Pit Disaster Memorial, in the centre of Burslem.

****

As we rode, I reflected on the decision to go a few miles out of the way to set off from that spot. Sneyd Colliery was not the first pit in the area to suffer major loss of life during the war. Eleven men had been killed at Mossfield Pit, Longton, in March 1940. Mining was a dangerous business whether the nation was at war or not. Add to this, the general hardships of war, the shortages and family tragedies and you have a perfect recipe for communities to look to themselves and take care of their own. Though mining wages went up during the war, there was more attractive employment - hence the need for the Bevin Boys in 1943 - and industrial relations were not good in the coal mining districts.

Today we can see the names of the victims of the Sneyd Pit explosion on the memorial in Burslem Market Square. All over the age of fifteen, but twelve aged twenty or younger.

I remembered, too, looking at a list of the Lidice children who had been separated from their mothers, fathers, elder

17

brothers, cousins, aunts and uncles. Czech is by no means an impossible language to read, but it is unfamiliar to the western European eye in its patterns and the unusual frequency of accents draped across apparently vowel-less words. I wonder how many, if any, of the miners of North Staffordshire could have done better than me; tongue-contorting names of people whom they did not know, in a country far away. At least, that's how the UK government had seen Czechoslovakia a few years before, when it was effectively handed over to the Germans.

Yet, the miners of North Staffordshire did care. And they acted, regardless of their own hardships.

Chapter Two

Susan, Mark's wife, met us at the Sneyd Pit Disaster memorial in Burslem, along with their children, Isabel and Will. We'd hoped that someone from the local newspaper might turn up, but they didn't. We wondered if a personage from the City Council might show, but the only council vehicle that pulled in was a street cleaning van - there was, of course, no real reason why anyone from the Council should have turned up, though it was good to see the guys keeping the place tidy.

Burslem is the "Mother Town" of the Potteries and, although the Market Place is not as grand as it once was, it is easy to understand that this was once the flourishing heart of the Potteries, the "Bursley" of Arnold Bennett's Five Town novels. The grandest feature is the Town Hall - actually the second of three - with its magnificent columns, deep front entrance reminiscent of an entrance passage into a medieval fortification and, literally above all, a wonderfully eccentric tower topped by the Angel.

Across the road - Wedgwood Street, Queen Street, Chapel Bank and Fountain Square all seem to merge into the Market

Place - is the third Town Hall; known as the Queen's Hall (Stoke town has the King's Hall), it was used mainly for theatrical performances and concerts. Mighty columns supporting and hefty stonework; early twentieth century civic pride in stone and mortar. Completed a year after the six towns became the Federation of Stoke-on-Trent, it was a flourishing town that could afford such an edifice.

Then there's the Wedgwood Memorial Institute, a short distance off, currently the much debated object of a restoration project supported by the Prince's Regeneration Trust and the School of Art, both wonderful buildings redolent of the skilled workforce that laboured in the potteries. A little way down the hill on the Trent and Mersey Canal is the Middleport Pottery. A completed restoration project - funded by the Prince's Regeneration Trust - it mixes working pottery with museum and contemporary galleries. Bounded on one side by a street of beautiful terraced houses; proximity was typical of life and work in the Potteries. Back in the Market Place, right opposite the Town Hall and Queen's Hall, are pot banks: Royal Stafford and Moorland.

Josiah Wedgwood was born in Burslem, where he set up his first workshop. Perhaps the biggest name in ceramics, he

20

dominates the topic so much that "Jerseyah" often gets the credit for the inventions of Josiah Spode, as well as his own. Wedgwood was not just an inventor and innovator, he was one of those bustling entrepreneurs - but one with a strong social conscience. It was in The Leopard, an eighteenth century inn on the Market Place, that Wedgwood first met with the Duke of Bridgewater's engineer, James Brindley, to discuss the possibility of building a canal from Burslem to the Trent and Humber, to give access to Hull. This eventually became the Trent and Mersey Canal.

The Leopard's upper floors have seen better days and are out of use, though the ground floor rooms are brimming with colourful tiled floors, wood panelling, mirrors and old photographs. Full of atmosphere and original features, it has been described as one of Burslem's hidden gems. I'd go further; Burslem town centre is one of England's hidden gems.

Ho, ho! I know. Heritage is to be found in stately homes where everyone speaks nicely and the servants tug their forelocks and we can pretend we are in a period drama, rather than in the lines of terraced houses gathered around the civic buildings of a midlands town that has seen better days. In

Burslem's Market Place you are in the centre of a unique landscape; and the town has a beautiful park too. Another one to put down to civic pride and, more recently, a grant from the Heritage Lottery Fund.

****

Next to arrive, to see us off, were Alan and Cheryl Gerrard. They deserve a special mention, they really do. As memories of the strong links between the City of Stoke-on-Trent and the people of the Czech Republic have faded, these two have laboured to revive and strengthen them.

The strong links? Well, miners are miners. My first teaching post was in North Nottinghamshire - during the strike of 1984-5. The area was split between solid strike action in the pits that were administratively in the South Yorkshire Region and the working miners in the Nottinghamshire Region. It was a thoroughly awful time. As a teacher one remained neutral. At the rugby club the topic was banned; miners paid their membership and match tax if they could - lack of overtime meant significant loss of earnings for working miners - the same applied to striking miners, with only their strike pay to live on.

There was a time when miners stuck together. Most were unionised, but their identity was also shared by their colleagues around the world. Working underground in Czechoslovakia was much the same as working underground in Burslem, Longton, Fenton, Hanley, Tunstall, Stoke, Talke or anywhere else. Miners were miners all over the world.

Of course, they'd argue and have the odd punch-up outside the pub, but when a shift began they knew that they'd face common dangers and looked-forward to seeing the light of day again - as would their families.

Yes, miners were miners all the world over, even in wartime. In 1943 Will Lowther, President of the Miners' Federation of Great Britain put it like this in his Presidential Address to the Annual Conference;

> *The life and work of a miner gives him an outlook that is only understood by those in close contact with him. Yet it was from our ranks, in those far off days of the Fascist attack on Spain, that appeals were made to those in authority to make a stand against the aggressor. Often we thought we were talking to the deaf and maybe blind.*

23

Miners, unlike many of their critics, never gave praise to Mussolini, Hitler or Franco, and from that position we will not retreat. It is for those deep-seated, human reasons and faith in Freedom's cause that we link our demands to today's needs. We hate Fascism and Nazism with the same intensity that we love Liberty and cherish Freedom. It was this Trade Union that on May 1st, 1942, convened a Conference of Miners from every nation, allied or enemy, to weld a force that would give the greatest amount of support for our faith and cause. That day there were gathered miners from Great Britain, Czechoslovakia, Poland, Belgium, Luxembourg, Austria and Germany, to show their deep detestation of the Nazi methods. Messages of support came from the USSR, USA and the Swedish Miners, and of their unity of purpose with us. The French miners sent a message through an underground source with other French workers, as some of their leaders had collaborated with Vichy and gone Nazi. Since then we have heard of the French miners, and they wait the freeing of their nation from Nazi domination. It was a German miner who spoke at that Conference saying to the miners of the Ruhr: "I want to tell you to trust these British comrades and comrades in other countries now because they are fighting against the same common enemy. I call upon you to resist and to profit by every raid of the R.A.F. in order to reduce production in the mines and in the workshops. I ask you to smash Hitler's war machine." The work of that Conference has been carried through, enlarged and developed with the help of the International Transport Workers and the International Metal Workers. Broadcasts are put across every weekend of what we are thinking and doing in to-day's struggle. The truth is put across to Hitler's victims frankly and fearlessly so that they know that the free workers of the United Nations will keep up the supplies of guns, planes and tanks to blast the guilty criminals off the face of the earth. There is no misunderstanding as to what those crimes are. Apparently there are some people in the Labour Movement who want us to forget the horrors practised by the Nazis at

Lidice, at Rotterdam and wherever they have set their feet.

Thus, when Lidice had been destroyed in 1942 - and it was obliterated - and Adolf Hitler declared that "Lidice Shall Die Forever!" and news spread, it was the British miners who took it to heart in a way few could have expected. This was especially the case in North Staffordshire.

****

So, what had happened in Lidice?

There are numerous accounts of the atrocity, which was, conveniently, filmed and photographed in detail by a Nazi film unit. Amongst the scenes of death and destruction are numerous shots of smiling Gestapo and SS officers along with shirtless, strapping men of the Reich Labour Service. Their satisfaction came back to haunt them when their own film was used at the Nuremberg Trials.

The bare bones are these. Keen to show the occupying Nazis that they were not immune from the consequences of their actions, the Czech government in exile, a number of Czech military officers and the British Special Operations Executive wanted to make an example of a senior Nazi.

Hitler had recently appointed Reinhard Heydrich as Governor or the Protectorate of Bohemia-Moravia - as the Nazis referred to the north-western section of Czechoslovakia. Ordered to boost flagging industrial production, Heydrich increased rations for workers whilst carrying out a murderous onslaught against any resistance, tangible and potential. He hit, especially hard, at those who might offer leadership. As far as Czech officers in exile were concerned, Heydrich had to go. A plan was hatched and though reprisals were expected and dissenting voices were raised in the light of that certainty, the decision was taken to go ahead.

Though the plan was controversial, Operation Anthropoid was successful. Heydrich died of wounds inflicted by a grenade thrown by Jan Kubiš, after his colleague Josef Gabčík's Sten gun had jammed.

Heydrich's deputy, Frank, was ordered, by Hitler, to "wade in blood". Arbitrary arrests and executions followed, but even the Gestapo failed to find a suitable target on which revenge on the grand scale could be exacted. Kubiš, Gabčík and their colleagues all died in a shoot-out in the crypt of St. Cyril and St Methodius' Cathedral in Prague, contacts and other members of the resistance were arrested and executed; but that was not enough for the Nazis.

When a boastful letter had arrived at a Kladno factory and was opened by the manager rather than the addressee, the Gestapo got its first link to Lidice. The letter was intended to impress a girl. Neither intended recipient, Anna Maruščákova, nor sender, Václav Řhía, had anything to do with the plot or much to do with Lidice, but he claimed to have "done what he had to do". Just a sad, stupid boast, but that did not prevent the murder of both of them in Mauthausen Camp in the autumn of 1942.

During interrogation by the Gestapo, Maruščćková mentioned that Řhía had asked her to pass on best wishes from Josef Horák to his family and friends in Lidice. One can imagine the eyes of the interrogator lighting up with glee, though it is very unlikely that Josef Horák had made any such request. Perhaps Řhía was just trying to boost his credibility in the eyes of Anna. The power of love, or lust, or whatever. It certainly boosted his credibility with the Gestapo.

Josef Horák? There were many Horáks in Lidice, but Josef had disappeared, along with fellow Lidice resident, Josef Stříbrný, and a friend, Václav Student. Horák and Student were officers in the Czechoslovak Air Force; Stříbrný was an infantry officer. All had secretly left the country on December 28th, 1939. They'd gone to join their native armed forces in exile, eventually making their way to France and then the UK. Fatefully, the Gestapo had also learned, from a captured Czech airman, that Josef Stříbrný had received parachute training in the UK.

Relatives of the exiled soldiers were rounded up and interrogated in the best traditions of the Gestapo. All they could say was that the men had disappeared in 1938. Truth did not satisfy the inquisitors. Despite their persuasive methods, the Gestapo got nowhere. Threatened, beaten, petrified with fear for their loved ones, the Horáks and Stříbrnýs had nothing to tell.

This must have been a time of deep concern to the people of Lidice and the surrounding area. The occupiers were wading in blood, as instructed - hundreds of Czechoslovaks were being rounded up and murdered - members of the resistance active and potential, and this murderous revenge was being

29

made manifest in their little, tight-knit community. It must have been the talk of the village and its neighbouring communities. It was no surprise that the miners assumed that the Nazi "raging" on June 10th was something to do with the Horák's and Stříbrný's exiled sons.

The inability of the families to provide their brutal interrogators with anything to add to the spurious letter meant that even the Kladno Gestapo had to report that it could find no evidence to link Lidice to the assassination. Of course, whilst justice or legal cause may have exercised the minds of lawyers in Germany, in the occupied lands anything went. Neither Hitler, nor our helpful ally, Josef Stalin, paid more than passing attention to any legal process, other than the purely symbolic. Despite the ignorance of the Stříbrnýs and the Horáks, Lidice's fate was sealed.

In fact, the German authorities were fully aware that Lidice had no link to the assassination of Heydrich. Karel Čurda, who had been parachuted into the country along with Gabčík and Kubiš, had told them so. An active collaborator, unbeknown to his superiors or the British, he received one million Reichsmarks for betraying his colleagues. Executed for treason in 1947, he explained that he did it for the money.

Shortly after Heydrich's Wagnerian state funeral, whilst compulsory national mourning was underway, Frank, Heydrich's deputy, reported to Prague from Berlin that The Fuhrer had ordered the following with regard to Lidice;

1. Shoot all the adult men dead.
2. Transport all adult women to a concentration camp.
3. Gather all the children suitable for Gemanization and place them in SS families in the Reich, and bring the rest up in other ways.
4. Burn down and level the village entirely.

Thus it was, Lidice would die, forever.

The personal instructions of the Führer were not to be ignored or questioned. Whilst he took only limited interest in the detail of most things, Hitler's will was the weathercock on which ambitious Nazis kept a keen eye. One might not know exactly what he wanted, but taking the opportunity to follow his will or even amplify on it, were sure ways to get on in the jungle of competing ambitions that was the Nazi regime.

So, Lidice was to die.

The village was sealed off on the evening of June 9th. Travellers were allowed in, but no one was to be let out. Böhme, head of the Prague Security Police, Geschke, head of the Prague Gestapo office, Weissmann, head of the Kladno Gestapo, and Vit, the commander of the local Gendarmerie, set up HQ in the home of František Hejma, Mayor of Lidice. During expulsion from his home, Hejma was forced to hand over to the Gestapo all documents relating to the village.

Chapter Three

A few years ago the towpath of the Caldon Canal, which has a junction with the Trent and Mersey Canal at Etruria, not far from the Roundhouse - the only remaining building of Wedgwood's Etruria Pottery - was surfaced as far as the edge of Stoke-on-Trent. Later, the sealed surface was extended to the Flint Mill, built by James Brindley, at Cheddleton. It is easily cyclable from there to The Churnet Valley Railway's Cheddleton station, though the cycle route leaves the canal with an eccentric leap up and over the bank.

It is the little things that count sometimes. Several miles of good cycling - even if the path is in need of some maintenance in places and there is one very pointless gate - and what do we remember? The lack of a drop kerb. Well what I really remember along here is looking at the road to Leek already carrying a stream of traffic. Not so busy that a confident cyclist could not use it, but how much pleasanter, if a trifle slower, to wind along the contours of the canal, leaving the city behind and entering a world of gritstone houses and walls of rough pastures.

Yep, a few miles outside Stoke-on-Trent and one is into the Peak District. Often spoken of as "Derbyshire", The Peak District is also in South Yorkshire, Cheshire and Staffordshire. I have heard it said, no doubt only with the tip of the tongue directed towards the cheek, that the best bits of "Derbyshire" are in Staffordshire; in Macclesfield they might say "in Cheshire". There are some very good bits in Staffordshire; the Roaches, Lud's Church, whilst the area around Three Shire's Head, where Derbyshire, Staffordshire and Cheshire meet, is as wildly beautiful as anywhere in the southern Pennines.

Anyway, there we went, off up the hills and down the valleys, though generally the former, towards Ipstones - pausing only to admire a locomotive in steam at the Churnet Valley Railway. Railways were very much a part of my childhood. We had a complete set of WH Awdry's books in a beautifully bound series, published sometime in the 1950s.

So much for great literature of the past. In fact, so much for great literature of the present - this is all that is on offer here. Anyway, there's me and Mark pedalling off towards Ipstones. Any signpost for Ipstones could be replaced with the instruction to head up-hill, or almost all of them. It is possible

34

to descend into the village, but you have to go a long way up first.

We acknowledged the beauty of our local area. An isolated house built against a vast craggy outcrop, peaceful fields where hay dried in the sunshine and near views that changed with every turn. Britons are fortunate in the countryside that surrounds them; a comparatively gentle countryside that has such splendid variety, occasionally turning wild.

Though we moaned at the hills, as cyclists do - whilst secretly loving the uphill's more than the descents (though, I'll admit that this may be an exaggeration and that I may be in a minority) - a couple of days later, as the Netherland's flat acres became a little tedious, we welcomed the small climbs around Arnhem. Later, despite everything being new to us, we came to appreciate our everyday countryside much more than we usually do.

Stopping in Ipstones to buy some food, Mark headed for the fruit - a banana and an apple - and some nuts. I headed for the fruit - a banana and an apple - and the bags of sweets. Mark was surprised that I had consumed the entire bag by the time we got to Hull at the end of the second day; I was surprised that such moderation had been shown.

For me jelly beans and fruit gums (of all types; midget gems, sports mixture et al) are the kings of the road and my jersey pocket is rarely without some such. Energy gels and protein bars are fine, but, to my taste, they just do not satisfy the soul. Riding Land's End to John O'Groats several years ago, I put two quarter pound bags of sweets in the bar-bag each day and never had any left when the night's accommodation was reached.

Mark is more of a lunch-picnic-cyclist - which has equal merit - I am very much a grazer. A picnic of bread, cheese, tomatoes and other salads became the norm as we moved on. No doubt very good for our health, but taking a good hour out of the cycling day. Truth is, that one should not go on a long cycle ride to lose weight, so you need one feed or the other, or both. Returning home lighter in body is a likely consequence, but should not be the purpose. You'll be fresher in mind too.

Truth was that much of the first day was on familiar ground. Until one reaches the half-way point of a decent day ride, one will often find oneself riding from the front door along lanes one knows well. Familiarity can breed undeserved contempt.

The truncated hill around the Cauldon Quarry came into sight before the race down to Waterhouses. Here one will always catch the crowds on a sunny summer's day. For here beginneth or endeth, depending on where one starteth, the Manifold Trail. Following the former track-bed of the Leek and Manifold Light Railway, built to carry the produce of farm and mine from Hulme End and the valley of the River Manifold, it is now a tourist hot-spot.

Bikes can be hired at Waterhouses and one can roll down to the Manifold along its tributary, the Hamps. This little stream is usually more of a weedy rockery than a babbling brook. Even the Manifold is a dry stream bed for much of the year, shortly after it passes Wetton Mill. Limestone geology with all the sink holes, caves and fissures; this is a classroom for geologists.

All very familiar territory to me, but still spectacular. A deep gorge, crags that beetle above the river of people on the tarmac. The track is not technically all traffic-free, though the sections where road took over the track-bed usually sees walkers and cyclists outnumber cars and motor bikes. There's even a narrow tunnel, before a final run into a bowl in the hills and the end of the line at Hulme End.

Along the way there were numerous pedestrians and cyclists. Too numerous to get up much momentum. This is a good, relatively level way to explore the countryside - in the White Peak, the dales are often more spectacular than the hills through which they burrow.

How many groups of children and teachers on bikes had I led down here on outings from schools in Stoke-on-Trent? Though part of a job, I'll have to become very stony-hearted not to recall those school trips and smile.

I reported each term to Sustrans and Stoke-on-Trent City Council that I had led so many groups of so many children and so many adults for so many hours on a ride on the Manifold Trail, as part of a wider programme developed with the school, to encourage active travel. I could report how some children who could not ride a bike six weeks before had now completed a trip of six, ten, twelve, sixteen miles. I'd sit for the twentieth time, feeding the ducks, near Wetton Mill, while Andy Barrett - a generous enthusiast for cycling and encouraging others to join in, with whom I had the pleasure to work - would lead a group to Hulme End and back. We could report that we had arranged tandem rides for children with severe balance issues.

The adults - teachers, teaching assistant and parent volunteers - would tell us how much the children had enjoyed it and how much it had benefitted them. Yet, we already knew that. You only had to listen.

"The best school trip ever." "I'm getting my Mum and Dad here." "Can we do it next week?" "Look at that bank, don't go up it do we?" "I fell off into the nettles, but I'm not stopping." "I couldn't ride that far, but I did." "Thanks, Steve." "Thanks, Andy." "Thanks, Miss." "Thanks, Sir." "What's that smell?" "Wild garlic." "Can we go up Thor's Cave?" "Where's water gone?" "How far's the ice-cream?"

Officially, some of those schools were in areas of multiple deprivation. A few children had tough shells, some genuinely troubled by life, let alone the prospect of learning; all were just young people with hopes and dreams. Like all children, they could easily have those knocked out of them. Yep, I hope they enjoyed cycling and want to do more of it, but I hope they learned resilience and determination as legs began to ache or saw that they had done something they had not done before, even if they weren't as good at it as their mates.

Teaching someone to ride, developing the bike skills of a group, learning to communicate and cooperate on the move, building independence and responsibility, and then riding down the trail singing, ringing bells - generally wrecking the peace of the countryside - stopping for a picnic, buying ice-creams and setting off for home. Well, I enjoyed it.

****

At Lidice there stands a remarkable sculpture, a group of bronze figures. It is the work of Marie Uchytilová. Twenty years of her work. Eduard Stehlík quotes her explanation of how this potent, terrifyingly tender life-work came about in the years after 1971;

> *I was at home alone... I was looking out into a genuine All Souls' Night, thinking to myself - right now little lights are lit on all the graves around the world, but not on the children's graves. Those 13*

40

million children have no lights (referring to the estimated 13 million children who died as a result of the Second World War)... *and thinking along like this, I got the idea. I thought that if I made a group of the Lidice children being put to death together, it could be the right symbol for those 13 million children...*

Later that day, she stood in the mist where the village of Lidice had once stood. Envisaging the spot, she decided that she would create a tight knit group of eighty-two statues, each an individual, conjoined by fear, love, disbelief, in a common and awful doom.

The Lidice children had grown up in a village, in an era when life was simple, but in many ways, hopeful. The village school was well established, there was work locally and, away from school, Lidice life, no doubt like numerous other villages in Czechoslovakia, gave freedom and security, friendships and, equally doubtless, arguments and occasional tears.

It is easy to sentimentalise life in the past - especially rural life. In Lidice there were children who lived in, what today, we might call overcrowded houses. There may have been times

41

when some went hungry. There were those in families that were comfortably well off, there were those who were not. But that was their life and the life they knew. Notions of progress need to be carefully formed and imposing our present imperils understanding the very past we wish to discover.

Being sent to fetch tobacco for the adults meant a trip to the hut that graces photographs of the scene in front of St. Martin's Church. There Augustin Popíšil sold newspapers, cigarettes and shaved the men of the village. Milk toffees - Stollwercks - were there too, though at ten hellers they were a real delicacy. A photo in Stehlík's "Story of a Czech Village" shows a sturdy looking man in a cardigan, wearing a cap, cigarette in one hand. The shop counter obscures the fact that he had returned from the Great War with no legs. One could imagine him telling stirring or gruesome stories to fascinated children, though he may not have done. Fifteen Lidice men had not returned at all in 1918.

In 1923 Lidice had built a memorial to the men who had been killed in the war. Surmounted with a bust of Jan Hus, the medieval scholar whom many Czech's regard as one of the founding fathers of the nation. The inscription was remarkably similar in sentiment to the Kohima Epitaph.

"When you go home, tell them of us and say, for your tomorrow, we gave our today." "To those who secured happiness with their lives, sacrificed for the freedom of this country." Though the Kohima epitaph has become associated with the Second World War, it had its origins in a set of epitaphs written for the Great War, 1914-1918; though it expresses the same sentiments as the inscription on the memorial to the dead of those years in old Lidice, the latter has a more nationalistic tone; they both share the attitudes and beliefs of those who remember their war dead - especially as the result of that sacrifice was a positive one for the nation; but they grew from very different histories. Along with most of Lidice's memories, the memorial was destroyed. Like most histories it is half-forgotten or, maybe, half-remembered.

****

Off the bikes at the café in the old station yard at Hulme End, I was worried that the group of cyclists - about twenty or so - on a Sunday club run would have decimated the cakes. Most cyclists are legendary eaters, only, in my experience, heavier on the cake are silver-tourists sallying forth from a tour bus. How often have I been overtaken a mere mile from the café

43

by a tour coach? Hard to say. Worst example was when slogging up from the Spittal of Glenshee - back in the days when I was much faster - looking forward to a millionaire shortbread in the café at the Ski Centre at the top of the pass, I spied one of the UK's best sneaking up the hill behind me, bent, no doubt on cheating me of sustenance. Desperate efforts failed to maintain my lead which was whittled away. Sweating profusely and breathing quickly, I arrived to find contented coachees carrying plates of cakes of all types. Only macaroons were left; what use is such a thing to a cyclist? Good job it was all downhill to Braemar.

After some ups and downs and a brief trip along the Tissington Trail, we rolled through Youlgreave and down to the A6 just south of Bakewell. Great summer weather fills the Peak District with cars and ramblers and amblers. We sweltered along the main road and halted to take a look at the creations in a gallery in Rowsley. Mark recognised some of the work and schmoozed the owner. I enjoyed cooling down.

Cool is not the word for the climb from Beeley up to Beeley Moor. A youth on a light-weight racer sped past me as I twiddled slowly on up. The good weather brings the crowds and the crowds generally come by car. Every now and again I found a short convoy passing me when the twists and turns allowed. Eventually hitting the open moorland, leaving the last of the shade, I noted the youth loading his bike onto the rack at the back of a car. Guess he'd been training, he'd miss out on the descent.

Dragging myself to the summit, I waited for Mark. The views were great; hazy, but great. The White Peak in the foreground, the far moors on the western flank of the Peak just visible in the shimmering distance. Mark came up before long. We were crossing a line. We were now looking east, for the first time; I felt as if we had made some progress. Actually, we were still getting into the ride and had hardly been moving rapidly, but behind us was home and the Peak District; ahead in the mind's eye was Chesterfield, North Nottinghamshire and, eventually, the long rural miles of Lincolnshire.

Yet the best laid plans do not survive contact with the enemy. The enemy, in this case, being the maze of roads in Chesterfield. No offence meant to Chesterfield: it is true of most large towns that finding a pleasant way out is usually the hardest part. No, Chesterfield is a fine town in which I once spent many happy hours, usually watching the home county and whoever Derbyshire were taking on at cricket at the lovely Queen's Park ground. Memories of the famous crooked spire of the grand parish church rising above the trees that surrounded the ground came flooding back.

And therein lies half the problem of getting out of town. Misleading notions of familiarity with half-forgotten landmarks - we are talking thirty-five years ago - started to come back to me. We wandered a bit and then, purely by chance, came across a sign for NCR67. Initially this followed the Chesterfield Canal, which is undergoing restoration, with some stretches open for navigation.

Much beloved by cycle route designers, canal towpaths and old railway lines can make great cycle routes, especially in hilly areas. The Derbyshire-Nottinghamshire border is lumpy cycling country - lots of ups and downs, with no really major climbs. Amongst the old mining communities, pits long gone, is some lovely countryside. However, we missed our way. We'd left the canal - which had disappeared anyway - and joined the old railway line along which NCR67 continues. Wanting to leave it just after Renishaw to head for Sprinkhill and Hartshill, that nasty feeling that the going has been good and we'd gone too far began to grow. If there was a sign, we missed it; the other strategy of counting bridges failed because we had not bothered counting. There'd been more than ten, probably, in any case. Making a best guess it turned out that we were not so far out of our way, a fact confirmed, as we pushed our bikes up a muddy path, by two ladies taking their dogs for an afternoon stroll.

We'd gone about a kilometre out of the way and were on the edge of Killamarsh, a former mining village. It brought back memories of hearing the village's brass band playing in, of all places, the Grote Markt in Ghent. Visiting that beautiful city, the incongruity of the mellow sounds of old favourites, coupled with talk in strong north Derbyshire accents, struck me as I sat outside a bar sampling one of Belgium's multitude of beers.

Truth was, that even though we'd crossed the backbone of England, I, at least, was back on familiar territory. Having taught in North Nottinghamshire for nearly ten years, I had a pretty good idea where we were going, though things looked very different. The collieries that dominated the landscape when I'd lived there had gone, new housing estates had grown up around the villages. Mind you, the pub gardens were full of families enjoying the late afternoon sunshine, much as they always had been. That we did not join them was really down to the fact that, first day out, plenty of hills and a good few miles in our legs, we were looking forward to propping the bikes up, having a beer and a shower, something to eat and some more beer - probably in that order.

This was to be my first experience of warmshowers.org. Ha ha, I do actually wash more than once a year, despite what some people might put-about. No, www.warmshowers.org is a cycle touring community in which you either offer to host, seek hosts or both. You are expected to arrive by bike; you might bring some food or drink, but there is no financial cost; the host might provide food, though I have had guests cook for me; you chat, sleep and set off the next day, almost certainly having shared traveller's tales and learned a lot. A bit like Couch Surfing, it is not the province solely of young people on a gap year budget; it is helpful, interesting and, yes, good if you are on a budget.

Mark was especially keen - not, I add with libel lawyers in mind, because he pays more than usual attention to maintaining a frugal budget - but because he is very well-travelled (seriously well-travelled, really) and loves to meet people as well as see places. Exuding a warmth and amiability, quickly at ease with most people, one can see why his digital social networking is so successful. He would say that the latter is all about business, but is hardly ruthless. My wife says that I, on the other hand, travel to see places.

But where were we? On our way to Prague? See, there lies the danger when people impede the daily mileage and natter instead of pedalling with a sense of discipline and iron purpose.

So, we had arrived in Shireoaks on a hot summers evening and met our host on the bridge over the once-again-water-filled Chesterfield Canal, next to the village shop from which we had purchased suitable drinks for rehydration and to thank our benefactor.

The night's billet was perfect. Beer, shower, dinner and beer, chat about all sorts of things and beer. Our host was into mountain biking, though he also rode a tandem when his girlfriend was about. He was not a local, but had moved to the area for work, renting a house until his contract either finished or was extended. So much for meeting local people. Not really a fair comment. After all, we were still on familiar

49

ground in England. Mind you, when in Prague we stayed with a Slovak and, only later, with a wonderfully helpful - and local - Czech family.

Chapter Four

As the German soldiers prepared to shoot the men of Lidice on June 10th, 1942, the women and children were taken to a school in Kladno. Amidst scenes of distress and terror which were hard to bear or fully understand, they were separated. Remember Srebrenica? Bosnian women and children removed whilst the men were massacred in one of Europe's most shameful post-1945 episodes? History did not repeat itself, people did.

The Lidice children were taken from their mothers, aunts, grand-mothers. Babies were sent to an orphanage in Prague. The rest began a journey which only a handful were to survive. The older children tried to care for the younger, but they were unprepared and alone and, almost all, totally surplus to the requirements of the Reich. Almost all. Three children, Dáša Veselá, Hanička Špotová and Vašik Zelenka, were kept behind, though separated from their mothers. They disappeared in a grey car.

The pathetic cargo of eighty-eight children was dispatched and eventually arrived in the Polish city of Lodz. Stowed away, with instructions that no special care was required, in a former textile mill, the children began a dull routine of hunger, dirt and deprivation. Their sole relief came from remembering Lidice and their families.

Kindness came from a Polish nurse, Julie Makowska, and her husband, who went so far as to take one ill child into their private accommodation and to try to help care for the "miserable" youngsters. A group of Polish prisoners who were kept on the floor below, shared food they had hidden - mouldy though it was, it was welcome. A Polish doctor, Jan Zielina, organised a food collection amongst his colleagues and friends. Mrs Makowska then prepared the food for the younger children and ensured it reached them. Zielina testified to the bravery of the Lidice children during his acquaintance with them. He describes how they not only cared for each other, especially, the younger children, but praised their dignity and the way the older boys displayed hatred towards the Germans.

Apart from the post-war testimony of the Poles, we know something of the children's Stations of the Cross because there was a handful more whom the Reich decided might be of use to them.

The children had arrived at the "camp" on June 13th. About two weeks later they were assembled in a room. Two uniformed men in jackboots inspected what must have been a tattered bunch. They walked up and down the lines and pointed at some children. Those selected had to go and stand away from their friends. They chose six girls; Maruška and Anička Hanfová, Marie Doležalová, Emilie Frejová, Eva Kubiková and Vera Vokatá.

The Hanf sisters - Maruška and Anička - burst into tears; they had made a promise to their parents that they would not leave their little brother. Hard to believe, but the paragons of Aryan purity and ruthlessness to whom they addressed their tearful request gave-in. Eight-year-old Vaćlav Hanf joined his sisters amongst the seven children, waved off by the eighty-one left behind as a lorry took them away. Shortly after they arrived at a camp in nearby Sporna - bunk beds and straw mattresses amongst the improvements, though the lice were just as bad. About a month later they were taken to a children's home at Puszczykówko (Puschkau, in German). There they were reunited with Hanička Śpotová and Vaśik Zelenka. They were to know nothing of those left behind in Lodz for several years.

On July 6th children from the exterminated hamlet of Ležaky joined them in Lodz, along with little Dáša Veselá, who was no longer required by the Reich for Germanization.

****

Another sunny day greeted us along the Chesterfield Canal towpath as we headed into Rhodesia. Getting lost is almost inevitable on a cycling tour, but this seemed a little much. Geographically astray maybe, but surely we had not popped through the fourth dimension? Zimbabwe, perhaps, I thought? No, it really was Rhodesia. Having spent my early teaching career in the area, a quick photo of the village name sufficed, rather than a long look at a map or a resort to GPS.

Remembering the way from memories of nearly thirty years ago is not the surest base for navigation. So much had changed. The busy little town centre in Worksop had a new alignment of roads. Familiar pubs had closed, above all Manton colliery was no more. On the whole the town had a lively feel - for eight o'clock on a summer morning - but is very much part of the country where many people have seen their old way of life disappear with opportunity slower to catch up.

I have very happy memories of North Nottinghamshire. First job, first pay-packets.

Splattering sun-screen generously over myself, whilst Mark spread his on with rather more precision - it is all that careful crafting developing a deft touch in everything - was necessary before we reached Retford. Another hot, hot day in the saddle; wonderful; Good Old England.

I declined Mark's offer to take a look at some of my old haunts, though we cycled past a few. Both the houses I had lived in were still there. Two of my favourite pubs had closed. The vast new school that had replaced at least two of the old comprehensives in the town sparkled glassily. The tree-lined main street seemed narrower, but the Market Place retained an aura of grandeur that would not be out of place in a provincial Central European city. Once the scene of Friday night fights as the Half Moon and White Hart kicked the crowds out at closing time, the hand of modern day café culture had laid claim - at least during daylight. I can't comment beyond that. We coffeed-and-caked. Vital. We would soon face a challenge.

Waving goodbye to Retford (The Royal Borough of East Retford, as it should technically be referred to - once the scene of riotous elections in the days before 1832) and shortly after passing the first house I rented in town and the estate where some of my old pupils and their parents just about managed to keep things together, is a hill. It is not a difficult hill, but comes as a surprise.

Leverton Hill rises sharply. A steady pedal attains the summit. The road was busier than I remember from previous rides - I guess there is just more in the way of motorised traffic everywhere. A bike ride into Lincolnshire from Retford always meant crossing the Trent on Dunham Bridge or Gainsborough Bridge - occasionally further north at Keadby. Back in the day, I had often thought that the old Torksey Railway Viaduct would make a grand crossing point for bikes and pedestrians and equestrians. In 2016 my wish had come true, but, former Sustrans colleague, Ed Healey, had pointed out to me that the access on the Lincolnshire side was still a footpath and required an inconvenient "lift" to get through. One of those frustrations about cycle routes in the UK. Bit by bit they develop, working towards a long-term goal but, too often, with long periods when nothing happens.

Mark and I had decided to keep to the roads. I reached the top of the hill first - not a boast, honest - and had time to snap Mark with a lorry looming behind as he crested the hill, North Notts laid out behind.

Many of the roads around here were improved between the miner's strikes of 1974 and 1984-5. Railway workers traditional support for the miners made the three power stations of Mega-Watt Valley an easy target for disruption. The government realised this. Perhaps that is another reason for the faster flow of traffic.

From the summit of the climb there is a lengthy glide towards the Trent. Leverton Windmill stands as a testament to the power of the modern world, as distant cooling towers loom behind it, though still a good distance away. Further off, the Lincoln Edge emerged from the summer haze, though Lincoln Cathedral, mounted stunningly, above the city, could not be made out. Fields of yellow and green, patches of woodland before us, blue sky above.

North Leverton with Habblesthorpe has a longer than average name, but one of the attractions of it and other villages around here is their apparent ordinariness. Do not take this as an insult. Peaceful and attractive and functional; reassuringly so.

Major river crossings generally mean main roads. There is a cycle path alongside the A631. It narrowed and became more overgrown as the river approached and the road turns from dual-carriageway to busy single-carriageway. Hey-ho. When the infrastructure really needs to be good because space is more limited, the same factor seems to prevent it; infrastructure in the UK is rarely about giving cyclists and pedestrian's priority. Still, the simple fact is that the bridge over the Trent at Gainsborough is older than the road, and so the bottleneck.

The Trent was not the widest river we would cross by a long chalk. At Gainsborough sea-going ships used to come into port to take the produce of the area out. The rich agricultural soil on both sides of the river produced not only foodstuffs, but led to the development of heavy engineering businesses that served agricultural needs. Marshall, later Fowler-Marshall and Track Marshall, once had a plant in Gainsborough. In fact, when they branched out from steam traction engines, steam-rollers and tractors, they opened a second factory to build aircrafts. Nothing remains now of the old works, which I'd cycled past when I first came to the area. There's a shopping centre, Marshall's Yard, on the site of the old Britannia Works.

We skipped along the road that runs past the old river front warehouses, into the suburbs along the river bank. Then a swift right turn away from the Trent. There's no sudden valley wall to climb - the levees are steeper than anything else hereabouts. There is no sudden change of scenery, but having started in Stoke-on-Trent, left the river as it curves south-east and north, crossed it once more at Gainsborough, we were now leaving it until we returned home.

Despite the presence of the mighty steelworks around Scunthorpe and an extractive industry that provided the raw material, and though there are now refineries and ports along the south bank of the Humber, the area has a fundamentally rural feel to it. Away from the river, we ran along woodland roads, flat and shady, climbed the occasional small rise to pass through a village that was built above the winter-floods of the olden days and came in sight of the Lincoln Edge.

For me, the Lincoln Edge had always been one of those way-markers. The surprising climb up the steep scarp may not be long or too arduous, but it is there on any journey across the county. A farm shop at the base of the Edge provided a bit of shade as well as fruit and biscuits for lunch. Over-ripe bananas were so despicably cheap that we might have eaten more had it not been for possible ill-effects, causing abandonment of bike and a sudden rush into the undergrowth. Mind you, the gentleman who took our money seemed to be making up the cost of the goods as he went along. He obviously had a liking for Mark - or maybe anyone who reduced his stock of over-ripe bananas - and gave him a discount.

Once up on the Edge a long, very long, gentle descent takes you down the valley of the River Ancholme: ours ran past quarries on dust covered roads. Away to the south, out of sight, was Lincoln, its cathedral lording it over the city from the Edge. I recalled that I'd visited Lincoln with my parents, taking in the Lincolnshire Museum. My Father had stopped to gawp at a face-digger - a sort of vertical conveyor belt with steel edged buckets, pushed onto a quarry face to excavate. Back in 1946, de-mobbed from the RAF, he had got a job with Fowler's, engineers of locomotives, steam engines and so on. A face-cutter had been the first sale he had made.

That made me feel rather old. Growing up with coal, engines, heavy engineering - making things, made me feel as if I were from another age. Time has moved on and the future looks very different. Growing up in the modern world of virtual and digital may be mystifying, but it ain't as mystifying as being on the wrong-side of middle-age as technology runs away from you. I am not nostalgic about coal-mines on the basis that I would not want my son to work down one, but should he want to become an engineer and build machines or bridges, I'd be mighty pleased. I think I'll be proud of him whatever he does, but imagine seeing a ship on the slipway and being able to say, as it slides into the water, "My son built that". (Apologies to all shipyard workers who do the actual construction work.)

Fortunately, no quarry lorry had hit me whilst I drifted away into the realms of reflection.

We picked up the road for the old market town of Brigg, or Glanford Brigg, and got our heads down for a rapid few miles. The town centre is now a pedestrian precinct and a very nice one, too. Boats dating from 900BC or thereabout have been found here and the town's past has much to do with the river - well, a ford and a brigg (derived from a norse word for jetty, but here referring to a new medieval bridge). Once the main town of the area, it is now dwarfed by the very different urban Scunthorpe. Still, it is a pretty place at the foot of the Lincolnshire Wolds.

I always like passing through Brigg, or even by-passing it on the motorway; this is because I know an "interesting" fact about Brigg. Would you like to know it? Is anyone interested? My wife, who is usually driving, was the first time and pretends to be on each occasion; my son no longer lifts his eyes from Zombie Cabbages Versus Melon Robots War XXII, or whatever his latest download is. Mark was the beneficiary today.

The first sound recording of an English folksong was made in Brigg. In 1906 Percy Grainger recorded Joseph Taylor, carpenter, steward of a local estate and parish clerk of Saxby All Saints - a village at the Wold foot a little to the north of Brigg - singing "Unto Brigg Fair". Brigg Fair was held on August 5th, if the song is reliable, which is my birthday, isn't that interesting and well-worth cycling halfway across England for, Mark? Alright.

Now, fascinating though this sort of thing might be and, please note, my wife says that she likes to cycle tour with me because it is interesting, there is only so much trivia one can take. A cycle trip with another person must involve a good deal of chat about all sorts of things, but there comes a point when enough will have been had of the other. Without resorting to Les Dawsonisms about mothers-in-law, there are few people who can converse constantly day after day. Even fewer can natter on as the miles roll past without causing mental fatigue. Put simply, every cycle-tourer in a group reaches a point when they need to be alone. That does not mean left behind or lost, it just means opening a gap wide enough to be with one's own thoughts for a few miles.

Mark let me get to the Wold top first and I tried to get a photo of him panting up the slope in the fashion of one of Marshall's old traction engines. He wasn't, so I didn't bother. So, we turned off the main drag onto a balcony road that stuck to the crest of the hill, with the open Ancholme Valley to the left, and before long, the Humber ahead.

Nearly coming to a standing stop as a right-turn took us onto an unexpected ramp up, we soon sped down one of those lovely valleys one finds in limestone country. Though gentler than the Yorkshire Wolds, the Lincolnshire Wolds are smashing for cycling and walking. At the end of this valley stood Barton-on-Humber, at the southern end of the Humber Bridge. Another progress marker on a cycling trip, it is genuinely iconic as the Gateway to Hull and the East Riding or The Gateway to Barton-on-Humber. Note: ask my good friends Simon and Ann Hawksley, residents of Hull, which is the correct description for the bridge. Ann comes from a family of Hull fisher folk; her opinion would be a strong one.

Mark wanted to take a look at the Ropewalk, in Barton. Once just that - a vital industry along the Humber bank - it is now an art gallery. Needless to say, Mark knew some of the artists, but also had some of his work in the gallery a few years ago. He did not quite get as far as sealing a new deal, but things looked good for further dialogue.

The Ropewalk provided a real sugar spike in the form of some of the sweetest cakes I have ever tasted. Having much more experience in this field than in Mark's orbit of art and, needless to say, being a bigger consumer of cakes than Mark, I can vouch for the effect.

As we left, we fell in with a local cyclist with whom we rode over the bridge, which ushered us into the outskirts of Hull. Our newly acquired friend took us to a famous viewpoint beneath the bridge deck, where one can admire the view directly between the piers that support the towering suspension system.

I'd actually seen this before. Emma, my wife, had been swimming across the Humber and I'd wandered round, eventually finding this spot. Swimming the Humber can be treacherous; tides and currents make this powerful slab of water - calm though it might look - potentially very dangerous. A lifeboat station - manned by volunteers - sits close by the bridge. The swims across are organised by the lifeboat volunteers. Mind you, someone has walked across the Humber - not using the bridge either. Details of such behaviour are to be found on information boards. Ferries once plied across the Humber between many of the towns and villages that lined the banks. Famously, Daniel Defoe spent several hours wallowing around in a rowing boat as the oarsmen attempted to reach Hull.

Loitering under a bridge could be dangerous too, or, at least, construed as suspicious. The peculiar viewpoint has its merits, but we did not spend too long there. Our guide said that he'd take us in to the city centre, though it was beyond his destination. An easy journey - Hull is fundamentally flat - I soon recognised the area where my friends, the Hawksleys lived. Sadly, we were running out of time and wanted to buy some grub to consume on the ferry.

We'd thought of stopping for fish and chips, with that Hull delicacy, chip spice. Even there we were stymied.

We arrived right in the city centre, where Queen Victoria, or rather her statue, stands atop the public lavatories in a fitting tribute to her beloved Albert, who said that if he were not a prince he should like to have been a plumber.

Hull was "undergoing regeneration". This is a phrase used by many councils for having the road and path surfaces of the city centre lifted and replaced, probably with some nice stone setts. Actually, that is unduly cynical. Hull was to be City of Culture the following year; for years it has been redeveloping itself. There is some very good cycling infrastructure - notably on the way to the ferry port - and use of the bicycle as a means of transport has never dropped as pathetically low as it has in many parts of the UK. A flat, working-class city;

cycling has always made sense. It will not prepare you for cycling in the Netherlands, but there is a tradition of cycling just as there is across the North Sea.

At the ferry port we rolled up the ramp, met a small group of local cyclists who turned out to be making one of their regular trips to the Netherlands - on this occasion to Amsterdam. More exotically, a group of young cyclists on well-laden touring bikes, were stowing their machines alongside ours. We had a little chat.

They had arrived in Hull the week before and had cycled north to Whitby, thence across the North Yorkshire Moors and the Pennines to Carlisle; through the Lake District and across the Dales to York, and returned to Hull. Not bad for a six day trip. They would load their bikes onto two cars in Rotterdam and drive home to Zwickau, in the east of Germany.

"Ah," I said, "We will be in Dresden in ten days' time." They replied that it was not far from Zwickau, but that they would be there quicker. I tried to cadge a lift, with tongue in cheek, but something was lost in translation and they looked concerned. I rushed to explain that it was a joke and that we

67

were riding to Lidice, near Prague. They knew of the village's significance, but we spoke mainly about their tour.

Many cyclists in the UK look to the near continent to find cycling Heaven, citing much more considerate driving and greater legal protection alongside all the charms of travel in foreign lands. Feeling that too many British motorists are either ignorant of cycling and cyclists or deliberately, aggressively disrespectful or even downright dangerous, they hear the gentle "toot, toot" of a French car horn as the amiable warning that a car is coming past as a breath of wind blowing from paradise.

The Zwickau posse had loved touring in England. They remarked on how friendly it was and how safe the roads were and that the drivers were generally very considerate and that the mixture of scenery was glorious. They'd even got a good word for the beer they had sampled - quite something for a German. York had been a bit too busy, but the moors and the hills of the north had been wonderful. Men after my own heart.

In our cabin we began the cycle-tourist ritual. Two hot June days in the saddle and sweaty socks do not make for happy times in a small cabin with no openable port-hole. Add shorts and shirts into the brew and action is needed. Bodies are easy to wash with just a little soap and water or a few wet wipes, but cycling gear can be a pest.

Most technical gear should dry quickly, even when hand-washed in the sink or worn into the shower and wrung out by hand. By the morning a cycling shirt will be easily dry given reasonable conditions, but padded Lycra shorts can take an age. They have a propensity to slip off anything they are draped over in the hope that air might circulate; they end up on the floor, leave puddles in the shower room or embarrassing damp patches on carpets. But the job must be done.

Scrubbed-up, a bit, we spread the laundry out as best we could and left the shower cubicle fan buzzing away. With the ship already gliding between the Humber's numerous treacherous sand-banks, we doubted that things would dry well. Were we able to utilise the outdoor seats, the railings or the mast, they'd be dry in a flash. I expected that, next morning, Rotterdam would see a mini-mobile clothes-horse passing through. Ah, real cycle touring, at last. At least the locals would be spared the sight of undergarments. That is one advantage of padded Lycra.

Getting out on deck to see Old England disappear can be done at a leisurely pace on a ferry from Hull. To the south, the Lincolnshire bank was a line of refineries and chimneys and wharfs. A far cry from the southern shore further west. Around Winterton and Alkborough, where I'd first cycled to the Humber bank many years before, it had been so quiet - yep, industrial Scunthorpe and the chemical plant at Flixborough - scene of a half-remembered disaster which I can just recall from childhood - were not far off, but at Whitton one felt that one was on the edge of the world and that one could go no further. For some strange reason - memory does this sometime - a bit of doggerel was brought to mind as my eyes turned to the northern agricultural, East Riding bank.

At Whitton Town End, brave boys, brave boys
At Whitton Town End braver boys,
At every door
There sits a whore
At Whitton town end, brave boys.

It must have come from some bit of social history I'd picked up years ago when I pursued a passion for the history of Lincolnshire and read avidly on the subject. Certainly, my experience of Whitton was very different. Utter silence.

70

Of course, Yorkshire is different to Lincolnshire, but those last few miles of farmland on the edge of the Humber and the sea looked likely to be equally short on activity of any kind. And then the land gave up, curving gently to expire as the lighthouse at Spurn Point flashed a brief goodbye as we finally left our homeland and slipped out into the open sea.

People write poetry and music about the sea; they do the same about their homelands. For the British, the two go together. The foreigners may or may not begin at Dover, but we know that beyond the sea are different languages, customs, attitudes, and that to reach them we have to cross the water. Rivalries between English, Scots and Welsh are rife; but, to my shame, I will always learn a few basic words to be able to be polite in France, Germany, Belgium, Italy or wherever I go, but I only know a few words of Welsh through regular visits - and I usually forget to say Diolch!

England, Wales and Scotland are old countries, with old awareness of themselves as nations. Along their borders blurring takes place - I have eaten deep-fried haggis in English Berwick-on-Tweed, and there are, I believe, even more significant cultural bonds - it is wonderful, what cycling introduces to you and gives you time to think it is worthwhile

71

pondering about. On the continent, many countries may have national awareness, but have often been nations for only a relatively short period or have had territory transferred along with more or less willing and happy populations. In some cases they have disappeared completely, permanently or temporarily.

The Netherlands has the oldest national anthem in the world. It celebrates William of Orange and the nation's battles to keep their independence and religious tolerance intact. The English and the Dutch have been enemies and allies; Dutch architecture can be found up and down the east coast of England and Scotland; we have much in common.

Leaving the UK a year after Scotland had voted to remain a part of the United Kingdom, but shortly before the referendum on the UK's membership of the European Union felt odd, in the sense that we might be returning to a country with a very different future to the one we were leaving. By the end of our tour the result would be in - in fact, we were in Prague when we heard the news that the UK had voted to leave. Of course, leaving the EU is not the same as casting off all ties with Europe, just as being part of it is not the same as sharing identical cultures. We can't ignore or reject centuries of cultural exchanges, of wars and trade. But it felt like that was what the UK was about to do. We had some interesting discussions about attitudes to the EU, right across Europe.

In one sense, at least, it was a pleasure to leave behind the divisive and patronising campaigning; Project Fear versus Project "Everyone else is part of an establishment conspiracy and we don't like experts" was pretty pathetic, with partial truths and insults being flung while anyone who tried to introduce some nuanced considered opinion based on a balanced assessment of the evidence could expect to be called a liar or worse, an expert, and be dismissed. Getting away from all this was a blessing. A putrid debate - whichever way one voted or whatever outcome one desired; the conduct of the campaigns and the behaviour of many leading figures in the political world during and after the vote was dismal, especially when one looks back at previous generations. But it certainly gave us something to chat about when important subjects, such as beer, bicycles and food were exhausted.

I wondered if we had become so unfamiliar with real political conflict that our sensibilities were shocked when the nastiness emerged, lulled by consensual stability in our prosperous Western European homes for many a year. Maybe, I just need a thicker skin.

Cycling is a voyage of discovery - not of judgement - but as we edged out into the grey night of the North Sea one wondered how much one's world might change during a short cycle tour.

Chapter Five

A British cyclist pedalling off the ferry at Rotterdam, if they are anything like me and visiting the Netherlands for the first time in years, may well go through a number of emotions fairly quickly. The whole experience can be disorientating, embarrassing, joyous and surreal. Those benighted foreign chaps do not do things like we do back in Blighty. They haven't for years. It's all because it is flat and they have a Dutch cycling gene and are just weird, high on cannabis smoked in Amsterdam's cafés.

The real reasons for the Netherland's magnificent cycling infrastructure are more sensible. Though Amsterdam may have a reputation for liberal attitudes to drugs, it is not widely shared in the rest of the country, as far as I have seen. Dutch people are no weirder than the British, and having been the only completely un-potty person in several places where I have worked, I should know. There is not a cycling gene in their DNA any more than there is a motoring gene in British DNA or a gesticulation gene in the make-up of Italians. True, maybe, that lack of ascents encourages everyday cycling, but I am not aware that cycling journeys are the norm in our own Fenlands. Cambridge has numerous other factors; Hull, too,

75

has decent cycling numbers by UK standards, but that is the result of a tradition of working people riding bikes as much as the flat streets of the city.

What the Dutch have is a tradition of cycling that has never gone away. At a time when motor vehicles were encouraged to take over British cities and those of many other nations, a series of deaths of children led to major protests against the way in which motor vehicles were coming to dominate Dutch cities, towns and villages. From the early 1970s onwards the Dutch decided that the built environment should be for people and not for cars; cycling was a vital part of ensuring that people of all ages could travel freely in a way that was good for the environment, community cohesion and health. They took on the car and have kept it in its place. Don't go too far. Many journeys in the Netherlands are made by car; there are lots of major roads; many Dutch people love their cars; but there are few people who have never or do not cycle at some point. Infrastructure to enable this, has been built into transport engineering in a way that is replicated in few other places. Consistently well-funded year-on-year, innovative, supported by road regulations and laws, at the forefront of every planner's mind; it is no surprise that people of all ages and abilities see that cycling is for them. It is everything that cycling in the UK is not.

The Hull to Rotterdam ferry arrives in Rotterdam in only the broadest sense. Europoort is some twenty miles from the city centre and there are several towns to cycle through first, and a ferry too. All - except for the ferry - is on wide, well-made cycle tracks with clear signage at every junction. You roll along amidst the sounds and smells of manufacturing and commerce served by the rivers and canals. It is the ships that get your attention as you ride, not the cars and lorries.

Priority is unnerving when you are not used to getting it. Motorists wonder why you do not just plunge on across the junctions. Almost all junctions that are not light-controlled or avoided by a cycle-subway, put the motor car in second place. But at the back of the British mind is always the belief that drivers will not grant you your right of way. British drivers generally are given right of way over cyclists and pedestrians. The Dutch driver has to, and they do; it takes time to get used to it, to be convinced. In fact, they often cede passage even on those odd occasions when the cyclist should give way.

I imagined that drivers were able to identify fresh-off-the-ferry-Brit-cyclists and clicked their tongues impatiently at our hesitant conduct. As for locals on their bikes, they must wonder what is going on when two middle-aged men, wearing cycle helmets, ride so quickly - these things being relative - only to slow so much at each junction, small children on the school run hot on their heels. The Dutch have a reputation for tolerance, but they can be equally forthright. However, odd looks were as far as it went.

A lady on the usual sit-up-and-beg bike, laden with a heavy-weight of cabbages in the forward basket and a sack of leeks strapped to the rear rack, whizzed past, quickly followed by a student who appeared to be taking the complete works of Shakespeare or Erasmus, or some voluminous scribbler, back to the university library. Something needed to be done to preserve my dignity.

So, I tagged on behind one of the quicker riders and learned all about inner city cycling and how the cycle lanes make it so much easier to ride than drive. By the time the glassy glitter of the hyper-modern city centre hove into sight, I'd got it pretty well off pat. My unknown and unknowing coach had taught me not to feel surprised that cars stopped for me.

Looking back, I think I was a little embarrassed by the way I could ride continuously and quickly into a major city - an impossibility in most British cities - even those with a modicum of decent infrastructure for cyclists and pedestrians. By the time we started trying to escape Rotterdam, any feeling of guilt was long gone. Dutch city cycling breeds freedom and confidence.

Our map did not really show the suburbs of the city. We knew the next towns, but these were not signposted consistently. Ah! We thought, something less than perfect. The last time I'd had such a good and pointless gloat was when an ultra-efficient - by which I mean stereotypical German-in-public-office - tourist office representative in Nuremberg gave me the summer public transport connections from the Hauptbahnhof to Playmobil Land. It turned out that the summer timetable had expired six weeks earlier. We walked the final two kilometres.

We did not have to walk much in Rotterdam, but a temporary feeling that everything was not quite so heavenly in the cycling paradise was reassuring. It did not last long. At major junctions there seemed to be large maps showing key routes, so we were able to break down the out of town destinations by checking the suburbs en-route.

Why not use the Satnav? Well, we did on many occasions during the trip, especially for escaping cities. Trouble was, the SatNav tended to go round the houses - sometimes - run out of charge or lose connectivity. Just as maps could be too detailed (an odd thing to say, but where there are so many cycle routes, specific routes can be hard to keep track of) and to take too many on a long trip consumes space and adds weight. Even the sun went in when we wanted to get a basic idea of direction. So, over the whole trip, we combined the primitive with the modern and got by with everything from downloaded interactive maps of the Czech Republic to asking passers-by and guessing. There were also natty examples of sharp-witted map-work. Despite all this, we always ended up in the right place.

As tourists, though relatively quick-pedalling ones, we needed to orientate ourselves, especially where diversions occurred. When a road or cycle path is under repair the Dutch do not just stand a warning sign in the cycle lane and dump everyone into the carriageway, oh no. However, when you have not seen this with your own eyes you may be hesitant to believe that all you are told is true. A lady of a certain age pedalled rhythmically past us as we stood eyeing up a diversion that went from cycle path onto a slip road leading to a major road as it approached a bridge. She stared at us, possibly wondering what we were doing hanging about there when surely we should know that the cycle path was just continuing. Feeling a little embarrassed, we followed her, noticing that further back, the slip-road had been closed to motor vehicles. Yes folks, the road had been turned into the cycle route. Even better was ahead. Toiling up to the bridge behind the lady on her shopper, we discovered that one entire lane of the dual-carriageway over the bridge had been given over to cyclists, pedestrians and builders. The cycle lane was narrower, but once again, the motor vehicle had been compelled to share the space.

It has to be said that when the Dutch decide to do something they are capable of great collective effort. I suppose that this comes from a history during which they have fought off the Spanish, French and the sea, especially the sea, and all-comers (including the English). When cycling infrastructure is built, as it always is, it is built to a high standard, consistently. It may not be quite as vital to survival as dykes and sluices - we rode past many and their scale is incredible - but it does give each small town on the way to Rotterdam (and I guess everywhere else) a sociable, human atmosphere. Rotterdam is the second-city of the Netherlands, but cycling into its heart is simple and no one seems to think doing so is either heroic or suicidal.

Largely, rebuilt after the Second World War, Rotterdam's commercial heart is a mass of glass. Reflections and a blue sky merge into a disturbingly surrealistic gallery of modernist art, with each piece on the grand scale. As a lover of medieval timber-framed houses jumbled around higgledy-piggledy narrow alleys, this is not really my thing, but you have to admire the scale and the foresight of the town-planners and architects. So impressed was I that my front wheel skidded against the kerb of the cycle lane. I attempted to avoid embarrassment only with a quick-witted lurch and a nonchalant survey of the cityscape. Neither fooled the onlookers.

Lots of infrastructure took us out into the inner, then the outer, suburbs. All very easy cycling, though it took us a while to get the right river crossing and to pick up the signs for the old town of Schoonhoven. Along the way, one could not help but wonder at the mind-set that builds broad cycle lanes next to largely traffic-free roads. Maybe everyone was lounging around with a cold beer as the flat-land wobbled in the heat haze.

It was not until we had left the docks, the suburbs and the ultra-modern city centre behind that I recalled having read about the destruction of Rotterdam in May 1940. It was a turning point in many ways and one which puts into broader perspective the bombing of cities such as Hull, which we had passed through, and Dresden, where we would spend our last night in Germany.

With characteristic determination the small Dutch Army and Air Force had put up much greater resistance than the German's expected when they invaded the Netherlands in May 1940. The outcome was inevitable, given the strength of the opposing forces. Such things had not cowed the Dutch in the sixteenth and seventeenth centuries, and the twentieth century descendants continued in the same fashion.

The defenders of Rotterdam held the German army. Whilst many civilians left, fighting continued as the Dutch attempted to hold a much stronger enemy at bay, with the river as their frontline. Although negotiations were underway for a ceasefire, a major bombing raid was planned, targeting the medieval city centre and the docks as well as, inevitably, residential areas.

The Rotterdam Blitz remains controversial, but does not get the same recognition as the later Allied air raid on Dresden. It seems that although a ceasefire had just been agreed, the planes were in the air and were not informed, either accidentally or deliberately. Red flares were fired, but since these were also used by German troops to identify parts of the city they had taken, any launched with the intention of recalling the bombers failed.

The raid lasted barely fifteen minutes. It would be easy to dismiss the death toll of somewhere around 900 - some of whom would have been combat personnel - as very low, compared to later raids on Hamburg, Dresden and the V2 campaign, or earlier attacks on Warsaw. Even if one casually dismisses this, as is easy to do at a geographical or chronological distance, the 900 or so who were killed could have been much higher. Around 85,000 people were made homeless, seventy schools and four hospitals were destroyed.

Flamed by high winds the next day, a firestorm developed, destroying almost all of the city centre. At the time, it was portrayed in Allied propaganda as typical Hun barbarism, whilst Goebbels blamed the Dutch for not surrendering when they had the chance. However, though a military target, the progress in negotiations and the ceasefire - which was imminent, even if news of its signing had not reached everyone, makes it hard to reject the notion that this was an example to encourage a Dutch surrender. German military units were needed further south, and when the government of the Netherlands did not surrender immediately, it only took a threat to treat Utrecht in the same way, to persuade them that they only had a choice between giving-in and seeing their country destroyed.

Just as importantly, for the longer term, the RAF altered its official policy the day after the raids. Initially stating that it would only aim to hit military targets - whilst accepting that civilian casualties were a possible consequence - two days later it attacked factories in the Ruhr, with the inevitable civilian casualties. It was a change of policy that was inevitable in any case; twentieth century war required twentieth century industry and the workforce were, albeit indirectly, just as important as the combat forces. In any case, heavy bombers were incapable of the accuracy neat distinctions between civilian, military and industrial, required.

On a journey into Central Europe, I could not help but ask myself why it was that the high casualties in the September 1939 air raid on Warsaw (the exact numbers are hard to discover, but are likely to have been around 20,000) did not cause the RAF official change of policy, but the 900 or so deaths in the Rotterdam Blitz did? Mind you it may well be overstating the cause of the change of policy. It is true that we Brits are brought up with a western European view of the Second World War and, in Britain, of our part in resisting Nazism. Nothing wrong with that, but there is, perhaps, a lack of the broader perspective. Thinking about these things without knowing the answers, is one way I pass time whilst pedalling along on a long tour. However, it only lasted for so long.

****

Time to Knooppunt!

Taking up the well-known Dutch cycling activity of Knooppunting brought a great deal of pleasure, as well as

86

further insight into cycle culture. Cycle touring is nothing if not educational. If you are unfamiliar with the Knooppunt system - to be found in Flanders as well as the Netherlands - it is, at least in principle, a work of true genius combining practicality and simplicity. A series of numbered points are marked on a map and posted on the ground, sometimes on a tall pole, others on a stubby little marker resembling a milestone. Look at your map, note down the numbers of the points and off you go. Reach one point and the direction to the next is indicated. Cycling by numbers. Easy. Well, it is, until, cracking along at a merry pace as we occasionally managed, one rushes by unnoticed. Or nature intervenes and lush undergrowth obscures the sign. Mind you, that does not often happen and with distance to the next sign marked it is easy to make an estimate or even an accurate measurement of the whereabouts of the next "punt".

The considerate designers had even placed noticeboards showing area maps. Hurrah! We could memorise lists of points and roll onward. Simple enough when the numbers are consecutive; harder when they leap about or reach the edge of another area where a number might be repeated. Healthy mind, healthy body, if you can manage it. Rather like trying to do Sudoku without pen and pencil, or grid, or in my case, ability. Still we had a good go and it worked pretty well.

We had decided to follow some "tourist routes" which turned out to be totally different to the broad cycle paths of Rotterdam and the roadsides. The purpose of these was to take one into "nature" and shun the trappings of smooth asphalt. They succeeded admirably. Sandy tracks made for slower progress. Lower gear, steady spinning and close attention to the occasional ruts. Pleasant enough, but things were getting hot. A return to smoother tracks was a relief; the setts of Schoonhoven a pleasure and the sight of cafés clustered around the old canal of this former inland port, akin to a vision of an oasis. Wonderful.

We selected the Blauwe Douve café in Schoonhoven, plonking ourselves under a large parasol at a table with a menu. The waitress arrived. Mark ordered water, I ordered beer and coffee (separately). We both went for sandwiches. Delicious. A discussion ensued on the merits of beer, water and coffee to hydrate. I maintain that whilst water may be best, the fact that coffee and alcohol are both diuretics does not mean that they cannot hydrate. Moreover, after two bottles of water, there needs to be something to satisfy the taste buds - my opinion. It was a fairly pointless discussion, but there was no time to order another beer to form a stronger conclusion.

More remarkable than the efficacy of the wares of the Blauwe Douve was the throng of cyclists who glided across the small square. Three MAMILS (Middle-Aged Men In Lycra) drew up to an adjacent café, but the majority of bicycle riders were on their way home from school. It seems that from the age of eight or nine children were allowed, by their parents, to risk their lives by doing the school-run alone, by bicycle and, Heaven forfend, helmet-less. Do they not realise they are about to die? Is their neglect such that they cannot, for the sake of their young ones' lives, ram their cars to within a centimetre of the school front door?

Of course they aren't; of course they don't. Instead, using the high quality infrastructure and amongst drivers who understand cycling, the children arrive in a healthy way, primed to learn, having been independent and responsible. Easy really. Teachers too, I shouldn't wonder. Skills and habits for life. How about it OFSTED? A bicycle is one of the few things a young person is ever fully in control of; and cycling is one of the few activities in which they are responsible, both for themselves and those around them. Talk about life skills and qualities.

And did this lot bear their sorrowful burden of getting to school with their mates lightly? Of course they did! They chattered in groups, they laughed, they rode across the square on bikes that were just everyday run-a-rounds, teenage boys on machines so uncool that were cycling not such an everyday activity they'd have died of embarrassment. Pink frames, wicker baskets, old black rattlers worthy of the veteran circuit, bikes too big and bikes too small. No Hi-Viz, no worry, no helmets, little traffic, good infrastructure, a culture of riding the bicycle as a perfectly normal activity. A little ironic for us, given our notion that cycling across Europe was notable.

We left the centre of Schoonhoven along the flower-box-lined banks of the canal that had once linked the river to the town centre - the artery of commerce in the glory days of a little Dutch town. The river we found ourselves cycling along the bank of, a few moments later, remains an artery of commerce. The Nederrijn is one of the five branches of the Rhine that fan out to form the delta of a river that has come half way across Europe. For centuries it has been a highway and even now, in the age of the plane and the long distance trucker, broad-beamed boats chunk along between ports inland and the coast, passing quietly, hereabouts, through the pastures and scattered copses. The bovines paid no attention to them, but for the middle-aged English midlander, boats bigger than the colourful narrowboats on the canal are a sight to see.

OK, I like trains too, not to mention, planes - well they are impressive, whilst trains and boats are things of beauty. Cars with running boards are fine, those without are not of any interest to me, though they can, admittedly, be very useful.

Bicycles? Can be things of beauty, but many are not. Still, so long as their owners like them, who am I to judge? Most Dutch bikes are a mixture of tradition and function, with an emphasis on comfort and utility for people on bicycles. The cyclists - the club riders and road racers spend a lot more and are as racy as any and, doubtless, as pricey. Then there are the amazing constructions of manufacturers such as van Huljstein of Arnhem. Carefully crafted steel sculptures on wheels, elegantly modest, but guaranteed to be the talk of the ride.

Riverside sights on a hot afternoon; teenagers swimming in the shallows, young cycle-racers hitting the road and small groups of ladies of a certain age steadily turning the pedals. The latter appeared to be returning from Kaffee met Gebacke or some such delight. Unrushed, they convoyed along in small groups, rather like caravans on the Silk Road; they approached at a stolid but regular cadence, passed by without a word, and disappeared with the same dependable rhythm en-route to an oasis.

A line appeared on the horizon, shocking us out of a heat-induced idyll. For once, it was not a dyke. It was a hill, low but real. The shock of changing gear transformed the ride. More trees, market gardens, very mild ascents and descents, but occasional gear changes! One no longer felt foolish for having more than a three speed hub. And shade!

We found two cars that were blocking a cycle lane. "God, these Dutch must really hate cyclists", we pathetically declared in unison. We weren't convinced and there was nobody else in earshot.

Time was passing by and a century of miles was on the cards. Dinner was a prospect, but Arnhem seemed to get no closer.

Riding past a roadside stall selling fresh strawberries and cherries, we both looked resolute to continue towards our goal - just as those ladies of a certain age seemed to be. A second stall soon followed and we looked at each other. We rode on, though both thought we might stop if there was a third stall. When the next, as it turned out last, stall appeared, I rode on, but was perfectly happy when Mark called out and I pulled over. Cherries and strawberries.

The stall-holder fetched some chairs. Perhaps we looked knackered. In fact, I am sure we did. The fruit was sweet, the best - a sure sign that we were knackered. How good does fresh fruit taste? Take a long ride on a hot day and relax at a roadside fresh-fruit kiosk in Gelderland. Then you'll know.

Approaching Arnhem, a longer climb or two dragged the journey out a bit, but getting through the suburbs and into the city centre was as easy as following the cycling infrastructure. Sadly, there was no time to visit the war memorials to our left as we entered the city. Dinner was what we wanted; history could wait.

Arnhem, like Nijmegen, was a strategic hub as the allies fought their way towards Germany in 1945. As a result the town centre is new. The inappropriately named Old Dutch Hotel stands amidst concrete and glass on the modern plaza opposite the railway station, where buses pull in and BMXers bounce about and twist in the air. Quite a show and very humbling when it comes to bike control. Please note, that there are many disciplines in BMX cycling and "bouncing" and "twisting" are not amongst them.

Comfy rooms, without being excessively expensive, city centre location, quiet road outside, friendly welcome and bikes stowed in the cellar. A satisfying, sweaty day. What more could one ask for? Well, disregarding the obvious - beer - what I really wanted was a hearty salad and some dinner.

What could be better than the restaurant next door? Well, we tucked in to the food and chatted to the waitress. We were both intrigued by a drawing on the wall consisting of caricatures of 70s and 80s rock stars with a few others thrown in. We began to identify them. Mark had been into punk rock as a teenager (guess it was a late teenager) and is still into a wide variety of more or less popular music. I preferred old style R&B and cool 50s Doo-Wop sounds and all sorts of stuff - though I prefer Sibelius, Elgar, Rachmaninov and Vaughan Williams for general listening. Still, we did pretty well and managed to argue only occasionally about some long-haired icon. When we were finally flummoxed and could manage no more, we asked. The waitress was unable to help, tending to question our positive identifications, so we had another beer and then went back to the hotel for a sound night's sleep.

Actually, we sat up for a while. Mark read and I worked on a blog post. We both drank copious amounts of water. Surprising how much one can dehydrate when cycling on the flat. By the way, blogging was something I had promised to do. So I did. It was a mistake and not a promise I shall make again when moving on every day and wanting to see a little of each day's destination. If I do, I shall invest in a hi-powered, small laptop. Waiting for the device to load the blog site, process a photo or simply gain access to the internet was a long-winded affair. Good job the blog was witty and well-informed, hey?

Eventually lights out, window open, I fell asleep to the gentle rattle of those BMXers bouncing around the square. There was barely any other sound on that Tuesday night in Arnhem. Surprise, surprise, not even snoring.

Chapter Six

Many a clichéd cycle tour blog, some written by me, has begun by stating that it looked as if it were going to be another fine day. So, here we go again. It looked as if it were going to be another blisteringly hot day. And, remarkably, it turned out so; there was no thunderstorm in the evening.

It was just the sort of day when I would, traditionally, have made a really early start and had a bit of a siesta around the middle of the day. There's always a bit of a delay when you are having breakfast as well as bed, and when you need to get into the cellar to retrieve your bike from its secure overnight berth. Even so, on many a tour - on foot as well as by bike - a pretty prompt start has paid dividends later. Hostels or campsites are even better; slipping away in the early light of dawn without waking later-risers takes care, but with practice has become a forte. There's nothing like a few miles before breakfast - or even second breakfast - and a mile in the morning is worth two in the afternoon...

I have trotted those phrases out to a number of cycling and walking companions. Most do not share my preference for early mornings. They seem to think it is just prejudice. There are practical advantages to early starts. In hot weather it is logical to avoid the heat of the day. If anything goes wrong during the day, there's more time to deal with it. And then there's the freshness of the air in the early morning, the dew scenting the air, the gentler rays of the rising sun...

It falls on deaf ears, in general. No telling some folk.

In any case, Mark has a more fastidious approach to breakfast. We've discussed the predominance of meat and pastry over fruit and dairy on my plate compared to Mark's. Savouring the flavours and trying a taste of everything on offer takes time, and Mark likes to take it. Important decisions have to be made between crème fraiche and Quark, not to mention comparisons with previous days' buffets.

Mark also has a much neater and more fastidious attitude to packing luggage. My method involves putting clothes into one bag, day stuff into another, books and maps into another, all the electrical gubbins I was carting about on this trip into a fourth, and so on. Each is then stuffed into the panniers. Clothes and so on at the bottom, waterproofs, lock and food at the top; maps, wallet etc. in the bar-bag. I stuff: Mark folds and places.

97

Early starts were out of the question. It is not much of a problem to adjust to later starts, though I still find late afternoon cycling harder than early morning riding. Yes, this could be because I have already ridden a long way. What I mean is that I prefer the morning.

Anyway, setting off from just opposite the main bus and train stations and getting out of the city centre and over the river held none of the nastiness that rush hour cycling can bring into the brightest morning in the UK. As the flow of cyclists came into town, we rolled easily out, crossed the bridge and picked up a cycle track towards Huissen. This was a little out of the way, but looked more peaceful than a direct route.

Arnhem stood across the river, modernly spruce on its low hills, giving safety from the swollen Rijn, re-crossing the river by chain ferry brought home just how much water was coming down from the heart of Europe. Car and bikes loaded, the shallow draught platform was hauled upstream into the current, a wide parabola bringing it safely across the wake of a heftily-laden barge and onto the landing ramp on the far bank.

Though surroundings were rural, there were views of the city over the river as we ran between the IJssel - as wide as the Trent at Gainsborough, but only a tributary of one branch of the Rijn - and the suburb of Westervoort. There'd been plenty of pleasant riverside pastures populated by contented bovines between Rotterdam and Arnhem, but there was a more rural feel as we headed eastward. Towns became smaller, local centres rather than suburbs and the electric grannies became more numerous. Mark coined the epithet "electric granny". To him goes the credit and on him be heaped the opprobrium.

Progressing at a rigorously steady pace on utility bikes with power-assist, the "electric grannies" moved in groups along the cycle tracks. None wearing anything that would identify them as a "cyclist" when they got off the bike to partake of the goodies in store for elevenses, they epitomise much that is desirable in cycling. It is something that everyone and anyone can do without buying any special gear - though a bicycle is obviously advantageous - as an everyday activity. Cycling does not have to be a gruesome challenge or require sponsorship for a good cause; it is normal, only requiring a café, a friend to visit, or a nice day.

"Electric grannies" predominated, but some of the posses had an "electric grandad" in tow. Without exception, the male of the species rode at or, at least very much toward, the back of the group. Male chauvinists might suggest that this indicated the simplicity of the Knooppunt system and the excellence of the signage. Given the steely visages of the electric grannies we passed, I should not care to say so - even if I were speaking in English and they only understood Dutch. No, these ladies are magnificent ambassadors for cycling - as are the men they drag along behind them. They are a testament to the success of Dutch cycling culture - and, at the same time, one of the reasons for it. The area is popular with German cyclists of a certain age too. Those Oms and Omas love their Omabikes.

Of course, cycle sport is popular, very popular, in the Netherlands. At the other end of the spectrum to the "electric grannies" the sports riders are the "cyclists" as opposed to "people on bicycles". Approaching the attractive riverside town of Doesburg, a mid-week club group crossed the main road opposite the cycle track we were emerging from. Being a Wednesday, I assumed that this was the equivalent of a "Wednesday Wrinklies" run. I take the phrase from the description given to themselves by a group of retired cyclists in North Staffordshire; I would not dare call them such, though, given his "Electric Grannies", Mark may be less restrained. We will both be amongst them soon -"Wrinklies" that is. Like this bunch, they ride as a tight group and, I guess this Dutch group cover similar eighty mile day runs. If they do not, then they looked as if they should.

As clearly as the "electric grannies" were casual, club uniform identified these wiry warriors as "cyclists" akin to any cycling club group anywhere in the world. They all wore helmets. Those who advocate compulsory helmet use often fail to differentiate between people cycling alone at a gentle pace and speedier club persons travelling at 20mph plus, inches from the wheel of the rider in front, in a peloton where one mistake can have an impact on the whole group. Yet, they, of course, used the cycling infrastructure too, where it ran along the main road into town, mixing with more disorganised, informal "people on bicycles".

How would that go down with cyclists in the UK? Would we swallow compulsory use of cycling infrastructure? To be honest, after weighing it up, the issue does not really arise. UK cycling infrastructure is neither extensive enough or of sufficiently consistent quality. Until it is, compulsion is

101

inappropriate. Whether it is desirable or not, is another matter. As some say, we already have a cycling network - it is called the road. A road, which many would-be cyclists feel is too dangerous to ride.

At Doesburg we turned away from the IJssel. Numerous cyclists used the cycle paths to Zehlem and Lichtenvoorde, but most were on their way to or from school, work or the shops. The leisure groups were replaced by individuals riding for utility - with a few notable exceptions, such as us.

I'd not like to give the impression that we were cycling through unattractive countryside. The cycle paths were often along avenues of trees by the side of almost unused roads. Yet, we'd spent a day and a half on the flat with attention held by the Waal or the Neder Rijn or the IJssel, by the swollen waters that were pouring down to the North Sea, by the barges chugging against the current or being swept along to Rotterdam. Visually I find such scenes compelling. However dimly some people might regard such behaviour, cycling along the banks of a big river is fun. They also stimulate mentally - helpful when pedalling steadily on; what are the boats carrying, from where, for who, to what destination; where did the rain fall, which spring or pool was the source of that stream, where had it lost its identity, merging to flow past castle walls, through cities and settlements?

Rivers give the impression of permanence in transit, as highways and barriers they unite and divide. In fact, there are few that have not been messed about by humankind - especially in the Netherlands. Water rules, it must be adapted to or guided, even mastered. Sluices, pumps, barriers and locks on a scale not seen in the UK, are the reason for the Netherlands existence in its current state. For the fan of civil engineering this is heavenly cycling.

Away from the rivers, the Dutch countryside was pleasant, as we headed slowly east. The big waterways were left behind; no more locks for the barges; no more vast sluices to hold back the water. I was ready for lunch.

Rolling to a halt in Zelhem, we found a bakery, selling all kinds of breads and pastries. Mark, as ever the good conscience, went off to buy tomatoes and cheese whilst I waited for a sort of sausage meat pasty to be warmed up. OK, he blotted his copy book by purchasing a bottle of beer, but no one was really too bothered and, he said, it was very flavoursome. We picnicked on some benches by the side of the cycle track, looking out over the municipal sports ground, shaded all round by tall trees that rustled gently.

Zelhem was full of witches, floating about above the high street or decorating the shops, flying round the church, sitting on brooms on plinths. Also clogs. Not real clogs on Dutch feet - I have never seen a Dutchman or Dutchwoman wearing clogs, other than in some bizarre folk-theatre performance at a tulip festival near Amsterdam many years ago - but ceramic clogs poking into flower beds and such like.

Actually, the statues, sculptures, representations, were not of witches in general, though the clogs were definitely clogs. No, they were of one particular witch, a Zelhem resident by the name of Smoks Hanne. The fact that her besom is flying brush first may be charm, or maybe she was just one of Satan's less competent offspring. Actually, she is remembered in car rallies, a cycle route and, it seems, at every opportunity in Zelhem and its surrounds, as a sort of natural healer. Apparently she lost her clogs whilst in flight, some say accidentally, others say in a fit of rage, around the tower of the Lambertskerk. Doves now occupy the holes they made in the roof.

104

I'd initially wondered if there was some link between Zelhem and Salem, Massachusetts. Seems that the name Zelhem derives from "heim" meaning "home" and "sales" meaning "house"; the "house at home"; a place where people feel at home. Good old Smoks Hanne does not seem to have been in the same situation as the tragic women executed in the famous seventeenth century witch hunt. She is remembered as a nineteenth century herbalist, very much the white witch rather than a victim of frenzied misogyny fuelled by religious mania.

The beer was not to blame for missing a hidden Knooppunt, with a subsequent detour until we retraced our steps to find it. Groenlo was the last town in the Netherlands for us. Rural lanes took us across the border, though we did not know it. The first clue that we were in Germany was the appearance of a street name in gothic lettering.

Cycling remained much the same; the gentle North European Plain stretches on. The arrival of gothic script alone marked another mental stage on the journey. A return shall be made to the Netherlands on another trip. I like it; and not just for the obvious wonders of water and drainage engineering. A shame they have to celebrate any hill that reaches over

100m, but amongst the flat-lands there's a lot of variety. It feels like a homely place where, despite there being political extremes, there is a consensus that common cause is a good thing in many spheres. Be it seeing off the Spanish, keeping the sea at bay, guiding the waterways to make them helpful or building a cycle network to keep towns and cities happy haunts for people rather than motor racing tracks or car parks. The Dutch seem to want to make things homely. Despite being densely settled by humans and intensively farmed, wild-flowers flourish, cycling and walking are genuinely popular; solar and wind-power are encouraged; water is managed.

This is not tree-hugging environmentalism, it is hard-edged practicality. Getting to grips with the situation as it is seems to me to be a Dutch characteristic. My wife once introduced me to some Dutch acquaintances, an elderly married couple. Exactly how these two had ever got together is not easy to fathom. She was a feisty Dutch Indonesian, a feminist and campaigner; he had been born into a farming family and ran a business, having already had a career as an artillery officer in the Dutch Army. Somehow they managed to tick along; I once heard her tell him to turn his hearing-aid on. He asked why. She said that it would enable him to have a conversation. He asked what conversations he ever had that were worth having. They had both made their minds up.

He once told me, as he tucked into his regular dinner of braised beef and gherkins (proper food for a Dutch farmer, in his opinion), how, during the Second World War, he had, as a teenager, got involved in the Resistance Movement. During the Allied invasion he and a friend had been sent to plant some explosives. Swimming back across the river in the dark, they were shocked to find a German patrol on the bank. Floating with the strong current, to avoid detection, they were pushed into the bank further downstream. To their even greater shock, it was an area they knew to be mined. I looked amazed, but a smile spread across his broad face; "We weren't scared. I was with my friend, Ton. I told him he could go first. Someone had to."

In every sense, the Dutch have striven hard to make their homeland homely and their cycling easy.

****

After being separated from their children, most of the Lidice women were taken to Ravensbruck Camp, fifty-five miles north of Berlin, near the town of Fürstenburg. The camp had been opened in 1939, as a concentration camp; political, social and racial prisoners. Victims of Nazism, all were used as forced labour. Death might come from exhaustion or disease, from a random beating on the whim of a guard, or by removal to a death camp when frailty, fatigue and age took their toll. Amongst these were some of the Lidice women.

There's not much to write about concentration camps and death camps that has not been better said by survivors and experts. There is no denying their existence nor that the Germans knew they were there - though death camps were initially situated outside the bounds of pre-war Germany. They are a blot on the World's history - though sadly not as exceptional as we might think. It is worth remembering that Britain's ally, Good Old Uncle Joe Stalin, presided over the Gulag system. The biggest concentration camp of the Second World War was run by the USSR, not Germany. But he was on our side. One might even consider that the British, Spanish and others, also made use of concentration camps, at different times. The worst European atrocities of the 1930s were undertaken by the Soviet Union, not the Germans.

Ravensbruck Camp grew as the war went on. In addition to the manufacture of clothing for soldiers on the Eastern Front - straw-stuffed boots and suchlike - major engineering companies set up factories building specialist equipment. Added to this, many women performed tasks such as cleaning, road-building (women were yoked to heavy rollers to flatten the surface) and so on. Able to work equalled allowed to live; unable to work bought a ticket on the next train to Auschwitz or Majdanek.

Able to work meant struggling by on a starvation diet, strength to face up to long hours of labour followed by sleep in squalid, disease-ridden huts, getting-by as best you could as your mother, aunts and grandmothers deteriorated, until a white card labelled them as unable to work and destined for the gas chamber. And all the time, there must have been distress at the unknown fate of the children and the menfolk. For three years the Lidice women fought through physical hardship and nagging mental anguish. Three years of desperate labour and fear, without knowing for sure what had happened to their homes and all those things that make a home.

Miloslava Suchánková recalled, in Eduard Stehlík's "Memories of Lidice", that she was not alone in dreaming of her village; on waking to another hard-day of labour, they'd often exchange the same story. They knew nothing. The prisoners detailed to organise new arrivals to the camp warned the new internees during their initial bath; there are women here from Lidice, do not tell them anything you know about the fate of their loved ones and their village.

Replies to the monthly letters the women were allowed to write also hid the ghastly truth. Relatives told them that the men were in concentration camps and that they had heard from the children who were in Poland. The latter was true - the children's sad last letters asking for clothes and a kind word and something to use as nappies for the youngest had arrived at the houses of aunts, uncles and grandparents who lived away from Lidice. As silent months dragged by with not another word they must have feared the worst, but maintained the white lie.

Exactly what the Lidice women held in Ravensbruck, or those sent to work in other smaller camps in other parts of Germany, believed had happened, is hard to tell. Whether they believed the news in the letters they opened each month

110

with so much hope and fear in their hearts, or not, they had hope; and the flame of hope burns, however much it flickers. From the day of arrival, delousing and the humiliating examination, to the day the Death March departed, they comforted each other and made friends with other victims of Nazism and misfortune, in the hope, even certainty, that one day they would return home and life would return to normal.

Miloslava Suchánková points out that Lidice women showed extraordinary resilience compared to other Ravensbruck prisoners; "… out of that spine-chilling number of 92,000 women who died in Ravensbruck, only 49 were from Lidice, which was one quarter; while it was two thirds for all the others who ever passed through the gate of the camp. At the same time, a great proportion of our death toll were very old women who had suffered from various diseases at home in Lidice."

Whatever hope they had must have been tempered by news brought by late arrivals. Most of the women arrived at Ravensbruck on June 14th. Seven women with children under one year of age had been promised during the awful scenes at Kladno High School that they would be allowed to stay with their children. They travelled to Ravensbruck via a

111

month's stay in the Small Fortress at Terezin (Theresienstadt). The place gained a terrible reputation for atrocities committed by Nazis to Jews and others. Here the very little children were separated from their mothers. The message for the rest of the Lidice women was that they had been utterly deceived by the promises of the Gestapo in Kladno.

Later on the four Lidice women who were pregnant on June 10th arrived at the camp; two in September and two in October. Leaving their children in a Prague orphanage, they could only confirm that the word of a Gestapo officer counted for nothing. The remaining woman from Lidice had arrived in August; Marie Rákosová had been in hospital on June 10th.

While some of the women may have feared the worst, they all still had hope. Failure to grasp how ruthless and inhuman the Nazis could be is a common theme. Much of Europe could simply not accept that the reported atrocities were possible or that anyone could stoop to such depths, even in war. False reporting of "Hun" atrocities during the Great War led to scepticism; propaganda in 1914-18 did not serve the victims of the Holocaust or the common folk of Europe well in 1939. The very existence of death camps, let alone their true function were initially too far beyond even the worst excesses of European history to be credible to the mind of the human in the street. Had Lidice been destroyed in 1939 and not 1942 and had the Nazis not made such a noise about it, reports of that too, may have been ignored by many.

None would have ignored the murder immediately after birth of the child born in Ravensbruck on October 28th 1942 to Františka Hroníkova, from Lidice. October 28th was the Czechoslovak National Day. There was no-one, of course, to tell.

The daily jeopardy of existence in the camp was made worse by random beatings by the SS guards. Having witnessed a Polish prisoner being bludgeoned to death with a large pair of tailors scissors, Miloslava Suchánková realised just how thin had been the thread by which her life hung at the hands of the guards. The Polish woman's crime a minor misdemeanour and a face that looked as if it were smiling.

The first Lidice woman to die in Ravensbruck was Marie Šroubková. Having gone insane, she was briefly used for medical experiments. She died in September 1942. In March 1943 Marie Hanzliková died in the camp. She was eighty-seven. Others were transported to death camps, presumably amongst them "Granny" Verunková; her daughters had carried her through the camp gates in a chair they had brought from home. Chronic rheumatism had prevented her from walking for twenty years. Such were the enemies from which the Herrenvolk felt the need to defend itself.

After the Red Army liberated Auschwitz in 1945 a gas chamber was built in Ravensbruck. Life became even more precarious. I once heard a Jewish survivor of Auschwitz say that such dire straits made them understand what it was to live for one minute and what they might do to survive for one minute more, and that if one has never been in that situation then one will never understand the imperative to survive for the next sixty seconds. The will-power of the survivors to hold on was tested again when, with the Red Army getting closer and closer, the prisoners were led away on, what became known as, a Death March.

One hundred and fifty women from Lidice were part of the Death March. Three did not survive. Only hope can have fortified them for the journey, even the old and frail, the exhausted and ill. With little food and poorly clad and shod, they were marched 150 kilometres to Schwerin. Three days into the march the SS guards fled. The women were free. Just like that. They did not even have to take a "single bound".

A few days later they were officially liberated when Red Army soldiers found them sheltering in the forest. No ceremony, no great decrees. Most headed for a "reception camp" for displaced persons at Neu Brandenburg. Amongst those millions of people milling around Europe seeking news of loved ones or a way to get back home, the Lidice women were driven on by their desire to return home and find their children and menfolk. Such was their ignorance and love.

Chapter Seven

Our German journey commenced at Zwillbrock.

No doubt, everyone will be desperate to know whether the cycling infrastructure deteriorated once we departed Netherlands Heaven. Well, you'll just have to contain yourselves. Same with regard to "electric grannies".

Stereotypical German persons exist to the same extent that stereotypical English persons exist. In other words, they do not really; but many of us have characteristics that we inherit or grow up with which are dependent on social mores and environment during our upbringings.

So, German stereotype number one; Germany is well organised. Nothing to be ashamed of there, you say. Quite. I always feel a sense of order in Germany. The public transport in Nuremberg always works smoothly and is seriously integrated; cycle lanes must be used, where they exist; Nuremberg Bratwurst are sold in threes; the beer is brewed within the laws of the Reinheitsgebot - only it isn't. No, I am not denying that the trams run on time, merely that things are not as simple as they seem. There are anarchists and those who would subvert conformity. When the Bavarian pure beer law was adopted by unified Germany in 1871, it caused consternation amongst brewers, especially in the north and west of Germany. In fact, even though it was not fully adopted until the time of the Weimar Republic (1918-33), it led to the extinction of many regional brewing styles (black beers, fruit beers, non-Pilsener style beers in general), though some demonstrated stubborn resistance to authority. Nor were the resistors crushed. Post re-unification, a series of court cases over the right of a monastic brewery to sell its "Black Abbot Beer" became known as the "Beer Wars". After a period during which the beer could be sold but not labelled as beer, the forces of uniformity were defeated; Schwarzer Abt Bier may now be bought in good conscience by both anarchists and conformists alike.

Cycling and wandering round bits of Germany, occasionally visiting bars and chatting to locals, one thing seems to unify Germans, beer drinking: disunity comes from the fact that they all think that their local beer is best. This can get quite parochial - beer pump rather than parish pump arguments are, in my experience, not uncommon, and can become quite vigorous. On one such occasion the only way to halt the rant about how much Tucher Weissbier was better than Lederer

Weissbier, was to point out to the enthusiast that he was sitting in the Lederer Kulturbrauerei and drinking the hated product. This was, he declared, "The cost of friendship with someone who could not be bothered to travel the six kilometres to Fürth to drink better beer in its native realm."

As a federal republic, Germany does have a strong sense of common culture mixed with strong regional, even very local identities. To some extent the same is true everywhere - we'd ridden from Burslem, in the heartland of the North Staffordshire oatcake; a culinary delight celebrated in songs such as Merrym'n's "I Want Oatcakes" (for My Christmas Dinner). Never heard of it? Just shows how deprived non-oatcake-eating communities are. As for those things some Derbyshire folk make - they may look like proper North Staffordshire oatcakes but they aren't. Probably cooked upside down, or something like that.

Anyway, if Germany seems, occasionally, to be riven by petty local differences it is a good thing. It reflects the history of a people who, having been united into a nation under the "Blood and Iron" of Prussia, have kept some of the precious pieces of Bavaria, Westphalia, Franken and all the other cities, towns and provinces that were once independent states united by a more-or-less common language and, often, culture.

I will admit to liking Germany and seem to get on well with most Germans I have met; almost all speak some English, many more correctly than I do. Needless to say that helps a great deal. The first time we checked directions, the response was in English - accent must have given us away; all we said was "Vreden, bitte?" with a final upward inflection.

There was no significant change to the landscape nor too much of the architecture. Names, signs, churches, greetings, all shifted to German, but for several miles one might not really notice the difference. There is something to be said for the Schengen agreement, even if the UK has never been part of it. Of course, free movement of labour and open borders are very different things. The UK's only open border was, and at the time of writing is, with the Republic of Ireland. As for us, we weren't intending to set up shop in Germany, but we were going to cycle across it, and we intended to pop out the other side nine days later.

Vreden is a small town, largely indistinguishable, on passing through, from many other small towns. It sticks in my memory

119

because of a yellow helicopter mounted on a platform over the river, as if it were waiting to catch fish. We entered the town via a park full of families enjoying the afternoon post-school sunshine. Not so radically different to Hanley Park or Burslem Park, back in good old Stoke-on-Trent, or the families riding down to the riverbank near Schoonhoven.

This part of Westphalia is pretty rural, but we followed the cycle route signs. We quickly learned that D-Netz Route 3 was very much a leisure route. It wound into Stadtlohn and then took a roundabout ramble on forest tracks and roadside cycle paths in the general direction of our destination. When our own dear National Cycle Network was in its early years, the out of the way course taken on some occasions became known as "The Grimshaw Way", in a rather unfair side-swipe at the then Chief Executive of Sustrans, John Grimshaw. A true radical activist, he generally preferred a nice ride to a direct route, if the two did not coincide.

Well, Germany has a very well-developed network of cycle routes and many roads have cycling infrastructure, even when not part of an official route. The D-Netz network has been designed to use the best of the signed routes to create a vaguely grid-like east-west north-south network of prime routes. The ADFC (Allgemeiner Deutcher Fahrrad-Club) maps show all routes and roads (though Autobahn's fade into the background). There is a vast amount of detail. Almost too much.

Still, with the map and the signs, all seemed to be pretty easy. Then we noticed that some of the signs showed the same destination in different directions. Worse followed; successive signs had distances that increased and decreased or decreased and increased in the same direction. What was the point? Not of the signs, but of the European Union. Though neither EU Commissioners, The Council, European Parliament nor Court of Justice had anything, as far as I knew, to do with the signs, the mess over kilometres signalled a fundamental and pertinent question. Never discussed by Leave or Remain campaigns, it would have swayed me had I not already cast a postal vote. The question was this; if Germany has lost the ability to organise cycle route signs properly, what was the point of remaining in a community where the Germans were the chief organising force?

Eventually we came to a cycle sign for Legden. Pointing away from where we intuitively believed the town to be, stating an improbable distance considering how far we had already come. We dismissed it. Trouble is, following route signs de-skills in the long run and, short-term, tends to reduce awareness of where you actually are. We tried the GPS, but there was no signal; we studied the time and the position of the sun; then we checked the map. Blimey, even for an "old school" chap like me this came as a surprise. Back to first principles; last known point, where had we turned, what was around us. At 1:150000 detail is not great, but, it seemed a fair bet that turning left - the opposite direction to the sign - cross the autobahn and the railway, and we'd be there in ten minutes. Good old map-work came up trumps.

With a few turns of the pedals we were in downtown Legden, the quietest place in Westphalia on a Wednesday night. Probably not quite, but no cars moved, the main street was empty, but there was our accommodation in the heart of town, the Alt Legden.

The owner was everything a German innkeeper of yesteryear should be - very much what one of today should be too. Cheery, broad in the beam, extensive moustache elegantly waxed and neatly trimmed, and standing behind a bar. We stowed our bikes safely away and he showed us to a large twin room, almost a suite. Despite its narrow frontage, the inn was immense - and as silent as the Legden outside its walls.

He offered us dinner. I am always happy to tuck into a schnitzel or a good hunk of Westphalian ham, but we had agreed beforehand that, for reasons of attempting to stick to a budget, we should find a supermarket and dig into a supper of whatever fare we could lay our hands on.

We searched Legden. We would have asked, had there been anyone on the streets. We walked round the town to end up back at the inn. A silent evening in a little German town. Across the road was one of those narrow, medieval houses, brick and timber, of which one wonders how it has remained intact and why someone built it like that in the first place. Better food for the mind than the belly. Historical note, if it is of interest. Rent on plots with a frontage on the main road were high, therefore narrow, high buildings were preferred. At least, that is the most common reason given for this type of medieval design.

In desperation, probably to avoid another history lecture, Mark headed off - but he did not escape. We walked in the one direction we had not yet taken. At a crossroads, first unseen around a corner, were: a take-away pizza shop, a kebab shop, and an Italian restaurant and take-away. It was wonderful. A choice. The Italian restaurant won, hands down.

We settled down, ordered drinks and prepared to tuck in to a hearty pasta dish. The owners of the restaurant told us that they originated from Sardinia, but did not have time to tell us more. Two, then three, then four more people came in. Legden was coming to life.

Between the assembly of eight, we managed to converse in a mixture of languages. Given a few courses more we could probably have re-invented Esperanto. As it was, we tried to find as many drinking toasts as we could in as many different languages. Then came the big question. We had explained that we were on a trip from England to Lidice, near Prague. Very good, but what the others wanted to know was, "What are you doing here?"

We had no prepared answer. Mark looked at me, after all I'd booked accommodation and come up with the schedule. Well. Really it was just on the way, in the right direction, on a gentle rural route avoiding the hillier industrial belt further south. All true, but not very flattering to the little town some of these folk called home. Why should it be? Getting off the tourist track is a good thing, in my opinion. Would we have been enjoying the company of some locals in a big city bar in the shadow of the Eiffel Tower? Possibly, but less likely. No, local bars are best for a bit of a chat and a few beers at a sensible price.

A single car broke the silence of the high street, as we strolled back to the Alt Legden. Mark went off to read, but, shamelessly, I headed for the bar to undertake further rehydration. Quiet night? Yes. The beaming landlord stood smiling, one hand on hip, the other grasping a beer pump. In conversation with him were a barmaid and two other customers. I bought a Bitburger - if I recall correctly - and was immediately identified as being English. Guess what? All who could, began speaking English. Mein Host spoke some, the barmaid who was Hungarian, spoke none, the other customers - a German - spoke quite a bit - and the young man at the other end of the bar spoke a lot of very good English. He had lived in Germany all his life, was of Polish-Turkish parentage, but saw himself as a German.

And so we embarked on a discussion of beer and Germany. The young Turk-Pole-German explained that he was in

125

Legden because he was working on a maintenance contract at a nearby factory. He headed home each weekend to the Ruhr area. He explained that the barmaid was in Legden on a sort of work experience and language course. He translated my English for her, obviously welcoming the opportunity to chat to her and make himself useful. The other customer explained that he lived in Legden.

There was a clear theme. Everyone felt it necessary to explain their presence. I explained mine, briefly, adding that Legden seemed to be a pretty quiet spot and a bit off the beaten track. All but the barmaid smiled. Pole-Turk-German young man translated. Barmaid smiled.

They must have spotted that I had not got the foggiest what the joke was. Those English, no sense of humour! Mein Host spoke. "You know nichts of Dorf Munsterland?" He was right, "Nein, I know nothing. Nichts." I was getting into the multilingual spirit.

"Ah." The landlord searched for words. "Partying."

Young Pole-Turk-German intervened. "A few kilometres from here there is... like a lot of clubs... disco... people come to

126

party." The other customer grunted disapprovingly. "From all around people come there to party at each weekend. Hundreds and hundreds. Stay here 'til Friday and you will see."

Up spoke Mein Host, "Sixty beds all full. Every weekend. Weekends are not quiet for me, but for business they are good."

I had unhealthy visions of taxis dumping hordes of wild party-goers in the early hours of the morning; entwined couples and others staggering up the stairs, whilst Mein Host prepares hang-over cures and twiddles his moustache. Good job they wash the sheets, I thought.

The door opened and another customer came in. An elderly gentleman, the others pointed me out to him. I was a cyclist, and this chap had just returned from a trip down the Weser cycle route - on a power-assisted bike. Wonderful! It seemed that here was a genuine, real-life "electric grandad". I felt I should fetch Mark. Knowing, I'd be unable to explain what that was all about, I managed, remarkably and to my great credit after another couple of rounds, to keep my joyful thoughts to myself.

He asked about our trip, but, uniquely, did not ask me to justify my presence in Legden in the middle of the week. "There is no German city, I think, where there is a big river, that you cannot cycle through on a riverside cycle path."

We then decided that we should have another drink because we were all jolly good people and we would not discuss the Brexit Referendum nor the EU, but celebrate our good-heartedness. Instead, we felt that we had spent too much time speaking English, and, for reasons of good manners we should all try to learn some Hungarian. Mein Host excused himself - to tidy up and prepare for the morning - only to reappear instinctively when we all agreed that we had not had enough beer to master the Magyar accent successfully.

Eventually, time came to head for home or bedroom or both, arrived. Next morning I could remember no Hungarian at all. If only we had had another drink, I am sure I would be speaking it like a native to this very day.

Chapter Eight

Why had we gone to Legden? The town's page on Wikipedia tells the reader that it is a town, its area and region - and that it is in Germany. When we headed out of town the next day, we found a community garden to stroll round, circumnavigated the church and ambled off in the grey drizzle. Still, we had a good time in dear old Legden - despite not being there at the weekend, or, maybe, because of it. We had comfortable lodgings; a pleasant dinner with good conversation, Mark had enjoyed his book, I'd done my bit for international relations and, narrowly in my opinion, failed to learn some words of Hungarian - anyone can manage gulyás and paprika. All this just proves that getting off the tourist trail is fine and you can have the best time in a little town that modestly asks, "Why are you here?"

It is not a long way from Legden to Münster. Fundamentally a rural ride, we did not follow any signed route, unless it combined with our way. More traffic was on the cycle paths than on the roads they ran alongside. Not that there were many people about at all. There were low hills to be seen, but any incline encountered was gentle. Even so, there was a jarring note.

Horrible to say, but Mark had a squeaky cleat. An unpleasant phenomenon. Generally, pedal related squeaks are amongst the most annoying. They cannot be escaped and are not usually amenable to bodgery. Thus, we looked out for a bike shop. On the edge of Münster we came across what may be the largest bike shop I have ever seen. It had everything, almost. All sorts of bikes, stacks of helmets and saddles, tools, accessories, the whole caboodle, except SPD cleats.

We rode into the city and found Bike Corner, colourful and bright, even on a dull day. Turned out that it specialised in selling bells. The colourful, designer-brand, idiosyncratic goods included items other than bells, but nothing that resembled an SPD cleat. At least, they knew a shop that would sell one. The internet did its stuff and we rode amidst the flow of local cyclists into town, turned off at a couple of junctions and found salvation.

Time for lunch, before seeking out our hotel and a bit of sight-seeing. We joined the stream of riders in the city centre and found a bench in an avenue of trees. In the centre of the path was one of those pieces of public art that German cities seem to go in for. A tribute to a Münster anarchist, a statue covered in newspapers. To be honest, the whole scene appeared anarchic. Cyclists came from all directions. They cut around the bins, swerved in front of us, mixed with pedestrians and all of them seemed to pay no attention before scattering in various directions.

I watched as I ate. This was not Dutch style infrastructure. Yet there was a rhythm to it all. Strangely, at least at first, there seemed to be no conflict. Surely there must be collisions, I thought. I did not witness one, but the segregation of pedestrians so common in the Netherlands, was less common in Münster. Mind you, where it did exist take care; stand in the bike lane and expect no mercy.

As we carried on eating, a cyclist pulled-over and pointed to our bikes. In excellent English he - as do most fellow cycle tourers - asked us where we were going and where we had come from. We fraternised. He, too was a cycle-tourist. He enjoyed cycling in the islands of the Caribbean. Had we ever been? Would we like to go?

He explained to us how a few years before Münster had been bedevilled by car culture, dirty and choked with traffic. Now it was a different matter, because the campaigners had persuaded the City councillors to improve things and invest.

131

This was not the case in the Caribbean, but the cycling was still fabulous. Had we been? "Would you be interested in cycling there?"

He explained how Münster's main roads now had segregated cycle lanes and that there were many cycle routes around the city. As we could see, it had all been worthwhile. This was not necessary in the Caribbean. "Have you been? I can recommend it. I will be going soon. You must go."

At this point I noted that Mark had sidled off to sort out a non-existent mechanical problem, maybe to polish his new cleat. I continued the conversation, introducing places where I had toured. None of them, apparently, matched the Caribbean.

Our friend gave us directions to our hotel, at first along a main road - segregated cycle lane with the odd piece of street furniture obstructing it, but well-used nonetheless. The signed route - for this turned out to be none other than D-Netz3 which we had first encountered on entering Germany near Vreden - took us through a quiet church yard and past a cemetery. And there, right on route, was our hotel; Hotel Haus vom gutën Hirten. An undertone in an English reading of the name suggesting "good pain" were dispelled by a warm welcome and a comfortable room.

Travel in company over a period of several days can reveal many things that one never suspected about one's companions. "That was a very well-kept cemetery, quite beautiful," said Mark, or words to that effect. It was kempt and peaceful, I had to admit. This was not the last time he noted the state of burial grounds. Mind, a man needs interests and cemeteries are no worse than many things. They are full of names and sculptures and tell us a lot about the people of the area. Or maybe they are just pretty and peaceful - there was no sign that this one had ever been the scene of anything that was not.

At the time I was getting ready to pursue my interest in the various ways that Germans prepare dead pigs so that they can be eaten. This is physically less healthy as an interest than wandering around graveyards, but may be more popular.

We were both keen to pursue an enthusiastic interest in the ways Germans brew beer - and maybe take a look around, unencumbered by bikes. We'd stowed those safely away in the hotel's bike shed. Walking into the city, we managed to avoid all those "bloody cyclists" buzzing back and forth.

Admiring the Lambertkirche, we headed as directly as we could to the Pinkus Müller brewery and the "brewery tap" nearby. This is a tourist attraction in its own right. The brewery produces organic beer, claiming to be the first to be totally organic in Germany. The Müller family came to Münster in 1816 and set up as brewers and bakers, later leaving the baking behind. The name Pinkus comes from a rather eccentric advertising ploy. One of the family, when a student, and his friends decided to see if a gas-light could be extinguished by urinating on it. Success gained Carl Müller the nickname "pinculus" or, in English rather than Latin, "little pisser". He later spotted a good opportunity for a founding legend, shortened it to Pinkus, and so preserved his name for ever. The beer is generally just known as Pinkus.

The beer tends to tartness. Perfect for a hot afternoon when the sun has come out and you have nothing to do but sit about. You'll be pleased to know, if you have ever, or ever intend to have a half-litre of the stuff, that the tartness comes from combining a fresh altbier with a more aged altbier that has been deliberately infected with lactic bacteria. So much for pure beer laws - actually all beer relies on bacteria more or less; but some more than others. Accompanied by a platter of Westphalian goodies, this was perfect. A real work of art.

Then we went to the Pablo Picasso Art Museum. It just shows what a refining influence artists are, though a good guzzle of beer may have helped. Generally, once ensconced in such a fine example of social and cultural history as this particular pub, the only way to get me out would be to go and find another. However, be it Picasso or Mark Dally - a combination rarely found in the same sentence (so much for Picasso) - there are good influences to build the mind and soul. Mind if some of the pieces displayed were anything to go by, some of the artists had drunk more of something much stronger than I had.

If there had been Legdeners present, they would probably have asked, "What's Picasso doing here?" So did I. The museum does not just exhibit Picasso's works, but those of his contemporaries. Many were collected by a wealthy local lady who was not only a patron of the artists, but was their friend.

On the whole, my taste in art is traditional. You know those vast landscapes with a Prussian Blue sky and a few dark storm clouds covering ninety percent of the canvas, a strip of dark colour at the bottom, which on closer inspection depicts the slaughter of a battle which the artists claim is the heroic moment of his nation's founding and that the dead and maimed chaps were either only too happy to die in the cause of national destiny or should not have been so stupid as to stand in the way of history. There's usually a bunch of Generals and their staff looking jaunty whilst admiring the scene. Well, I'd love to have a room big enough to hang one in.

However, my more artistic friends always say that the thing to do is to spend some time looking, and, in the past I'd done this and had some enjoyable times in galleries. Even more convincing that Picasso and his buddies would be worthy of a perusal, was carrying Harry Davies's "Waiting for the Magirus" in my pannier - or rather the afternoon I'd spent looking at it and then researching a few things, before blogging. After all, art is communication; whatever message is intended and no matter how attentive the receiver, the impact may not be that intended and the meaning may be little more than a Chinese whisper when processed. Art is a dialogue. The same was true of the ceramic artwork Mark had created and wrapped, padded and wrapped, that sat in his pannier.

So we stayed in the gallery and admired, until kicking out time.

Harry Davies is an artist based in Stoke-on-Trent. With some of his work already in the Lidice Gallery - alongside many world renowned artists - he generously provided a new piece based on an element of the Lidice story. "Waiting for the Magirus" was dark, very dark, making a great impact on me when I first saw it. Alan Gerrard, co-owner of Theartbay and, along with wife and co-owner, Cheryl Gerrard, a driving force in the movement to re-establish links between North Staffordshire and the Czech Republic, had asked Harry to undertake the work. Alan sent me a scan of it one wet Saturday afternoon. I looked and looked again and saw more and more. This is the blog that resulted;

> On Saturday afternoon, rain pouring down and family at the cinema, a mail arrived in my inbox telling me that Harry Davies had mentioned me on Facebook. Logging on, there it was. I was

137

stunned. The text was a plug for the Burslem to Lidice Bike Ride - very kind of you, Harry. But the image was a hollow-eyed, desolate face, a distinct touch of the crucified Christ about it, but superficially more childlike, though desperately sad in a way no child should ever be - the face of someone who has seen too much.

That was my initial response. I claim no knowledge of or skill in art, but, here's my five penn'orth - my personal reaction. You'll judge whether I have missed the point or not.

I downloaded the image and enlarged it. The more one looked the more there was. Here it seems was a face resigned to death but held in some kind of limbo in which life carried on though an inevitable death awaited, imminently. And unlike the crucified Christ, with no resurrection and no purpose. Little flecks of colour began to appear; the tracks of tears, stains of blood, the discolouration of death? And the mouth, set without fear or shut in eternal silence? Looked again at the eyes; sunken and baggy, closed or plucked out or raised to Heaven or rolling in death-throes? Does this face see or hear or just exist for the moment, its inner being to be snuffed out by a power with no care or compassion? Could it speak, or utter a sound? Is there nothing to say in its hopeless, helpless world? No anger or accusation; of this world, but beyond it; alive, but dead.

So, the above is my first and second take - untutored and simply my own. And each time I look, the face seems older, though the victims, we know, never aged.

Back to the image. Harry had entitled the piece, "Waiting for the Magirus". I'd tried to think about the image before thinking about the title. What did it mean? Well, search "Magirus" and you get a page full of results about a truck manufacturer in Ulm, Bavaria. Digging deeper and it emerged that they had a specialism in fire-engines. Indeed, they were credited with producing the first ladder on a rotating platform, so important in rescuing people from upper storeys.

A little deeper and a website explained how the SS adapted Magirus trucks (not fire-engines), as well as trucks made by Saurer, Opel and others. There is no suggestion that these companies built vehicles to be used as "gas-trucks" where a simple adaptation or two meant people could be killed using carbon-monoxide. It was the SS who chose them because they could take up to seventy people at a time and converted them into murder machines.

Interviewed after the war, several locals stated that they had seen these vehicles operating in the forests around Chelmno in 1942. The "Black Raven" revved gently for ten minutes and then drove away to some crematorium or pit. It seems that such was the fate of the children of Lidice, and Ležáky and countless others. I believe that gas-trucks were first used, within the Third Reich, to kill the handicapped and congenitally ill, removing them from the blood-line of the Herrenvolk.

Is the "wait" of the title for its arrival, for its task to be done, or to reach the final destination? I hope it is something that we are not all waiting for. It can't be our world, can it?

Hard fact and art both disturb us. Yet, as my jaunt across Europe approaches, I suddenly felt uplifted. Why? Harry Davies' work hangs in the Lidice Gallery alongside that of artists from around the world. What a privilege to carry this in my panniers. More so, what a wonderful act to trust such an emotionally-charged creation to me. It made me feel like some sort of conduit of goodwill - albeit one that will still enjoy the ride, despite the added responsibility. My wife suggested that it would be safer to send it by post and pick it up there to pass on. To me that would miss the point.

Harry Davies has put an extra swagger in the pedal-stroke as I ride to Lidice. In the past I have ridden many a mile, often with a theme in mind. When I decided to ride to Lidice, it was because of my own personal interest and a vague desire

141

to support an excellent cause. Now, I have a real
purpose!

Mark Dally is an artist working in ceramics. He came to the Potteries to study and has remained in the area. His creations are often in black and white or cream - even his Shand Stoater bike is black and white - though creamy shades furnish a setting for bright colours to jump out of his creations. I'd say that there is movement in his work, though it is made of clay. Drunken-legged clocks? Well, Mark makes them.

The piece he made for Lidice was an abstract piece. Here's my take on it:

> *Celebrating the hope, the joy that people were determined to bring by the rebuilding of the village of Lidice - both physically and as a symbol for all those communities destroyed in wartime atrocities - here is Mark Dally's ceramic piece that he is probably, even as I type, packing carefully for its journey on the back of his bicycle from Burslem to Lidice.*

Abstract flowers blooming? Buds opening to welcome the light of peace? Could be. "Lidice Lives" in a celebration of gold and titanium. Even so it is a solid little thing, reminiscent of a cuddly teddy-bear with arms outstretched to welcome, or offer, an affectionate embrace. Or raising its arms in triumph and shouting news that good can conquer bad? Mind you, the slight incline - it is not symmetrical - forward, when viewed from behind, resembled, a little, a boxer braced to give as good as it received or more; "Yes, I'm gentle and amiable and welcoming - but don't push your luck, because I can stick up for myself and I know I'll have friends who will stick by me."

Mark promised a contrast to Harry Davies' sombre and provoking painting, "Waiting for the Magirus". And he has created one. Mind you, it is not without its provocative message. Just as the people of many countries took up the banner raised by Barnett Stross and the communities of North Staffordshire, the vigorous, sturdy piece of ceramic art reminds us that for good to triumph over evil is not a matter of luck. Kindness and

143

hope and love need to be backed by grit, determination and commitment. Lidice lived because "ordinary, kind people" said it would, rolled up their sleeves and got stuck in to make it happen. They could have ignored Lidice, but they decided - even when fighting a war - that they'd do what they knew to be right.

Let's celebrate that!

If Legden had been more miles from Münster and we had arrived later, which one would I have chosen; Picasso or Pinkus-Müller? Well, you can find Picasso all over the place can't you?

Let's get back to Münster and wonderfully named Schoefferhoffer beer - one beer that I could have a pretty good chance of pronouncing accurately enough to get another, even if one had a skinful of it already. Well, a skinful is not recommended in any cycling handbook if you have good distance to go the next day. So Mark, went off to find a couple of bottles of beer for a night cap and I wandered off to the hotel to drink water. For accuracies sake, I should point out that Mark did offer to share a bottle.

Münster had, I thought, changed for the better since my previous visit, which must have been in around 1988. I recalled, allowing for the fact that the whole day had been as wet as this day had been in the morning, a city centre choked with traffic, grimy buildings and narrow pavements. There may well have been some people on bicycles but I do not remember any. They'd have been pretty courageous. The improvements could not be put down entirely to cycling; good public transport, cleaning buildings and creating car-free areas will have played their part. However, all are elements in creating cities for people; a city that is good for cyclists is likely to be good to live in - even if some of the residents would prefer Jamaica.

****

Religious fervour has played an important part in the history of Münster. During the Reformation, in the sixteenth century, the city came under the control of Jan of Leiden and his Anabaptist followers. Martin Luther had never envisaged a social revolution - in fact he had not really intended to see the Catholic Church overthrown, but having taken the lid off the pot, others were happy to dip the ladle in deeper. The Anabaptists were far more radical than the Lutherans. In

145

Münster, they took no time in kicking the Catholic Bishop out and overthrowing the established city government. When the city was retaken, revenge was equally swift. Jan and other leading Anabaptists were executed and their bodies hung in cages from the steeple of St. Lambert's. The cages are still there.

Anabaptists saw no child baptism in the Bible, so they rejected its validity, insisting that only an adult could profess their faith and, therefore, be baptised. Communal ownership and social equality were also key elements which the propertied classes and the established Church found alarming. As ever, leaders did not stick to their guns; power corrupted. Jan of Leiden declared himself "King of Münster" and the Anabaptists were accused, by their enemies, of polygamy, orgies and the usual sort of lurid stuff that opponents can be charged with.

More recently, it was from the pulpit of St. Lambert's that Cardinal Galen preached protests against the Nazis. Clemens, Graf von Galen, Bishop of Münster, was the progeny of a long-established Westphalian aristocratic family. Socially and religiously conservative, he sympathised with the Nazis desire to destroy the Treaty of Versailles that

146

had crippled Germany after the Great War and with their opposition to socialism and the liberal values of the Weimar Republic (1918-1933). He was a patriot. Mind you, every political party in Germany and every coalition government had wanted to overthrow the Treaty of Versailles. Some had tried to show that Germany could be trusted or that paying reparations was impossible, the Nazis took a more direct approach. There were also many Germans who were opposed to socialism and, in particular, fearful of the spread of communism. There were conservatives who would have restored the Kaiser. It was entirely possible to sympathise with some of the Nazi goals without supporting the Nazi Party.

So, when Galen spoke out against the Nazis it was not a per se attack on them. Most famous for three sermons, he preached against the Nazis, his hand was all over a Papal encyclical entitled Mit Brennender Sorge (With Burning Concern) published against the Nazis in 1937. He had commenced his criticism of the Nazis in 1934, attacked their apparent worship of racial purity, criticised the Gestapo for lawlessness and ridiculed Nazi "philosophy". Then in 1941 he preached three sermons; two against Nazi attacks on the Catholic Church, and a third against the programme of euthanasia for invalids and the mentally ill. Illegally circulated in print, they are credited with inspiring opposition groups, but their impact on Nazi programmes is another matter.

Walking back to the hotel, I was pleased to have remembered that German history is as much about social and religious radicalism and reaction, violence and vulgar advertising, as it is about two wars and a dictatorship. Plus, Pinkus Müller is still going strong; so is the Roman Catholic Church.

Chapter Nine

And this is where Chapter One began, on June 10th in the wheat fields of the North German Plain, patches of woodland green dotting the canvas, the blue of cornflowers mixing hazily into the golden fields. It reminded me - though cornflowers are rarer in the UK these days - of the East Anglian Breckland. The broad, wide skies are the same and the peculiar light that, on a sunny day, arcs between the distant horizons, is also similar. Likewise, the small towns and villages, almost all of which D-Netz 3 avoided, until we reached Warendorf.

Approached on a traffic-free cycle path along banks of the artificially constricted River Ems, we found a town busy with shoppers on its broad pedestrianised high street. The River Ems is not one of Germany's best known rivers, but reaches the sea in a major estuary at Cuxhaven, beyond Bremen. Here, amidst the pastures and fields it is little more than a fenland dyke. Even so, it has its own cycle route, the Ems Radweg.

Warendorf likes horses. Around the town were painted ones - models; striped, spotted, green, red, gold and blue. It also

149

likes real ones. The Nordrhein-Westphalen stud farm is based there, as is the German Olympic Committee for Equestrianism. Any similarity to Newmarket would be purely coincidental, but it certainly seems prosperous, benefitting from proximity to major cities (Münster, Osnabruck and Bielefeld) without being dominated by them.

It is an old town, though two "Great Fires" destroyed many of the original buildings and its old and new churches. Yet, as is often the case in German towns, tradition is at the forefront of the image. Above one shop doorway a woman held a scrawny child by its neck - both were made of iron, I guess, and were supported by a short beam that projected above the street. At this point we made what I assumed to be Germans laugh out loud in public. Whilst pondering on what this gruesome scene was all about, I remarked that the dangling figure might be her husband. Two passers-by laughed, one smirked and another snorted; all were men. That German sense of humour. Maybe one of them really was her husband, or her lover.

We spent time in a gallery, where a young artist was mixing traditional themes with pop-art. On the verge of making a living from his creativity, he looked forward to a time when he

150

could turn down some of the more prosaic work which had kept his business turning over. So interesting was his work that, when we went to shelter from the sun in the shade of the trees around the church, we discovered that the old building opposite was both brewery and bar. Had the artwork been poorer, I'd have been annoyed. As it was, it was too early in the day for me to have a beer. As for Mark, it is never too early in the day for a mooch round a gallery and a chat with a fellow artist.

Quiet country roads took us onward, towards the more urban, busier, industrial area to the south of Bielefeld. A sign stated that the route into Gütersloh was blocked, but no diversion was signed; Nederlands 1, Deutschland 0. Easy enough to pick up was another route, but, despite the signs, it seemed to get muddled. Eventually we searched out the SatNav and it guided us through industrial estates, alongside busy roads, on what felt like a tour of light industry. There's no doubt in my mind that it took us a long way round, but it got us there in the end. Guessing that this depended on the settings we had put in (for example, avoid main roads), we decided to do things differently next time, but we can't complain.

Reaching Oerlinghausen, the SatNav directed us along a street surfaced with setts. Then another set of setts and a hairpin bend and a grunt in granny gear, before reaching the top of the Tonsberg. When views could be caught through the trees, it was clear that we were now in a different landscape; yes, we had climbed a hill, a darned hearty one. Forested ridges rolled away north - they went south-east too, but we could not see those. This was the Teutoberg Forest or Teutoburger Wald.

There followed a ride along forest tracks. A handful of mountain bikers looked perplexed as we trundled along. Mark's disc brakes proved their worth on the descents as I clung on and hoped that the cantilever brakes would grip before hitting the next sharp bend.

Still in one piece when we hit smooth tarmac, the descent ran on into Detmold, before leaving a final haul up to the Youth Hostel or Jungendherberge. We'd made it just in time for dinner and the warden was happy for us to grab some food and fulfil the formalities after. Bikes stowed, food consumed, beer bought; "Yes," said the warden, "they are all at the top of hills. We put the berg in herberge." More Teutonic chuckles.

The modern hostel had clean airy rooms with large windows. Perfect for hanging out shower-washed bicycling gear and hoping it would dry by the morning. Needless to say it didn't, but it had done pretty well by the time we were ready to leave. There were a good number of folk staying at the hostel, including a large group of singers. Despite this, there was no clutter or feeling that a quart was being stuffed into a pint pot. Sadly, the choristers had punished their vocal chords enough during rehearsals, so there was no entertainment.

Detmold is an historic town, popular with walkers exploring this part of the Teutoburg Forest. In some ways this is the heart of German history and identity. A short distance from the hostel is the Hermannsdenkmal; the memorial to the first German encountered by name in history. Great achievement though that might be, he actually got that honour by ensuring that Roman writers would enshrine his name in their chronicles.

Hermann of the Cherusci, Arminius as the Roman historians called him, led an alliance of tribes against a Roman Army in AD 9. Whilst the battle of the Teutoburg Forest probably took place nearer to Osnabrück, the Hermannsdenkmal near Detmold commemorates German victory and Hermann himself. The sword at the memorial bears the inscription "Germany's unity - my strength, my strength - Germany's might". The message is clear; here we have the origins of the German nation, distinct from those Latinized people within the Roman Empire. On the other hand, some have suggested that it really marks the failure of the Roman Empire to spread civilisation into the land's east of the Rhine. Truth is, we do not even know if Hermann thought of himself as German or Cherusci or both, or whether the alliance he led had anything more in common than respect for Hermann and antipathy to the Romans. Strangely, it seems that Hermann was actually rather proud to be associated with the Romans. Scrape away at the surface of even the grandest national monument and things appear more complex than the shiny gold lettering initially suggests. The same can be said of almost any nation's founding story. The memorial, like so many others of its type, really speaks for those who built it rather than for those whom it commemorates.

****

At the time we were sitting down on the benches outside the hostel with a cooling bottle of beer, but seventy-one years earlier, people would have been making their way home after the first commemorative event held at Lidice to mark the destruction of that community. Estimates number the attendance at as many as 200,000 people. Film from the time shows vast crowds assembled around the wooden cross circled in barbed wire and a stone memorial which had been erected over the grave of the men by soldiers of the Red Army - the memorial that stands on the same spot today. Ominously, the Soviet memorial replaced a simple Czechoslovak flag and wreath which had marked the spot just one month earlier.

President Beneš gave the main address; dignitaries filled the grandstand; uniformed servicemen stood guard. It marked the disgust at the destruction of the village of Lidice and the murder of its inhabitants, so symbolic of the invasion of their country by Nazi Germany; it was also a great national occasion, proclaiming Czechoslovakia's restored, if temporary, independence following the expulsion of the unwanted invader.

Sitting in rows, in black dresses, holding bunches of flowers were some of the Lidice women who had returned. What they were thinking is hard to tell. Some clearly are desperately holding back tears; some clutch the flowers in hope, maybe;

how many would have hurled the sprays into the dust had not the eyes of the crowd been on them, had they not already gone through so much and had they still not hope that their children would be found? Such things are not recorded.

The women had gotten home by various means. Those on the Death March from Ravensbruck were liberated when their guards fled and after a few days hiding in the forest, they saw some Soviet tanks pass by and, without any great sense of elation and certainly no ceremony, discovered that they had been liberated.

Miloslava Suchánková described how things progressed. It must have been the same for many people of all nationalities in the hubbub of refugees, exploited slaves seeking to return home, those hiding their identity, those seeking loved ones. A heaving sea of humans needing to eat, drink and go to a place where they felt safe, be their journey in hope or despair.

> *We were free after three long years! But, as I say, it happened as if unwittingly, no great joy or jubilation. None of us had any idea what the upcoming days might bring. Yet our situation improved at least a little because some of the*

men (they had joined a larger group of inmates from Sachsenhausen camp) arranged with the Russians to move into some deserted houses in the town of Kriwitz, from where we moved to a chateau later, then to some wooden blocks in some labour camp, to end up in Neu Brandenburg, where a reception camp for foreigners had been set up in the place of the local barracks - a kind of transition station before repatriation.

Meanwhile, we managed to send some information to Prague saying where we were, including lists of names of everyone who was staying at the camp. And the Kladno factories dispatched two buses to collect the Lidice women. The rest of the women and the eldest of the men left for the home country together with us. We crossed the border at Cinovec on June 2nd 1945. Soldiers from the Kladno garrison awaited us there: they were guarding the border there and had a special ceremonial welcome ready for us. We were standing on one side, Soldiers and First World War veterans were on

157

the other side. They raised the flag and played the Czech anthem. We cried for joy to be home again and even saw the soldiers and legionaries cry. And mother said all of a sudden, "Girls, this is going to be worse than we thought."

Amongst the soldiers was a former colleague. She asked him about Lidice and he told her the news.

After liberation, when most of Europe was rejoicing to have shed the burden of war and regained its freedom, I learnt that the men had all been shot and the village torn down, and that I would never see my dear father.

When they reached Kladno they were met by relatives who would not allow them to go to the place where Lidice once stood.

Some of the other women had already arrived home. Anna Kohlíčková and her mother-in-law were amongst a group who had given the guards on the Death March the slip. They reached the border on May 22nd.

There we were halted by some Czech soldiers asking us where we were coming from and where we were going to. We told them. They suddenly turned into minuscule statues, and some of them shed a tear or two.

So we said, "Don't cry, boys: you don't know how much we look forward to being at home again. We have been looking forward for years, and now we have finally had the good luck. We are just very sorry that not all of us are coming back, that many of those who wanted to come along simply stayed behind. But we are very glad to be coming home."

The commanding officer had them taken to a former monastery at Česka Lipa, where they had the joy of a bath, but received no news of Lidice. Next day, on a crowded train to Prague, no one told them anything of their home village. The bus driver did not stop to let them disembark near Buštěhrad. In a small shop in Kladno, where they got off the bus, they decided to walk to Lidice. Other customers heard them and refused to let them go. Amongst the customers was their Uncle Kohlíček, who took them back to his house. On the way he would say nothing of their home.

The wall of silence was broken the next day. A car arrived to take Anna to Prague in search of her daughter Venuška at the institute in Dykova Street where she had given birth to her on Friday, June 19th, 1942. There was no sign of anyone, German or Czech. On the way back to Kladno, the driver turned off at the Buštěhrad cemetery; the spot where a group of miner's had given their bicycles to their friends before walking to their deaths.

Anna recalled how she could not see the tower of Lidice's Church.

> I didn't see the tower at all. We went all the way to St. Salvátor, a little chapel still standing there today, and there, instead of going on straight to Lidice down the hill, we made a right turn. And there were no trees around us, only crops growing tall. It was a rye field.
>
> The moment we made that right turn into a road going straight into the field, I felt such a pain in

160

my head as if I were hit on it with a blunt object, a very strong surge of pain. It was only then that I realised we were going through a place which had only been fields before, no road at all. And the trees went no further than there. Before, the road had been lined with walnut trees on either side... but there was nothing there. I don't normally suffer with headaches, I never had, but that was a fierce headache that made me feel that I would collapse. But on we went down a hairpin bend and then another, until we arrived, I recognised the place, on the road going from Hrebeč to Makotrasy via Lidice. That was where the old cemetery was supposed to be, but it wasn't. And that rye growing tall, and a little path mown down through that field branching off the road, just a narrow path not to spoil too much of the crop. Down that path Mrs Kubrová was leading me, saying nothing. I was so dismayed and desolate to see nothing at all there, not even the cemetery. First we would have to pass the parish house, of course.

But the only thing there was the path; until we reached the brook running from Hrebeč through Lidice and on towards Makotrasy; there was just a little makeshift footbridge which we crossed, and the path was mowed all the way to the common grave of the dead men. Only there did I learn the truth; Mrs Kubrová told me that at that point all the Lidice men had been shot on June 10th. After the women and children had been taken from Lidice to the high school, only then did they start to shoot the men. In that very same place I learnt the entire truth. What I did in that moment I can't tell, I can only hear Mrs Kubrová again and again saying, "Anička, be brave, your daughter must come back to you. Keep yourself alive now that she's lost her father, for her to have you at least to bring her up. Be very brave. I know it is terrible what I have just told you, but unfortunately it is true, all of it."

Fathoming what the rows of black-clad Lidice women at the first commemorative ceremony for their dead menfolk and their annihilated community went on and the politicians and others spoke... where could one start, let alone end.

162

In Eduard Stehlík's "Memories of Lidice", is a striking image of a woman addressing the crowd. Unbowed by her years in labour camps serving the needs of her enemies, soberly, sombrely, simply clad, is Anna Hroniková. The hope that she would return to her home had been dashed, the hope that she would again see her husband, her father, dashed; all those hopes which had driven her and other Lidice women to carry-on in spite of the hardships of the camps, in spite of the beatings, in spite of seeing their neighbours and relatives transported to death camps, in spite of hunger and seeing three of their like die on the eve of salvation, had been taken from them: except one. Her message to the crowd was simple:

> *Help us find our children. Without them life would not be life!*

Surely, even the Nazis would not have harmed the children. Things seemed hopeful; one had already returned. Eva Kubíková had and was there at the first commemoration event. She had been selected for Nazification, along with six others. Her aunt, who lived in Germany, had claimed her from the Lebensborn and she lived with her German relatives throughout the war. She was promptly retrieved by an uncle

163

when the fighting ended. She was soon followed by six of the children who had been under the age of one on June 10th, 1942. Would not the rest surely follow – eventually?

Chapter Ten

D-Netz 3 runs close to the hostel on the outskirts of Detmold. Countryside was reached in a few turns of the pedals. The theme for the morning, and much of the day, was hills and trees. Lots of both. Trees shaded the way, giving mental glimpses of deeper forests in the German heartland, obscuring signs. Wonderful things, trees.

The D-Netz route is very much for leisure cyclists or those who like a good bit of roughish stuff to spice up the day. Needless to say, we were not the only cyclists enjoying the morning sunshine, though pedalers were outnumbered by walkers. In the valleys stood ancient mills - shaded beer gardens indicated that they were put to even better use today.

The switchback riding of the first few miles was left behind when the ridge of hills turned south and we headed eastward onto a broad plateau with long, gentle climbs and occasional deeper valleys. Rounded hilltops with wooded escarpments hemmed us to the north. When rolling through the cornfields such views were idyllic.

165

So happy was progress along well-surfaced country roads that we enthusiastically went off course on a couple of occasions; admiring the view and not looking for signs or looking for signs and not paying attention to proper navigation. We knew where we were, but could not quite work out the right way to go. Actually, a bit of map study soon sorted things out, but Mark confirmed things with a couple of ladies who were chatting outside a shop. When GPS fails, rely on the locals. It took a little while for them to get where we wanted to go out of us. "Yes, Marienmünster, this way." They pointed down the road we had picked out on the map.

Marienmünster is not one of the largest towns in the area. In fact, blink and you'll miss it, or rather blink and miss the sign hidden in the bushes and you'll see it twice. Yes, astray again. Having climbed out of the town on a cycle track, passing a piece of public realm art - in this case a series of crosses that performed a trompe d'oeuil - we descended into a hamlet. There we were greeted with a wondrous sight. Blocking the road - honest, we could not have passed - was a baker's van with only a short queue. The cakes looked too good to ignore. We had to obey the "Law of Torte". Balancing calorific creation on my bar bag, so as not to disturb the soft cheesecake top garnished with fruit, I glided. The smoothness of that glide would have pleased the most exacting insurance company's good driving gadget - perhaps this method should be adopted. Better, it brought the cakes safely to rest at some benches in a playground.

Whether it was the soporific weather or the soporific cakes, when we headed off we followed the D-Netz signs and soon realised that things did not quite match up with expectations, despite the D-Netz signs we found. Remarkably, against both map and instinct, we descended a slope - up which were labouring several cyclists - and noted a second troupe d'oeuil made of crosses and exactly the same as the one we had seen on our way up the hill. We had a brief discussion about whether we had gone full circle or not. I was sure we had, so headed back up the hill, passing the spot where the bakers van had been, past the benches and down the road by the church once more. A few yards further on, what appeared to be a cart track turned out to be a surfaced road. Hidden amongst the twisted branches of a tree was a sign, pointing our way. Telling myself off for not sticking to basics, I vowed faithfully to obey the map.

The hidden sign pointed us back to the hills for a long climb through woodland and a wonderfully long descent - much of it on wide, smooth cycle track that swept around small pastures, dipped into the edge of the forest and coupled up with a babbling brook. Once again there was barely a car to be seen anyway, until we reached the edge of town - Höxter - in the valley of the River Weser.

On such a beautiful day, you'd expect an old town in a lush valley with a fine, broad river, to be busy. So, it was. Looking above the hubbub, the timber-framed houses were decorated exuberantly with gothic script; with emblems and badges, doubtless belonging to the merchants who had once called them home. I like the colour and tradition these bring; they shout out the confidence of the medieval burghers of Höxter. No doubt they made a good deal of money shipping goods in and out along the river. Their descendants seemed to have diversified into coffee, cakes and ice-cream.

The Weser was the biggest river we had encountered since leaving the Netherlands. Needless to say, those cunning German tourism promoters had made it possible to cycle all the way along the river, with much dedicated infrastructure: the Weser Radweg.

A decent bike ride north of Höxter is the Buckeberg, where, during the Nazi era, Adolf Hitler came to address the farmers and peasants in a celebration of Aryan "Blüt und Boden" - blood and soil. I'd walked along the hills a few years before; a Sunday walk ending in coffee and cake - very bourgeois, very German. We had visited the Schloss Schaumberg in the morning and were tucking into a mighty slice of Black Forest Gateau in a café set on the hillside. As the autumn sun sank, I recall, a hang-gliders silhouette floating across the orange sky. We then drove to Hameln and walked amidst the timber-framed houses in the old town. Better known to the English as Hamelin: a town of medieval buildings to match the legend of rats, children and piper.

Höxter had much in common with it. Both reek of mercantile prosperity in a bygone age; both have many decorated buildings; both names begin with the letter "H"; both would be ideal places to spend a night on a long cycle tour. The Weser valley could have been scooped out with a woodworker's curved chisel; roll with the flow and get in the groove.

For us in 2017, it was a much shorter stretch of the riverside track to Holzminden (another small town beginning with "H"). Riverside mills that had seen some big ships in the past and had also seen many better days, dominated the right bank. A regular parade of cyclists proceeded in alternate sun and shade along a marvellously surfaced riverside cycle track. Unlike the Netherland rivers, there were no craft for pleasure or work - though it was a lazy Saturday afternoon and everyone who was not in the informal bicycle parade, angling or walking, seemed to be sitting in Holzminden's riverside bars. We joined them and caught a bit of the European Football Championships. England were due to play that night. Neither of us was overly bothered about watching the game.

Others had more leisurely ideas. One pair of cyclists had placed a bottle of Riesling in each of the rear pannier back pockets. Nice idea, but some might feel that exposure to the sun would put the flavour at risk. Maybe the pannier was packed with ice. Or more bottles.

D-Nz 3 left the Weser, taking us to a series of dirt tracks. In the end, we got fed up with these pretty routes and decided to hit the tarmac. The scenery was just as pretty and Saturday late afternoon was not a busy time on the road. Peaceful countryside on a steady climb to Stadtoldensdorf and a trickle of shoppers lent a real lazy evening atmosphere. We pulled in at a supermarket. Stock up for Sunday lunchtime - we had no idea if the joy of Sunday shopping was as glorious in Germany as it was in the UK and we'd be pushing into old East Germany, so the prospect of buying the usual ham, cheese, tomatoes and bread felt even more obscure. All very exciting. Life on the edge.

The great question on a cycle ride across a country in whose name a terrorist dictatorship had carried out an atrocity that had wiped out the population of our destination was "can we buy bread and cheese on a Sunday once we cross into the former Soviet Bloc?" As for an EU membership referendum in the UK, well, we'd long left that behind. Even the fascinating questions surrounding German Reunification were of little account compared to our picnic. Cycle-touring is often, like political revolutions, a "knife and fork issue".

Keeping to the asphalt, the direct route to Einbeck saved time, as the day was drawing on. With the sun on our backs, sweeping curves of silk smooth road, ripening grain glowing against a background of shadowy green-black woodland. Cool air soothed sun-screen soaked flesh; a shower and dinner were just the other side of the next town; a cold beer to wash it all down, with any luck.

So, inevitably, we had one of those finding-your-way-out-of-town moments. Even a town of moderate size can be awkward to escape from when names on signs are unfamiliar. Einbeck is not a large town, but as we had SatNavised the destination, we were taken past the correct road as the GPS insisted that we should go up a slip road and join a section of main road forbidden to cyclists. Cyclists are always banished from autobahn, motorway and suchlike, but there are sometimes other sections of road that are closed to them. This time the map won out. We checked it out and headed back towards Einbeck to swing off along a broad, quiet riverside road that skirted along the foot of another thickly forested hill. Thank Heaven we did not have to cycle over that one, we agreed.

Then we spotted a sign to Greene, where we had a room booked at the Landhaus. So we began to climb over the shoulder of the hill we had celebrated missing out on. The road went up with an end-of-the-day gradient and hurled itself down to a sharp bend under a narrow railway bridge. It emerged at a main road junction next to a large white building - the Landaus Greene - and the river. Next morning we noted a sign by the bridge next to the hotel, indicating the Leinetal Cycleway. We could have missed out the last climb; we had followed the little River Leine out of Einbeck and the stream would have taken us on to Greene. But what is cycling without hills to climb? Or building an appetite to be sated?

The sturdy and amiable gentleman who greeted me, whilst Mark watched the bikes, was not quite the perfect Teutonic Mein Host as the paragon of Legden, but he ran that notable gentleman a good race. Stating that his English was better than my German is barely necessary, however, between us we had managed to confuse the booking process. He was surprised that there were two of us, because he had but a single room. Top and tailing, despite the fact that Mark's sweaty feet would have been treated in the shower, would not be something that either of us would have looked forward to and might have spoiled the prospect of breakfast. I'd have to offer to sleep on the floor. Being a gentleman, Mark would naturally refuse. Or would he?

"Ah! Ja, dare ist anozzer. Heff der sveet." He locked our bikes in a vast garage that may once have been a barn. "Englant vill play fussball soon. (He was obviously an optimist.) You vill vont to vatch? Or heff dinner?" Dinner beat England... as could have almost any plate of meat and salad involved in the competition.

173

Sitting room, four beds, bathroom and kitchen - all for the price of a twin room. Very good. We spread ourselves out, merrily scattering our stuff around, deciding first on one bed, then another. That is the trouble with suites, they invite disorganisation.

I have to say that the schnitzel in paprika sauce with fried potatoes was immense in size and very, very satisfying after a long cycle. It was matched by the salad that I ordered with it. Pickles, salad leaves, tomatoes, onions, cucumber and egg revealed themselves as one ate through the layers. Perfect, and at least over half healthy. Can't remember what Mark had, but there did not seem to be much of it.

Whatever it was, it came with a jolly refreshing Einbecker beer. And another. And possibly a third. What better way to end a day of fine German cycling, than with a fine German feast.

Chapter Eleven

There is much more to cycling than riding a bike and food plays a big part in it, at least for me. I'll admit to occasionally carrying an energy gel in a jersey pocket and sometimes finding one in the bottom of a pannier, unused and long-forgotten. I don't like them. They do not satisfy either belly or soul. As an aid to getting over the last hill they may have virtue, but as an incentive to reach the top of the pass they do not. Don't knock 'em, many people who cycle faster and further than I think they are wonderful, but I have rarely met a cyclist who prefers them to a jam sandwich. Maybe that says more about cyclists I might meet - perhaps we just travel at the same pace. I know serious road racers who prefer a nice jam doorstop to a hi-tech gel or powder, however scientifically-proven or well-advertised.

Sweets for energy boosts can easily be picked up as snacks along the route; caffeine is preferable in coffee bought from a café; true, it means stopping, but never mind. I suppose that is why I have never been a winner at cycling. Much as I admire the professional cyclists and enjoy watching the major tours, I can't help feeling that it would be much better if they had to carry their own gear and have a plat de jour with half-

175

bottle of vin rouge at lunchtime. There could be a King of the Cheese jersey. Alright, let us leave it there, it would not work. Mind you, if anyone could attack the Galibier after a plateful of steak and kidney pud that would seriously be something to put in the hall of fame.

I once attempted to continue for a further fifty miles in mid-Wales after tucking in to a most generous suet pudding stuffed with steak in an ale gravy. It was not successful, or rather it was unnecessarily uncomfortable. Since then, on a cycling day, I like to eat in the morning and look forward to a hearty evening feed. During the day, I'll graze - on a long ride - or just drop off for a cuppa. I hate cycling on a full stomach.

Despite that, breakfast was hearty. It always was. Sunday morning breakfast with the sunshine glaring through the breakfast room window. I do enjoy a buffet breakfast, but was beginning to crave a couple of rashers of bacon or some kippers. No pleasing some folk, is there? I've often been told by cyclists that continental hotels don't do proper breakfast for a day on a bike. This may be true of some, but I have rarely been disappointed on any European tour. The buffet means variety; bread and cheese one day, fruit the next, ham, eggs, salami, yoghurt - or different combinations on different days.

In the British Isles it is hard to avoid the full cooked breakfast. Hard because, when I spy other guests getting a round of black pudding, mushrooms and fried tomatoes, I lack the will-power to say, "No, just toast and marmalade, please." The ubiquitous full-English, full-Welsh, full-Scottish or full-Irish is wonderful as a set-up for a day in the saddle - just the ticket for a chap or lady on a cycle tour.

Amongst those benighted European lands there was never a rasher of bacon to be seen - a host of hams and salami and fried and boiled sausages everyday - but they just do not do bacon. Vegetarians have told me how the smell of bacon on the grill is a challenge to their principles which needs devotion to overcome. Well, for some strange reason I craved bacon, but had to be satisfied with fruit, yoghurt and bread, beautifully made bread. Hey-ho! The craving subsided and did not return. I do love well-made fresh bread.

Setting off, traffic was negligible when there was any at all. Bash along the road we thought - and quite right too. Cycle routes are fine, but round the houses is not always the best way. We'd got some interesting places to see and getting a few miles in had to be a good idea. Rain was due later on as well, so getting on had to be a good plan.

Bad Gandersheim was the next town. Being Sunday morning it was very much closed for business, despite the sun-shaded tables outside the bars in the town centre. It looked like it was festival time too, or was just about to be - expertise in German does not extend to tenses. In fact it falls a good deal short of that. Bunting and posters proclaiming the bill at the theatre gave the idea of what, if not when.

Turns out that in early July the town is home to a major theatre festival. An influx of 55,000 visitors fill the seats and, doubtless, the tills. The festival grew out of the town's status as an official spa. Three springs spouted curative waters, making the town a popular resort in the late nineteenth century. Visitors flooded in, though official spa status did not arrive until the 1930s. The second spur to theatrics came later, from Nazi desire to contrast German Kultur with "Jewish-Communist Decadence".

Behind this lay the towns origins. An Abbey was established in the ninth century by the Duke of Saxony, the town growing

178

up around it. Hrosvit or Roswitha, credited as being the first German poet, wrote there in the tenth century. I wonder what a medieval Christian poet would have made of being a Nazi icon? Given the attitude of the medieval church in Western Europe to Jewish people, one shudders to think that they may have been quite happy about it. Perhaps that is unfair to Roswitha, though not to the medieval Church. It was a different age; a backward age, unlike our own in which racial prejudice could never flame into violence, could it?

That Sunday morning, the place had that homely, small town feeling. Not complacency, but a liveable familiarity enhanced by the pretty, unspectacularly beautiful surroundings. The valley is broad and the dark, witch-ridden forests flanking the slopes of the Harz, a safe distance off. In places like this one can understand "heimat". Heimat; that relationship between a person and their surroundings, a positive feeling that may arise from birth or be acquired in some other way. Initially reassuring to those who were dislocated by the exodus into cities during the industrial revolution, it was patriotic but not nationalist. Despite that, it was a feeling that could easily be shifted into "blood and soil" extremism.

Today, that era seems that it should be as far away as Roswitha, though it is far from dead.

The gentle hills rolled on as we found our way through peaceful villages with almost no-one to be seen. We guessed that they had either had a good night out or were preparing for a big day in Bad Gandersheim. Happily this left the main drag almost totally to us east-bound cyclists.

We re-joined D-Netz 3, which at that point was also the Harz Cycle Route. At times the number of different emblems indicating cycle routes was bewildering. The Harz Cycle Route is designated by a witch on a broomstick. Such a sign directed us onto what, quite clearly, had once been a main road, but had been abandoned in favour of a new one that rumbled a short distance to the north. Guessing that this had been since the unification of East and West seemed reasonable, but it is surprising how rapidly nature can reclaim things. OK, some of the patches where the surface and underlying hard core had disappeared may have been down to human action. But the woods on the south side were edging their way across, bit by bit. Ice and snow of north German winters had lain open the surface. Rideable, but you'd want good, very bright lights after dark. An old leather saddle in contact with a leathery old arse aided comfortable progress.

Primal forces in the heart of medieval Germany. The old road may be disappearing, the witches of the Brothers Grimm and Walpurgisnacht may be present only on cycle route signs, but here, one felt, things had been different in the recent past. It began to feel, whether through prior knowledge held in a corner of my memory or some innate quality, like an old land with a much deeper past than the shallow pits that held the posts that bore the wire that kept a nation apart for forty years. One wondered how separate they might still be. The rest of the day provided some answers.

Signs took us along a quiet route into the old city of Goslar. Here it began to drizzle, so we sheltered under a tree outside the old cathedral, ate to the accompaniment of the muffled voices of the choir and congregation, and hoped that the rain would cease. It was the first rain of the tour, but not the last. To demonstrate that we were not going native, we discussed the rain; a penetrating, drizzly mass. Overshoes and jacket needed.

Goslar is a moderately sized town set under the brooding Harz Mountains, marking the edge of the North German Plain. The Harz Mountains may brood on sunny days too, but the trouble with moving-on touring is that you really don't get to know. Rain and cloud and forest could be seen merging over the spires, and brooding they definitely were.

In those dark slopes was the source of the wealth of the town, once a favourite residence of medieval German Emperors. The town was founded by Henry the Fowler, first of a line of Holy Roman Emperors from the Saxon and Salic dynasties. In the hills, to the south, silver, copper and other minerals were found, bringing wealth to the city and to the imperial rulers. Another area to come back to.

Tourists under massed umbrellas were guided past us to view the historic buildings and find out more about the quiet town's much noisier history. For the first time, I felt that it would have been pleasing to leave the mission and take a longer look around. No cycle tourist minds rainy day riding too much. You can't if you want to get somewhere. Yet, I recalled reading about medieval German history and Goslar had always featured on my list of places to visit. Once again, a definite venue for a longer stay. The area is a UNESCO

World Heritage Site - from its ancient mines and their drainage systems, to the city they paid for.

Spotting an illusory lightening of the rain, we headed off, passing out of an old city centre, full of modern shops, their lights shining in the early afternoon gloom. Goslar was no longer a Free Imperial City, but it was prosperous - obviously prosperous and able to preserve its past. Things were about to change.

There was no indication of where the old internal German border was. Maps make interesting reading for the cyclist, the historian, the geographer and the politician. Nations use them to assert rights or justify claims; winners redraw them; international treaties amend them. Take a look at maps of Poland from 1400 to the present day and you'll see it disappear. Try to tell a Pole that those maps of Eastern Europe where Russia, Austria-Hungary and Prussia cover modern day Poland are legitimate, or observe how ambitious Poland was in the fifteenth century. Take a look at the tangled history of Germany between 1945 and 1990. The maps tell all, with one big exception. Those border changes split families, friends, changed where people could shop and what they could do. All done by the drawing of a line on a map.

183

The seamless progress of roads and routes on the ADFC maps would not have been there when I started work in 1982. Somewhere the border must still be visible, in the Harz Mountains, perhaps. Yet, the difference between prosperous Lower Saxony and Saxony Anhalt was as sharp as any line drawn by a drafts-person across a blank sheet.

Though she lived far to the south, I could not help but think of how different life might have been had twelve year old Else Kalb found herself on the eastern side of the border. Seven years old when war broke out, life became increasingly hard by 1944. Yet, at least in the wooded valleys of northern Bavaria they could get wood for the fire and scavenge for mushrooms and forest fruit. A different branch of the family, in Thuringia, were, like her, "liberated" by the American's.

The American's were good news, on the whole. They might be enemies to be cautious of, but, to the mind of a girl brought up on Nazi propaganda the Soviets (Russians, Cossacks, and all) were barbarians capable of any sort of brutality. They were the real enemy.

Then things changed. That area of Thuringia was swapped by the Americans and the Soviets moved in. Soviets is accurate, but Russian was how she would have described them, so Russian it will be from now on.

She recalls how quickly things impacted on life. On one occasion she was told that she would represent the Bavarian branch of the family at a wedding across the border. This was before walls and fences had been erected, but travel was impossible. She would have to run the border. Her brothers were thought to be more at risk than she was... surely even the Russians would not harm a teenage girl.

So, having found enough money to buy a new pair of shoes and a nice dress - her father was temporarily unemployed and the families money came from making string bags, vests and suchlike, which her elder sister took to Munich to sell (by bicycle, a journey of over sixty miles each way) - off she went by train to meet a cousin who would guide her across the new dividing line.

It was mid-winter and deep snow sapped their energy as they approached the ridge above the forest. Against the moonlit sky, two guards were silhouetted as they chatted before moving off in different directions. The cousin had done his homework. Perfect timing took them across and down the other side before the guards returned to their meeting point.

That was the easy bit.

On the day of the wedding she dressed neatly in her new clothes, but was immediately told that she could not wear them. "You will be spotted. No-one here has new clothes or shoes. They will know you are from the other side. You must put on older clothes." Even in that short time, the material gap between the West and the East was becoming very obvious.

Fresh snow falls made it impossible to travel cross-country on the return journey. They would have to take the road. Wrapped up as warm as could be managed and with a gift for the border guards, she set off with her cousin. He'd take her as far as the guard post and help carry her bag with her nice new shoes and dress and a lot of string. "I don't know why," she recalls, "They did not have much but they always had lots of string. Each time I ran the border, they had lots of string."

Near the summit of the road stood a guard post. A light shone in the window and a guard was visible, standing by the door.

Her cousin left her and she walked on alone. Remembering what she had been taught about the Russian's she did not expect to be allowed to pass unmolested. These were the monsters which the war had been meant to destroy. Now they were in charge.

On she walked and the guard raised his head and told her to come into the hut. He prodded his sleeping colleague and they looked her up and down. She'd expected him to kick his comrade awake.

Reaching into her bag she produced the bottle of diluted meths mixed with bottled cherries; Germans, it seems, were convinced that bored, homesick soviet guards - in fact, any Russian - would drink anything alcoholic.

The men took the drink and gestured her on her way. She walked alone to the nearest station and headed for home. Things had changed rapidly; her view of "Russians" was modified, the family in the east would soon be out of reach and it would be many years before Germany was reunified. String for the vests would have to be found elsewhere, though when her father returned to work, it was not necessary.

187

Else is my brother's mother-in-law.

Lines on maps matter, though we had only had to show our passports once on the trip - in Hull. Not until we reached Prague Airport to return home would we need them again. With the debate on EU membership continuing in the UK, I wondered if, amongst all the noise about trade, sovereignty and cooperation, that the thing people would notice most would be queues at airports, ferry terminals and any other border crossing. Maybe Brits will need a Schengen Visa. Who could tell at that time?

Bad Harzburg was the end of the line in Cold War days. Just beyond lay the Eastern Bloc.

With the rain becoming thicker, we stuck to roads - more obvious signposting allowing the map to stay in the bar bag, where it was meant to keep dry. It was in a little village called Wasserleben that I spotted that the houses were dull, sometimes decrepit, versions of their former German Federal Republic counterparts. Casting my mind back to brightly decorated woodwork in Hoxter and in sunny villages along the way, Wasserleben was dull and, literally on the day, weather-beaten. The miserable afternoon curtain of rain seemed appropriate in a village whose name translates as "Live Water".

Cracked window frames encasing hollow-eyed windows, disconsolate empty houses in the heart of the village. If there was life, it seemed to be limited to the three women who eyed us warily as we passed. Mind you, cycling for pleasure in the rain is one pastime that may well deserve a wary eyeing.

Even so, Wasserleben should have been a sepia photo of times gone by; a rustically overladen ox-wagon blocking the turning in the heart of the village, a mountain of hay brushing the upper storeys of the grimy buildings. This afternoon, there was not even a Trabant to disturb the splash of rain on the patches of tarmac and uneven setts. A Gothic scene, a set for a peasant rising in a Frankenstein movie. In the light of a bright sun, it may have looked very different.

In fact, Saxony-Anhalt, the province we were to cycle in for the next couple of days, has been economically out-performing most other German Lander in the last few years. The almost total collapse of its Soviet era state run industries has been retrieved by massive infrastructure investment, by the German government. Unemployment is down and farming is on the up as well. Despite this, the population continues to decline, partly because of migration, partly due to a mismatch in the death and birth rates. Assertions that Saxony-Anhalt has overcome all its problems since re-unification looked overstated to me.

Still, of all the German Lander, Saxony-Anhalt has, proportionately, the most World Heritage Sites. These are not given away. This province owes the multiple honours bestowed on it by UNESCO to those good old Saxon and Hohenstaufen Kaisers and a disgruntled cleric named Martin Luther. Quedlinburg Castle and Old Town is a UNESCO site; that was our destination for the day. But, before then, we made a serendipitous discovery that was unwanted but salutary.

My introduction to Saxony-Anhalt was not ideal. Sure, the little villages were probably pleasant enough, but determined rainfall that seeks out weakness in waterproof defences put a literal dampener on initial impressions. Yet of all the memories assembled as we trundled across Germany, it was Saxony-Anhalt that provided my strongest. On that Sunday afternoon I just couldn't get over the feeling that, in the Land with the lowest immigration of any German State, the highest level of depopulation and the lowest religious identity in Germany, that its people might have lost faith in Communism, Capitalism and God. I was heading that way.

By the way, that does not make it a bad place full of miserable, deprived people. Not one little bit.

We took roads all the way to Langenstein - none of them cobbled, sett or with patches of sand - but there we knew we'd need to take to a cycle route. Trouble was that the signed route did not seem to be signed in the right direction and looked anything but welcoming. Had it been covered in a foot of dung, some of the tangled mass of setts would have forced a sharp corner through the surface. So we left the little bridge where this brookside "cycle" route embarked from and ended up in a quaint, but quiet village centre.

Then we spotted a sort of social-cum-sports club. It was open and had a pretty good crowd of people coming in and out. So, we asked. What was the best way to Quedlinburg, please? Was there a cycle route?

Clearly cycle sport was not amongst those pursued by the Langensteiners, or maybe the cyclists were out training in the rain. Neither did anyone seem to go to Quedlinburg by bicycle. At last, one helpful local said that he thought there was a cycle route on the left if we carried on up the road. He was unsure and so were we. Left would not, logically help, but maybe there was a right turn too.

Off we went. We rode to the end of the road. Yes, we passed a field track that crossed the road and, on reflection, a study of the map in a nice dry room at Quedlinburg YH, we should have turned to the right and followed it for a couple of kilometres before joining the brookside route of jagged surface. Yet, we did not; so unattractive did it's drenched surface look. Pouring rain deprives one of sense sometimes and we went to, literally, the end of the road, where there was a right turn onto a track. It was not signed, but we took it.

In a few metres we passed through a gate and spotted some noticeboards. We pedalled on. Ahead were some derelict looking buildings and what appeared to be an unheralded monument. Depressing weather and we had stumbled upon a concentration camp from the Nazi era. A small one. A satellite of the much bigger Buchenwald. Here only 7000 prisoners dug and laboured and starved in underground galleries meant to protect the manufacture of engines for new jet aircrafts. Only 7000.

Functioning for only a year, it was liberated by the US Army in April 1945. Most of the inmates had been marched off in the pointlessly cruel Death Marches so symbolic of SS determination to drag everyone into their own perverted Götterdamerung - those SS that did not run-away of course. It is estimated that a mere 25% of the Langenstein "marchers" survived their trip to Berlin.

Described as a camp for political prisoners of all nationalities, it also had a crematorium to deal with the inevitable deaths. There were 1100 hopelessly weak male inmates left when the liberators arrived. Few could stand. One leant on a door jamb, fleshless, his kneecaps the most prominent feature. Thus noted one of the American officers. That image stays with me as much as the images from the film of the liberation of Belsen when, with outstretched arms a skeletal figure lurches helplessly towards a soldier, vacant eyes staring, seeing God only knows what. Was there hope in his heart or what was left of it? Like the Lidice women, liberation staggered limply into their consciousness.

The memorial carries the names and nationalities of many of the inmates. Poles, Belgians, Russians, Czechs, Dutch, Germans and more. One can see why European unity has an attraction. Of course, not being in what some regard as an overweening, undemocratic bureaucracy, is not the only alternative to continental war. It isn't, is it?

A little beyond the memorial track, which we thought might be the one indicated by the people in the village, fizzled out. Retracing our tyre tracks past the memorial, past the handful of huts and through the gate, we agreed that it was a sombre, sobering spot to match the dingy light and the constant rainfall. So, we headed back to the village, once again ignoring the turning we should have taken.

Back at the social club, another bunch of friendly and helpful locals understood enough of our German to realise that they were going to have to use what little English they had. Generally, English speakers are less common the further east one goes in Germany, though amongst the younger generation it is common. Their parents and grand-parents learned Russian. Still, the mobile phone is international and without resorting to a translation app we were able to find that, according to their data, there was no road between

Langenstein and Quedlinburg, without going a very, very long way round. Not only were these people not cyclists, none had ever been to Quedlinburg along a local road, only on the autobahn.

"That is not a thing you can do," said one. We realised this, but the whole wet afternoon had been topped off by the diversion with its dismal terminus, so even taking on the speed of German motorists on a motorway might not be so bad. We could get a lift from the Polizei and pretend to be ignorant foreigners. That would not be so wide of the mark. With limited acting necessary, we might even get an early dinner and only a small fine.

Only joking. So, we turned down the lunar surface of the cycle route we had first spotted on our way in. Yes, a small sign indicted that this was it, The Harz Vorland Radweg. It was possible that a troop of highly skilled artisans had painstakingly tessellated each sett into place, tamping it into place with a specialist hammer. I imagined a troop of East Germans kneeling in line and advancing in the belief that pride in their work and the creation of a better socialist society would be reflected in the excellence of the short stretch of road they were building. Their labours being undone by the careless hand of capitalism as it spread, alienating the pride of the worker from the socially useful task he had performed. Equally, a lazy builder who had just demolished a farm may have, in order to maximise profit, tipped the debris out, kicked it round haphazardly and driven his van over it a few times.

Whatever their political era, these setts refused to accept the authority of their capitalist master or show socialist class consciousness and stick together in solidarity. On the other hand, there was no liberal compromise to rub along with their neighbours. These were the awkward brigade of any political system. They'd argued with their neighbours, rejected a common purpose and had each gone their own way. Fed up with the rules of geometry or the dictate of cycle-path building, they were forging their own individualistic future.

Fortunately, after a couple of hundred metres - it seemed much longer - we found ourselves on a relatively smooth, filthy wet, mud track. There were more signs and they pointed toward what we estimated to be roughly the correct direction. We climbed gently with unexciting views of wet crops and not much more. There was an incongruous level-crossing and more mud roads. But we trundled, as the map had led us to expect, almost straight ahead. It was not enjoyable. Rough riding, dirty bikes and Mark occasionally explaining the benefits of disc brakes. I prodded accumulated mud from between brake block and wheel rim with a stick. Neither of us was enjoying this, though it may have been very pretty under better conditions.

A mental fanfare sounded when tarmac returned in a hamlet named Börnecke. Relieved, we rode along a cracked tarmac surface and made a left turn following the HVR signs. A second sign pointed to the right along Westerhausener Strasse. For me that was enough. Mark wanted to ride down the hill to see if there was another route. I did not want to get the map out or go down the hill. I set off, demonstrating decisive route-finding, though it could have been interpreted as over-assertiveness.

A little way along Westerhausener Strasse, a short ride beyond the last house in Börnecke, there was a dog in the road and no sign of an owner. There were sheep in the open fields at the roadside. Dogs and cyclists do not always mix, especially farm dogs. We prepared to be nipped at and chased. Not always easy amongst straggling sheep.

As I watched the dog, it remained calm. Suddenly, I became aware that there was a figure on the bank to the left. I started and stared. Standing motionless and towering silently in a long shepherd's cloak was a man smoking a pipe. His hat reached its zenith at the rear and sloped gently to the narrow brim at the front. From it the raindrops dripped clear of his pipe onto his heavy, gaitered boots, which reached upward under the cover of his cloak. His lovat green get-up was almost a camouflage.

I wished him a good afternoon. He replied accordingly, though I think he added that it was not such a good afternoon in every sense. Then he was gone as we went on toward Quedlinburg. This was the second great memory from Saxony-Anhalt. No, not managing to wish a good afternoon and be understood. No, this shepherd seemed timeless in his traditional attire, doing a job that in many places such as this, would now be done by fences and an occasional visit on a quad bike.

He might have stood there when Germany was reunited, not even blinking at the news; maybe he witnessed the advance of the Soviet or American armies; maybe he had guarded his sheep as the Nazis took over. He could even have been on passing terms with Napoleon as he went on his way to Russia - if he went that way - or had a brief chat with Martin Luther about Indulgences. Mind you, if he had stayed that still Luther may have considered nailing a Thesis to him.

All that conjecture apart, the figure of that shepherd has stayed with me and shows no signs of going away.

A little further on we found an example of the kind of investment which has come into the east after re-unification. The smoothest of smooth tarmac sped us into Quedlinburg. Our lights flashed on the pure, black asphalt. A sign took us to the Altstadt and the hostel... if only we could find it amongst the labyrinth of cobbled streets and alleys between timber-framed buildings. I don't mind wandering in these places, but by that early evening, I just wanted to shower, put on clean, dry clothes and have dinner and a couple of beers. Where was that hostel?

We squared the compass and the hostel was not where it should have been; we SatNavised the location and could not find the spot; we asked some passers-by, who thought it was somewhere about; we looked down every street and on the third circuit looked up to see a sign on a wall against which I had propped my bike; Jungendherberge.

The hostel was empty that night - apart from us. It had been full on Saturday night. I think that is what the warden said as she took me through the various forms that needed filling in before we could be admitted. Dripping water on the forms, I had visions of having to do the lot in triplicate. I fetched Mark to do his bit, as one of us was not enough. Now, German youth hostels are organised on a State basis and this was definitely more what one expected from eastern Germany compared to the relaxed arrival at JH Detmold. Not unfriendly, no, amiable and welcoming enough, but it was the first taste that East Germany was finding it harder to adapt to the more relaxed customer care of the west. A tangible hang-over of more authoritarian times?

Formalities completed, the warden showed us round the hostel; our comfortable twin; showers down the corridor, bikes in the games room and the breakfast room across the courtyard. A drying room? Well, with no-one else in the hostel we utilised the corridor radiators - which were not on - as well as the shower room. Damp stuff draped, humans showered and dressed, we rapidly set off into that huddle of pretty houses and narrow cobble streets we had managed to find the hostel in an hour or two before.

The rain had stopped, but it was prematurely dark for a June evening. Actually, perfect. The cobbles reflected the glow of old street-lamps; pastel painted panels between the light timber frames were gently illuminated as if the evening sun was filtering through the thick clouds. It wasn't, but nor was it raining.

Wandering in such a place is not too much of a problem, but we were both hungry. A couple of take-away places on the edge of the Altstadt were not too tempting and the cafés were closed. Then, down a side street, by a rather grand stone building, we spotted a flood of light, a couple of wet parasols over some empty tables. The doors were closed but lights shone inside. Time for beer and grub.

Both were smashing. I seem to recall I had a pork based dish. A strong possibility, but the most memorable thing about the meal was that we had a frightful row. Well, being in each other's company all day for eight days, being of significantly different dispositions and having had a soggy, tiring ride, a bit of a barney was probably inevitable at some stage.

201

The chosen topic for disagreement was the state of the English education system. I think I know about education; so does, Mark. Exactly how we got into finger-wagging and so on. I cannot really remember - a sign of how little it really mattered. However, voices were raised. In the end we both offered to walk out of the restaurant. I apologised. Whether, Mark did or not or even needed to, I do not recall. It really does not matter.

The other customers missed the fun. They'd gone up into the gallery to watch football. We should probably have joined them and taken out the day's frustrations on whoever was playing that evening. Beer was very good, but a good night's sleep was needed. A sunny morning would be even better.

We admired the architecture on the way back to the hostel, discussing finials and decorative features, avoiding education policy.

We slept well and, in the morning, the sunshine had returned.

Chapter Twelve

In fairness to Mark, he did not gloat about disc brakes when I decided to spend some time adjusting my brake pads shortly after leaving the hostel. We'd eaten well, the sun was shining and the previous evening's vigorous debate had been followed by a very good recuperative sleep.

Clothes were dryish - those that were not occupied by rear racks and fluttered pennant-like in the breeze. Yesterday's rain was left behind. Moving on tours move on; the past is not forgotten, but the day's ride lies ahead and all that needs to be done is to turn the pedals and follow some kind of direction.

We'd decided to head out on the road to Hoym, from where we could follow a cycle route or roads to Falkenstein Harz and cut across country to Alsleben on the river Saale.

Quedlinburg seemed to be reasonably prosperous - there were hotels, tourists, shops and car sales, but Hoym was another matter. Arriving in a cobbled square on a cobbled street, all around we were spied on by dark windows looking out of flaking frames. Apparitions of shop names appeared faintly above some. Ghosts from the not so distant past. A butcher, a baker - no candlestick maker, though my German would not have gone that far anyway. Other unidentified enterprises too. Wiped out by Soviet era political ideology or by the challenges of competitive capitalism? Do not suppose it mattered much. Could just be the retreat we all see, wherever we live, from the village shop to the mega-market.

We alone moved - and that slowly. It came as a shock when a frail sash window rattled up and an elderly woman looked out. Her expression was a mixture of wonderment and concern. Why should anyone be here? Why were we on bikes? This was not Quedlinburg with its Altstadt and Castle, what were we looking for? Surely we could only be up to no good? Maybe we needed help? We must be lost? Or were we criminals? Guess Brits on bikes were a rarity in the village.

She called something as we moved off. Neither of us understood her, so we left her behind, with a friendly wave, unanswered. Why should we act differently to history?

Around the corner was a preserved watermill. A few miles on, during a brief, unintentional detour, a fully working watermill was in commercial operation. Green technology, lack of investment, inherited tradition or Communist inefficiency? All of them? Possibly. Maybe the "humble" watermill, one of man's greatest inventions, should be used more. After all, what is a hydro-electric power station other than a flashy waterwheel? Quite a bit more, I know, but not so different.

Hoym's version restored the village's still, silent persona after the rude interruption by the opening of a window. On the one hand, I wondered if that woman was the last inhabitant; on the other I expected to find a supermarket on the outskirts. Perhaps everyone had gone to work in Halle or Magdeburg, the two largest cities in Saxony-Anhalt, and one by one decided not to return. I hope I am not being unfair. I hope I'm mistaken, but Hoym seemed to personify some of the challenges being faced by Saxony-Anhalt; it could be beautiful, but it was run down and there seemed to be nothing for people to do to earn a living. Maybe, one day, it will go the same way as some run-down British towns and become the residence of choice for a flourishing generation looking to find a peaceful bolt hole from their busy lifestyles in PR, advertising or the Stock Exchange. Maybe.

A cycle track passed over a bridge next to the mill, signed with the logo we wanted. Mixed cart track, grass and the odd bit of concrete provided variety, but not great interest. All around, the land lay flat and featureless, until the Harz Mountains came back into distant view. In the meantime, I counted the cars along the road that ran parallel to the track, a mere few metres away.

Two passed us by the time we reached the next village, Reinstedt. Heretical this may be, but why bother about a cycle track of undistinguished condition with traffic so light? Being that there's no reason to assume drivers here were possessed of any greater homicidal tendencies than elsewhere and given that mass commuting to and from this rural backwater is almost certainly a fantasy - at least, at present - one must ask if it is really necessary?

We were actually back on our dear old D-Netz 3, though heading in the opposite direction to previous encounters. Explaining this without diagrams is tricky, but we were heading south toward the Harz, whilst our old chum having followed the foothills of the range was looping away north toward Magdeburg. I'd like to offer this as an excuse for a little wander into Meisdorf. Very pleasant, but unnecessary. Slavish following of routes without checking how far along it one is. Pathetic.

Yet Meisdorf was interesting, sitting at the Harz foot. The working watermill and a growing number of tourist orientated businesses made it brighter than Hoym. The sun was returning, after a cloudy spell. However, we were both overtaken by a feeling that we were heading into the hills, when we should be keeping east as the deep valleys curved away to the south.

What should really have given away our location was a whopping great castle standing on a prominent hill. The instruction, had we had a guidebook, should have stated, "pass the right of the immense castle that is impossible to miss and turn left". We had gone straight ahead.

The Konradsburg was remarkable and we actually ended up in the grounds after climbing and taking a second very minor - and, in this case - very welcome, unintentional detour. Castle and monastery; events are held here and the site can be visited - though not at the time we arrived.

The reason we arrived at all was due to a missing sign. The junction was obvious, but unpromisingly covered by long grass. A little way up, was a sign, invisible earlier. So we followed field tracks and soon arrived in Endorf, tiny, quiet

207

and rustic. Several of the buildings looked like the remnants of something more impressive. I'd have liked to have known more. They were old, but well-cared for and still in use.

Expecting storms later on - we'd been impressed by the accuracy of earlier weather forecasts - we arrived rapidly at a consensus; let's just follow the roads.

The roads we'd take kept south of Aschersleben, Saxony-Anhalt's oldest town - if you take monastic foundation charters as authority for that sort of thing. There was another of Buchenwald's satellite slave labour camps there, building Junker aircraft. Whether any of the Lidice women ended up here, I do not know. Yet Aschersleben does have a tenuous Lidice link.

****

Before the attack on Pearl Harbour, intervention in the Second World War was a matter of great contention in the USA. Whilst President Roosevelt was sympathetic to British requests for help, he played a waiting game. His opponent in the 1940 presidential election had been one of the few Republicans to advocate intervention on the side of the UK;

a businessman and lawyer named Wendell Willkie. Defeated, Willkie did not stop calling for the USA to consider its future safety and get involved in support of fellow democracies (and, of course, the thoroughly undemocratic USSR).

Following the Lidice atrocity, Willkie made an animated speech in support of action. His father had migrated to the USA from Aschersleben. I'd not even thought that Willkie was a German name; Scottish, yes, but German? So much for jumping to conclusions. Perhaps it was his German origins that inspired his interventionism; his great opponent in debates, the famed pilot Charles Lindbergh was also of German ancestry. Perhaps not. There's more to identity than ancestry and nation. Willkie's mother was born in the USA, of German migrant parents.

Of course, there were many Czechs and Slovaks in the USA too. Amongst that diaspora today is Toni Brendel. She has recorded how Lidice has been commemorated around the world, starting in her home town of Phillips, Wisconsin. This region saw many Czechs and Slovaks settle in the early twentieth century, and keeping traditions and links with their homeland has been a feature of civic life. One of those wonders of the USA; being American, but not forgetting the

209

old country. Many ex-pats keep old traditions from the homeland much more vigorously than those who stayed behind.

In her book, "Lidice Remembered Around the World", Toni points out that Pittsburgh and Chicago had large Czech and Slovak populations, and that there was even a Lidice in Illinois, now known as Crest Hills. Smaller Czech communities, such as Tabor, in South Dakota, also existed.

She describes how, when Phillips's residents heard news of the atrocity at Lidice on the wireless sets, they felt a very special bond;

> *Theirs was a very personal pain. They were sickened to hear about the indescribably inhumane events. Many surnames of the victims were identical to their own; Dolezal, Dvorak, Fojtik, Horak, Podhora, Popisil, Rames, Starka, Suchy, Urban, Vokoun, Zeman, Novotny, Novy. With a sense of anger, helplessness and despair, once heads began to clear, they made plan to memorialize Lidice in their own village.*

By 1943, they had erected a temporary memorial. The permanent memorial was unveiled in 1944, designed by Vaclav Hajny, whose miner father had once lived in Lidice. Crest Hills, formerly Lidice, had unveiled the first memorial to Lidice in 1943, with Wendell Willkie addressing the crowd which attended the ceremony.

However, Toni also points out that numerous communities in South America commemorated the events of 1942. Lidice and Ležaky became Christian names for girls. Prominently, a town in Brazil promptly renamed itself Lidice, but many others across the continent named parks, streets and squares after the distant Bohemian village.

Bremen, Germany, did too, but not until later.

Stoke-on-Trent had a small, but significant and active, Czech community before 1939. A number of children from the Kindertransport were relocated to the Potteries because of this. Some of the older residents of the area still talk of the "Czech children" with great affection. Amongst these children was Charles Strasser, founder of Photopia, in Newcastle-under-Lyme, one of the world's leading photographic businesses, at one time. There was also a small number of

Poles already established in Stoke-on-Trent, as well as a small Jewish community. Amongst both of these was Barnett Stross, General Practitioner, Councillor and, in modern parlance, Activist with a capital A.

Born on Christmas Day, 1899 in Pabianice, near Lodz, Poland, his family moved to the UK when he was three years old. Eastern Europe saw frequent pogroms and anti-Semitic attitudes were not uncommon. The UK had plenty of its own racists, but the family flourished in Leeds and Barnett went to University and became a General Practitioner.

Whether it was his desire or good luck that took him to North Staffordshire, or Stoke-on-Trent's good fortune, he certainly ended up in the right place for someone with a professional interest in diseases of the lungs. Opposed to smoking on the grounds of its impact on the respiratory system, he found a population living in a smoky bowl in the hills. Conditions such as Miner's Lung and Potter's Rot were common.

Often giving his services for free, Stross - known to his family as Bob - was christened Dr Bob by his clientele of miners and potters. He represented both the Potter's and Miner's trade unions in medical affairs, campaigning for better conditions

212

and for compensation for miners with serious work-related lung problems. "Media Campaign" has a modern ring, but Stross cut his teeth on campaigning for improved working conditions. When news of Lidice spread, it was almost inevitable something would happen, either through the Czech community's persuasion or the well-known Dr Stross's fundamental desire to challenge injustice, or both.

It was one thing to shout back at Hitler that "Lidice Shall Live". Going beyond the symbolic was another matter. It was here that his understanding of the local community was crucial. He would have been told about the villagers of Lidice, he would have known that his popularity amongst the North Staffordshire miners would allow him to appeal to that bond of kinship between miners, as well as to the sense of common kindness and generosity that is still such a prominent feature, in my experience, of the people of North Staffordshire.

Amongst his political and professional acquaintances, there must have been Arthur Baddeley, leader of the North Staffordshire Miner's Federation. A Methodist lay-preacher - with his moral roots in the Primitive Methodism that had such a huge impact in the mining communities and elsewhere in North Staffordshire - he was to be a key ally for Stross.

Both were eventually awarded the Order of the White Lion by the Czechoslovak government, for their leadership of the Lidice Shall Live campaign. No doubt honoured by the award, Baddeley's daughter, Muriel Stoddard, made it clear that his motivation was simple; "I suppose it was because it was to do with the mining community to which all his life he always belonged. It was to do with a mining community. He was very concerned with anything to do with mining." Stross, who had numerous achievements to his name, regarded the Lidice Shall Live campaign as his greatest success. Despite the amount of money raised and the rebuilding of the village, he felt that way because an act of terror and been turned into a weapon of peace and international cooperation.

Something we should remember today.

****

Cobbles may still be the order of the day on some eastern German roads, but the days when they were ubiquitous have gone. Slowly, they have been upgraded to asphalt, much to the relief of cyclists, no doubt. Having said that, when you do hit the cobbles, it is hard not to recite old jokes from the 1970s, referring to vulnerable parts of the male anatomy. I know better than to speak on behalf of women. A more important challenge is to resist teaching unwitting passers-by English vulgarities. Of course, the less common these cobbled stretches of road become, the more shocking they are and the likelihood of colourful language increases, though the chances of locals further developing their knowledge of English diminishes.

After several miles and a handful of villages without sighting so much as a pot-hole, we hit the road from Freckleben to Sandersleben. Patches of blown soil crept across the road and a peculiar breed of lumpen, bluish setts stuck out like miniature, rounded summits. The Observers Book of Cobbles and Setts may not have been written, but there were definite local variations on the theme. These ones were of medium size and seemed to have originally been parallelograms. Setts are quarried and worked into roughly regular shapes - though they may be far from uniform; cobbles are quarried and left as they are - or so I am told. So these were definitely setts, but they were radically uneven. Rattling over them risked dislocation of components, and not just the bikes.

By contrast, the tarmac after Sandersleben was a ribbon of tyre-humming carpet. And didn't the lorries know it. Rumbling setts cause everyone to rumble, race-track asphalt unleashes the beasts. It was the contrast that was noticeable, rather than the presence of any real threat, but by the time we reached the outskirts of Alsleben, things were getting busy - as can often be the case where there is a major river to cross.

A grassy bank surrounded by shrubs enclosing a service station, may not be the picnic location of dreams, but it was the best on offer before descending into the town. Unsure still of why we chose it, it turned out to be a fortunate choice.

We got the daily bread and cheese out. At that point I had a mysterious case of "Bothy Rush". For the uninitiated a bothy is an isolated shelter, generally in very remote country. Sometimes still used by shepherds or fishermen, they're open to the public. Carry out what you carry in; leave it tidy; maybe make up a fire in the grate; in all cases read the instructions about where to get fresh water and where to perform your bodily functions - there's a spade to dig. Maintained, in Britain, by the Mountain Bothies Association, in many cases, and in cooperation with local landowners, bothies provide valuable refuges. If you use one, take care of it.

So what is the "rush"?

At one time - still may be the case - there was, amongst outdoorsy folk, a propensity for use of dehydrated food. The effects of this often resulted in the alarming sight, in the depths of night, of a figure stepping rapidly over the sleeping denizens of the bothy, grabbing the spade and heading into the moonlit undergrowth.

Having that feeling in an urban area is a totally different experience - it was not as if I had touched dehydrated food. Public loos seem less common on the continent and the semi-industrialised edge of a small German town was unpromising. Jumping onto the bike and yelling to Mark that I'd see him shortly, by the river, I prepared to head into town. A glance to my right revealed a snooker hall of all things. They'd have a toilet, wouldn't they?

Caring not how I might explain my predicament to the lady in a polo shirt who was hoovering the lobby, I blurted something that had the desired effect. She pointed to a door at the far end.

A few minutes later, I emerged. She was smiling. Maybe it was quite common for middle-aged touring cyclists from the UK to burst into the room yelling "Toiletten, bitte!" It was only then that I noticed that there was nobody using any of the tables. There was no one else there at all.

She asked, in very good English, if that was better. Of course, it was. I explained my predicament and it was "no problem". As it turned out, her son had spent some time in Stoke-on-Trent, in Hanley to be specific. The world gets ever smaller. Naturally, as with almost every person we had met since Quedlinburg, she wondered what had brought us that way; it was not the traditional tourist route. Lots of cyclists came along the river, but not across country.

She had heard of Lidice, but not about the North Staffordshire mineworker's link to it. At this point I remembered that Mark might be down by the river by now, so said farewell.

No, there was Mark, nibbling cherry tomatoes - clearly some very nice ones, given the sounds of appreciation he was making. I'd noticed that sounds some adults would associate with the early stages of love-making were induced, in Mark's case, by ripe cherries, strawberries - almost any tasty morsel.

He was in no rush to leave an island of gourmet delight set between a busy main road and a fuel station.

When we did leave, it was with speed down to and across the River Saale. A few hundred metres further on and we picked up signs that took us down to the banks of the river and the Saale Cycle Route.

Strangely, I recalled some stuff from my ancient GCE O Level English Literature exam. Shakespeare's "Henry V" - Salic law and where it applied were a key legal debate in Henry's claim to the throne of France. Whether this was anything to do with the River Saale, I had no idea, but it came back to me and I nearly burst into a chorus of "Our King Went Forth To Normandy".

Had I done so, it may have mystified the cyclists who were pedalling along the neat strip of tarmac that ran by the river. As ever, German cyclists love the valley cycleway; they probably have a word for that particular emotion: Liebezumradfahrenaneinemfluss, maybe.

Late middle-aged, though not of the "electric granny" bracket, almost all clearly had some money. High quality gear - the sort that would be associated in the UK with people heading into the wilds or onto Ambleside High Street on a wet day - mounted on solid trekking upright bikes; these were the honest burghers who traditionally went on long Sunday walks culminating in vast plates of cake and cups of coffee followed by schnapps, who were helping to rejuvenate the economy of the Saale valley. Tourism, tourism, tourism.

The river at this point was broad enough to carry large vessels. Not steeply-sided enough to be spectacular, the valley is an attractive mixture of woodland and pasture, with occasional climbs, for the cyclist, over the low spurs that interrupt level progress. You can see why cyclists of a certain age and style love this kind of riding, and you can see why local government has given priority to building infrastructure here over some of the rougher, wilder cycle routes we'd followed between Goslar and the Saale.

As we found out later, hotels, restaurants and bars close to the river did well from cycling. Even so, not everyone had quite managed to adapt to the modern capitalist system. Taking a moment to shelter from a shower of rain, we suddenly realised we were under the eaves of a bike shop; a bike shop along a popular cycle route; no sign, no board

220

outside, no offer of a tune-up or availability of spares and repairs. Darkened windows added to the feeling that there was something either seedy or forbidden about bike shops by the Saale - or maybe the desire to make a profit still had not quite caught on amongst bicycle mechanics.

We took a few minutes to admire the castle at Wettin; not spectacular in style, but rising in best layer-cake fashion above the small town. A former centre of power belonging to the House of Wettin, who named the castle after themselves when they took it from the Slavic Sorbs. Eventually, the Wettins became Electors of Saxony and Dukes of Saxony, and later branches of the family became the Royal houses of Belgium, Portugal and the UK - amongst others. Wettin now seems to be a bit of a backwater, though clearly attracting tourists.

We admired it briefly and refilled bottles at the tap by the ferry.

On this day Wettin was wetted by a hefty storm. Great minds punning alike, the inevitable surfaced - Mark got there first, thus deserving the credit and responsibility; "We got a wetting in Wettin." Needless to say there were no hearty guffaws shaking our lungs to impede immediate progress.

Rothenburg-an-der-Saale sounded as if it should be pleasant. On the day, it did not look especially so. Trouble with the kind of moving on tour we were doing is, at least when it comes to forming opinions, that you really only see a little on either side of the track which you travel. An impression limited to whatever is visible on either side; a good high hedge could obscure an interesting sight. Existentialists might want to argue the point, but it is only introduced to serve as a ready excuse for the fact that what we saw of Rothenburg on a damp afternoon was not beautiful. Industrial archaeologists might have been fascinated, but the vacant look we got from a couple of guys sitting drinking beer on a doorstep did little to support the tourist trade. Having said that, there is a ferry and perhaps we should have sought out the Schifferhaus. Instead we saw a riverside industrial complex, elements of which seemed to be working, but it was hard to tell. Those with a strong realist streak might prefer this to Rothenburg-ob-der-Tauber, with its hopelessly romantic buildings and situation, but we pressed on.

There are numerous ferries across the Saale. There are bridges too, but much of the local traffic seemed to use the ferries. Paying the ferryman required scrabbling around for small change; ferries here are cheap. There might be impressive bridges for the main roads and old bridges in the main towns, but trundling between the villages a euro or less is money well-spent.

The Saale Cycle Route uses the ferry at Brachwitz. A short trip gave the ferryman time to collect the fairs and smile at our bicycles. He must do a good trade with cyclists - one suspects that on a summer's day his boat may carry more cycles than cars.

The route soon turned off the ferry road. Inundated by sand for several hundred metres, steering was a bit of a lottery at times. What really caught our attention, though, was acres of ground covered with prefabs and lean-to shacks. There were gardens too. Some buildings were scrawled with graffiti, derelict and squalid. Every now and again a sign announced, what I took, to be a "garden club". In these the prefabs were neatly kept, summer blooms, refreshed by the passing storms, filling the air with perfumed scent and the scene with bright colours.

We wondered whether these were squats that had, through a process unknown, become privately or collectively owned.

Had they been some kind of cheap housing scheme. We found out the answer later. Much later. We were told that these little pied-a-terres were created during the Communist era. With strict limits on travel and little money, city dwellers sought a breath of fresh air from what appeared to be akin to a Scottish but 'n' ben. Escape from the city, from the factory, from the tenement block. These were the lungs of Halle-an-der-Saale - or so we were told. Not that everyone had one, or even the majority. Even so, some have clearly caught the imagination of post-Communism Germans. Others were a tatty eye-sore.

They preceded the suburbs of Halle-an-der-Saale as the cycle route strayed away from the bank. Saale and Halle burst upon us at a gloriously wooded bend in the river, tree-lined parkland and a flotilla of colourful little boats. Sun-shining brightly, this could have been a holiday resort. We climbed up to the city to find Hostel Number 5, close to the very heart. Avoiding the tram-lines on a seemingly endless circuit of the town, we found it amongst an avenue of trees close to the city walls and just a short step, as it turned out, from the Cathedral.

Halle is Saxony Anhalt's second city, despite having a similar population to the state capital, Magdeburg. For British visitors the most obvious landmark would be the Handel Haus, birthplace and residence of the well-known British composer. In fairness, Handel settled in the UK after leaving Halle in 1703 and worked in other parts of Germany and Italy, as well. And, of course, from 1715 the British monarchy was German too.

We were too late to visit the birthplace of the composer.

After depositing the bikes at the hostel, we strolled along the broad streets and headed for the heart of the city. I'd heard that nearby Leipzig - over the border in Upper Saxony - was a great place to visit. Not having been there, I can't voice an opinion, but as one of the country's fastest-growing cities, many Germans clearly find it attractive. With a heavy-weight of cultural history - Johann Sebastian Bach is probably the most famous resident, but music, art and publishing all feature prominently in Leipzig's history - it probably dwarfs Halle. However, Halle was one of those cities to which I feel an immediate attraction.

Despite no great interest in Handel's music, I recalled "Raise the Alarm!" from Judas Maccabeus. My mother and uncles were all trained to sing and play the piano. Uncles have a habit of doing peculiar things and amongst Uncle Clive's peculiarities was a tendency, which he seemed unable to resist, to sing "Raise the Alarm!" in a resonant bass-baritone when someone rang the doorbell. It was far from his only song and his voice could be heard booming about the place during weddings, funerals, carols round the piano and so on. His piano playing was less successful, being scolded by my Grandma, I am told, for playing boogie-woogie whilst on leave from convoy-duty in the merchant navy during the Battle of the Atlantic. So much for culture.

A deep moat and old defences were crossed on the way to the city centre, where the appropriately named Market Church has a supermarket in the crypt, or so it looked from our approach. The Red Tower, two castles, Germany's oldest operational chocolate factory… Halle could keep the tourist occupied for a good long time. We were in search of food though, so the supermarket-in-the-crypt was all the culture we wanted.

Mark wanted to cook and magic up a salad. Having inflicted days of pork products on him, I went along with this. He does cook very well and it would save money too. Arriving latish, the square by the Market Church was quiet. Enough people to give it life, but not a summer tourist throng, as you'd find in Leipzig, Dresden or Prague. All to the good. I like cities where you feel that at least some of the people on the street actually live there or can afford to live close by. Yep, some of these people were off for a beer or were heading to the tram stop after doing the extra hour or so at work.

We searched through the supermarket. Mark concentrated on various vegetables. I sourced beer. There were all sorts of sausages, but did I give them a glance? Of course, I did. Did I attempt to slip one into the shopping basket? Did I consider putting a schnitzel under the bag of rocket and mixed salad leaves? No. What a fool.

Mark prepared a tasty meal in the hostel kitchen and we shared beer with a group of guys who were on a work trip. Their grub was not half as good as Mark's. I sliced salad and Mark slaved away at the pan. I opened the beer and wrote a blog as the finishing touches were put to dinner. All this domestic bliss was accompanied by a storm that would have knocked the spots off the Royal Fireworks, with or without music by Handel to accompany it. Then there was a rainbow, towering over the city.

We went to sleep as another storm approached. The air would be clear by the morning, we hoped.

****

Halle's musical culture goes back a long way. However, it's Conservatory of Music, Theatre and Teaching was founded only in the late nineteenth century by Richard Bruno Heydrich, an opera singer and composer married to the daughter of the Director of the Dresden Conservatory, where Heydrich had been a student.

In 1904 a son was born to the family; Reinhard Tristan Eugen Heydrich. He did well at school, was strong in Maths and Science and a fine athlete. Apparently he was bullied because of a high pitched voice and rumoured Jewish ancestry. At the age of fifteen he participated in a right-wing coup in Halle and from then on maintained links with nationalist and anti-Semitic groups. Joining the Navy, he had a string of love affairs and was eventually dismissed for conduct unbecoming an officer.

His wife, Lina, was a Nazi and it was probably she who introduced Heydrich to the party's ranks. From then on the career of "the man with the iron heart" sparkled. As he gained promotion after promotion he came to the notice of the Fuhrer, of whom he became a favourite. Tasked with destroying opposition to Nazi rule, he proved himself beyond doubt as the man to persecute, destroy and manipulate, but above all, the one who would hang his way to victory. The Final Solution was, probably, his idea.

In September 1941 he was placed in charge of the Protectorate of Bohemia and Moravia. Behind his appointment was a decline in industrial production and an increase in passive and active resistance. Increased rations for the workers and a campaign of terror against any political opponents or likely leaders of resistance ensued.

When, in the spring of 1942, he was warned of a plot to kill him, Heydrich refused to increase security and insisted on demonstrating the iron will of the Nazis to the population in general. He died from wounds a few days after the attack by

Gabčík and Kubiš. Others would wade in the blood of the Czech people, in general, and the villagers of Lidice and Leźáky, in particular.

As the men of Lidice were corralled waiting to face their deaths, a unit of the Schutzpolizei assembled in the village square by St. Martin's Church. Twenty were selected to form the execution squad. They marched to the orchard of Horák's farm. All had something in common with Heydrich. The great honour of shooting defenceless, innocent men and boys fell to a unit of the "Protection Police" from Halle. Three were of less hardy stuff than Heydrich. A pause in the executions - to drink looted beer - saw them decline further involvement.

With the removal of the women and children and the massacre of the men - a few exceptions were shot later - the mess needed to be tidied up and the village erased as if it had never existed. After all, that was what the Fuhrer demanded.

Destruction had already begun, so, pausing only to remove anything useful and to drink the villager's beer, all of Lidice was doused in petrol and set alight. As night fell, the village was burning; bereft of its people, it lived on in exile and name only. In the ensuing days everything, except a solitary pear tree, would be blown-up and bulldozed.

Chapter Thirteen

Whether you consider GPS to be an unreliable embuggerance or God's Gift to the Traveller, it does find ways out of cities really well. Getting out of an urban area is usually the most challenging bit of navigation of any day, especially when wishing to avoid the main roads where most of the signs are. Cyclists who know a city will tell you that the way you might go by car is rarely that which you'll follow on a bicycle. Back street cut-throughs and nipping across a park take the place of queuing on the main drag. Signed cycle routes might help, but to the eye of the stranger - with one or two notable exceptions - they can be hard to find and follow. Local destination signs don't always help when the town you want is twenty miles further on.

The good old GPS whipped us round some tenement-lined inner suburbs and across a main road and railway and we were back out into the countryside. Initially more stretches of bizarrely aligned setts made progress slow. Think, if Rubik had designed roads instead of cubes and left the problem half-solved; you'll be on the right track.

There was a muddy strip running alongside the road; a strip that narrowed and broadened, that changed place with odd sections of kerb. Trying to use this wasn't much faster, but saved the buttocks a bit of a pounding. Every now and again, the setts in the centre of the road remained smooth, but whenever we reached these a motorist came round a corner or pulled out of a drive, forcing us back to the edge.

The villages were immensely silent - by the time we got going the school run was done, commuters had commuted and the houses were shut. Cafés were not yet open and the setts rumbled on like distant thunder.

All of a sudden we left the historical throwback from the GDR and found ourselves in the white-heat of reunification road engineering. Symbolic of the new leap forward which has burdened the economy of the West and not yet solved the problems of the East, road infrastructure speaks of historic change. All I could say at the time was, "Thank God. My poor arse" - which wasn't the height of philosophy.

Not surprisingly we decided to accelerate and put in a sprint to the outskirts of Delitzsch, which we skirted via an industrial area next to a railway line. Minor confusion at the next

233

junction was soon dispelled and we decided that the best way for progress was to follow the road signs. No more cycle routes until late in the day - no, a list of village names from the map and the promise of decent roads all the way to the River Elbe. Mocherwitz, Krostitz, Kospa; the village names marked our progress, which felt all the more rapid because of it.

Eilenburg was busy, with people going about their business and sporadic waves of vehicles trundling along its wide main street. We searched out food and a bank. The latter caused a bit of trouble as we struggled to select the correct options from a list. All part of the joy of travel. Fortunately there was not a queue of Germans, either eager to help or to voice frustration at the incompetent Englanders who were wasting the lunchtime of busy people who had to get back to work.

Eilenberg is split into two by the little River Mulde. It wasn't a beautiful, deeply historic town, of the type so common in Germany. It had a pleasant, homely feel and the food shops and banks had definitely been appreciated. Green spaces by the river gave a feeling of openness and we were soon back into the countryside.

The plain rolled on, though a few more hills - albeit gentle - and more woodland began to cross our path. Storms rolled around. We successfully dodged them both by careful localised weather forecasting where alternative routes were possible and by good old luck. Rapid progress was made, halting occasionally to stare at the stork nests on telegraph poles and purpose made stork-nesting poles.

A feeling of greater prosperity crept up as the great river approached. Perhaps it was the farmland? But the fields were well-used, there seemed to be more livestock and the acres of grain were punctuated by copse and woodland. Even the surfaces of the country roads were smooth - even by comparison the winding rural lanes of home.

We stopped to eat our customary simple lunch picnic in Thallwitz. A delightful spot in a shallow valley. Here the River Lossa had been damned and sluices control the flow from a small lake. Sitting in the sun in the shade of trees by a pond built to power a mill? Could barely be better, could it? Thallwitz had a hotel, a small supermarket and other shops, a school; the houses in the centre were well-maintained, the nearby Schlöss and its park were still intact, the area around the central pond was cared for.

A few days before I had wondered if it was just the cloud and rain that had hung over the old villages of Saxony-Anhalt that had depressed the spirits. My question was now answered. It was not. Even if we had huddled out of a deluge, Thallwitz - and the neighbouring settlements we passed through - looked much more prosperous. This could have been superficial prosperity, but there was no doubt that there was more going on to propel money around the local economy. I could not help but wonder, if western Germans with money bought holiday homes or weekend bolt-holes? Maybe, but the amenities suggested more than just weekenders. Of course, it could well have been that our small selection of villages gave a biased impression. Saxony Anhalt had been interesting and full of history, but we were now in a land that was interesting and full of history and more able to pay for it. Mind you, this was not twee.

Our road followed the valley of the River Lossa; Lossa, Grosszscheppe, Kleinscheppe, Hohburg, Muglitz, Falkenhain, Borln, Bortewitz. All bucolic cycling, still successfully dodging the storm clouds. Sleepy miles, until a junction with awful sight lines in the traffic-ridden town of Dahlen. Nipping across the main road and selecting the correct route out, both took a bit of time. Cobbles... sorry, setts, can prove to be effective traffic calming. They also make it very easy to hear the approach of large vehicles. There were plenty of them passing through Dahlen, thundering along at no more than twenty-five mph.

A little to the north of our route, The Dahlener Heide is popular with hikers and hunters. Skirting around wooded hills, the scenery became more and more attractive, with the lake at Bucha catching our eye for a break. A long way from the sea, this lake makes Bucha something of a resort. Midweek on a sunny day, not a single boater, angler or swimmer made a ripple on the surface. Propping the bikes up against trees, we had a rest in the peace and the shade; by heck, the hotel across the lake looked nice, bet they had a beer garden just as shady and quiet as our roadside bench.

Instead of a half-litre of Saxon beer we opted to press on up the hill into the woods, passing a windmill prominent on a knoll. The cool of the woods dipping up and down into Cavertitz was joyful and, in seemingly no time, we popped out at the top of a valley side at Schirmenitz. Invisible, but obviously before us was the broad valley of the great River Elbe. A real stage-marker on our journey.

The Elbe is a very German river. On the map it slices across the country from Cuxhaven on the North Sea, through Hamburg, Magdeburg, Wittenberg, Meissen and Dresden, before cutting through Saxon Switzerland (nothing to do with Swiss territory, just hills and the mighty gorge carved by the river and a few romantic notions).

The Elbe Cycle Route is, I believe, the most popular German Cycle Route. However, the river does not rise in Germany. In fact it has travelled around a third of its total length - 680 miles - by the time it leaves the Czech Republic. It rises in the Krkonoše Mountains, or, in German, the Riesengebirge, close to the Polish Czech border. Here it is now known as the Labe (in Czech) and runs south out of the mountains. After Pardubice it heads west and north-west where it is joined by the Vltava (Czech) or Moldau (German) - or does it?

By some twist of fate the Elbe/Labe keeps its name when the, at this point, longer and wider Vltava/Moldau runs into it at right angles. Perhaps that is why the Bohemian river that flows through Prague, loses its name despite having drained, at their influence, a much larger basin than the Elbe/Labe.

In any case, whether the rain that filled the river fell on Bohemian mountainside or German forest, the Elbe we were joining was a thoroughly Saxon river. Lower Saxony, Saxony Anhalt, Upper Saxony; great states in their own right, at times in the past - especially the Electorate of Saxony and, after 1806, the Kingdom of Saxony. It would be a day's ride to the old capital: Dresden.

The Elbe was a landmark on our journey. We'd be with it until Ústi nad Labem, where we would leave it to ride on to Lidice. Before parting ways we'd travel through great enlightenment culture, disputed borderlands, tragedy and some beautiful scenery.

Needless to say, the cycle route does not always follow the river edge. It was a few kilometres before we ran by the sliding mass of water that makes the Elbe such a fine sight as it slews endlessly toward the Elbe Marshes. Pastures and water meadows, stooks and bales, boats towing barges, storks stalking fish or perching on the piles of hay. Bucolically restful, though not for the farmer or two who tossed the drying grass. I could almost have whistled a jumble of themes from Beethoven's Pastoral Symphony - one of my mother's favourites - and a celebration of the work of ordinary people and their importance. It was a sunny afternoon by a glorious river, the hardships of peasant life could barely be further away. Unless one was a peasant.

Sadly, we had but a cock-stride to enjoy our new acquaintance. Within a couple of kilometres we emerged onto the road just beyond Strehla. We turned back up the hill into the centre of this small, but lovely town. Through a cobbled, ochre-shaded square, and a few yards further on was our hotel.

Here was the perfect example of how cycle tourism was bringing prosperity. By British standards the tariff per night was low, very low; but by British standards the quality was high, very high. Friendly welcome, large comfortable rooms, hot shower, secure bike store. The owners of the hotel had clearly paid architect and builders a good deal.

A van arrived; a luggage wagon for a group of cyclists of the wealthy western German order, who arrived shortly after us. Services of a mechanic were called for - from the local bike shop. A visit to the nearby park in the grounds of the Schloss was organised, partly to visit the café-bar- restaurant. All very efficient.

Then came the question of where we should eat. It sounded as if the Schloss restaurant would be full and that there were limited alternatives.

"The Lindenhof is where we suggest for our guests. It is very good, but very busy. You should go now. Here are directions," said the lady of the house. We found the restaurant on one of the streets that ran off the square. In a broad avenue of villas, the restaurant stood out because of the tables and parasols - soon to be umbrellas - displaying colourful advertisements for the beer on offer.

A glance around confirmed the popularity suggested by the hoteliers. Groups filled all the inside tables, many gorging themselves heartily. This kind of behaviour is most inconsiderate when you have had a long day in the saddle and want to do exactly the same as they are. Shocking.

We wandered hopefully and studied the beer menu at the bar. "No, we have no table now," said the waitress. A waiter carried six foaming glasses of beer - wafting them almost under our noses.

"Perhaps we could eat outside?"

"Yes, I shall bring your menu with your beer."

Actually, the evening was still warm and sitting outside was pleasant. Then, it began to rain. Gently at first, breaking into a steady drizzle and then a momentary downpour. Good old German engineering extended to table-sun-shade-umbrella-parasol fabrication. Not a drop fell on us.

The waitress rushed out with our beer. God bless her! We don't want additional water in our pure German beer. Expertly, as, in my experience, with all German waiters and waitresses, the glasses were placed on beer mats flicked out from the hand much as a conjuror showing the ace of clubs to an amazed audience. Two menus appeared, as if from nowhere. She said she would return, or something like that. My German is not so good as to pick up rapid speech, so she may have said, "Bloody English, sitting in the rain." Must take local dialects into account.

There is something magic about having beer served at the table by experts. I struggle not to spill precious drops of Titanic Plum Porter on a short trip from bar to table. Stuffing the inevitable two bags of scratchings into the pockets should make it easier, but it does not. Yet these paragons swerve gracefully between tables, cart many glasses in one go and menus as well, let alone the drip mats. Puts me in mind of a walking trip when I drew a lot of smiles from the folk in a Norfolk pub when I asked for a pint of bitter and… but that is another tale.

We began our usual pre-dinner ritual. A deep draw on the beer. A perusal of the menu; me searching for the highest pork content - rather like punters in a cocktail bar searching for the mix with most alcohol - and Mark scanning for the fresh and new. A few more sips of beer. Misplaced queries to each other about what something might be and how it is cooked. In the East, an English translation on the menu is much rarer than back in the West. This makes ordering a lot more fun.

The rain stopped. The waitress returned. Smiling, she took out her note pad and waited. We looked at the menu again. "Could we have five minutes, please?"

Her smile disappeared. "No. You have one minute." Her smile returned, just as a villain does in an old Bond movie when decreeing that the trap-door to the shark infested pool should be sprung. Maybe she was expecting it to rain again.

Exactly which political philosophy her table-side manner had emerged from I'd not like to say, but, by the looks of her, I'd put my money on childhood in the Brezhnev era of Soviet stagnation.

Smiling, but leaving no doubt that we only had that one minute and not a second more, her manner suggested some training in the political police. We ordered with fifteen seconds to spare. She smiled politely again and brought us another beer a few moments later.

So, we tucked in to another hearty dinner. I have never liked leaving food on a plate, but on this occasion I made extra sure that every trace of vegetable was mopped up. Didn't want any unpleasantness when the "iron waitress" came to tidy up. You'll be amazed to learn that the beer glasses were empty too. So we had another, just to cement East-West relations and show we were really no threat to the established order of the Lindenhof. The sun was shining on a lovely evening.

At this point a lady and gentleman approached. She was walking and he was riding a bike. They hailed us, saying they'd seen us on the cycle route and asking what the beer was like. We got chatting whilst they ordered their drinks - with suitable alacrity.

Conversation began with them asking about our trip. They were impressed. They knew of the Lidice story, but knew nothing of Stoke-on-Trent. They listened with apparent interest. Then it was their turn. They did not regard themselves as cyclists. Yes, they rode for utility, to work, to the shops, to visit friends, when they were at home in Berlin. Once a year they took a cycling holiday, a tour by bike. They had seen us just as they arrived, spotting us turning off the track into the town.

They were heading downstream. Starting in Prague, they'd followed the Moldau/Vltava to the Elbe. The tour would end when they visited their daughter, a student at the University in Magdeburg. From there they'd take the train home.

Needless to say, there was an inevitable and very useful discussion of what the trail was like. We could contribute little, but they warned us that the path was generally good in the Czech Republic, but not always. If it rained some bits might get very muddy.

Fortunately for all, they had no interest in bottom-brackets, external, tapered, or otherwise, and did not want to discuss the merits of eBikes. Berlin, they said, was a great place to live and work. She had moved there from Munich; he came from a small town not far from the capital. Yes, Berlin had really come on, but they hoped to move away one day, maybe when they no longer had to chase the Euro.

As we set off back to the hotel, we walked with them for a while. We wondered where her bike was? She left it at their accommodation. Fact was that he could cycle more easily than he could walk. On foot he had to hobble, on the bike an old injury made no difference.

We reached the square and parted.

Chapter Fourteen

The next day, the eleventh of our trip, was a designated "short and easy day". Short, forty-five or so miles; easy, all along the Elbe Cycleway, so more or less flat and easy to follow. No need to SatNavise, get the map out or, quite possibly, change gear.

Behind the short mileage was Dresden. We wanted some time to look around this famous city. Some people like to build in relatively short days on longer tours. Personally, I'm not sold on the idea, but there are places I want to see and arriving in the evening would not allow even cursory visits to some of the most famous sights. An afternoon would.

The morning was sadly dull. Yesterday's gleaming swathe of water had lost its colour. The pastures were still there, re-invented as fields of dank sedge. As for the wildlife, the rain on my spectacles made that hard to spot. I stared over the top of them, in a poor imitation of a pre-war school-teacher. Actually, I remembered, I had been a school teacher - and quite possibly a parody of one.

Fortunately, the day was not to remain drizzly. However, for the first few miles there was little to see other than raindrops on my glasses, some impressive river-going barges and diversion signs where the route was being improved. "Raindrops on My Glasses" or "Lipstick on Your Collar" - a popular song of the late 1950s performed by Connie Francis, which I had heard on some radio show in the late 1970s. I did not burst forth. Strange what you think about on easy, wet, traffic-free mileage. Maybe there'd been more to the fabulous hotel buffet than met the eye. Wasn't just me. Mark had wanted to send photos of the table decorations to his wife. Bit more understandable, but far from normal.

As we rode beyond Riesa toward Meissen, the clouds parted. No biblical revelation, just some sunshine. A breeze got up and soon the delights of the previous afternoon by the Elbe had returned. Even so, at Meissen there was no delightful view of the Albrechtsburg Castle and Cathedral reflected in the river, as is shown on many of the publicity shots. We were on the wrong bank for that. Even so, the sight is a very fine one.

Although a castle has stood on the bluff above the river since the tenth century, the current affair is some five hundred years younger and had little military significance. Even its position as the leading residence of the Electors, later Kings, of Saxony, did not last beyond the life of its builder, Albert - he ruled Saxony along with his brother until 1471 when they split their territory by agreement. Dresden became predominant.

Even so, King Augustus the Strong, decided to found a ceramics works at Meissen and the town gave its name to the porcelain made there. The original name of the factory was Royal-Polish and Electoral-Saxon Porcelain Manufactory (Königlich-Polnische und Kurfürstlich-Sächsische Porzellan-Manufaktur). Bit of a mouthful. Wonder how they fitted that designation on the base of smaller pieces? Naturally, people called it "Meissen".

I had wondered if Mark would want to explore the ceramic paradise, though I guessed that it might all be a bit old school for such a creative chap. Fortunately I was correct, at least about him not wanting to explore. Too many tours of Great Houses where attention was drawn, by the guide, to very fine tea-pots, terrines and figurines of shepherdesses (one's that had never done a day's shepherdessing or even gone a-rambling in the new mown hay, as folk singers have it) put me off that sort of stuff when I was but a child.

Instead we opted to visit the supermarket and pick up our luncheon comestibles. We carried on up the river in the sure knowledge that there'd be a bench to sit at before too long. Half an hour later we were not so sure that there'd be a bench. We did see some interesting wild-west scenes of cowboys and tee-pees; lots of horses in paddocks corralled by tidy fences. No sign of the Mensch von Laramie, but all quite peculiar. I'd recognise buffalo if I saw one, but there were none and you don't want to know the distinction between one and a bison? Do you? In any case, we could not have sat on them to eat a picnic.

There were clearly some preparations underway for barbecues and such like; marquees, trailers and, of course, mobile bars - with German, not American, beer.

Just after High Noon a bench came into view and we slowed down, dismounted and leant our bikes against a rail fence that surrounded another paddock. Behind us was a smart villa surrounded by a wall and hedge. The river ran on the other side of the paddock, from whence a man wandered in our general direction. As we began to tuck in, he approached directly.

Older than us by a good few years, he looked to be of an age where he would have lived the vast majority of his life in the Democratic Republic of Germany - the ironic name for old East Germany. He spoke, but we did not understand. He spoke more urgently. Were we trespassing on his bench? Was there some obscure local by-law about eating in public? Was he after a slice of cheese and a handful of tomatoes?

I tried to explain that we spoke very little German. That is pretty much the little German I can manage in a coherent way, unless someone is selling beer, pork cooked in various ways or pretzels. This did not help. So, I exhausted my stock of conversational German by stating that I was English. The real hope of that is that anyone who can't speak English will give up or smile and assume that you really do not speak the local language. I should really be ashamed. In fact, I am.

Our acquaintance was made of grittier stuff and was not in the least put off by discovering we were English - there's always the possibility that I'd said I was something more exotic than an Englishman, but I don't think I did. In any case, my declaration that implied ignorance of German caused him to change tactics.

He began pointing at the bench, at our food - he was after a slice of cheese! You can keep your hands off our Dairy products, I thought. No, he then pointed at the ground around and began to imitate someone sweeping the floor. Ah. We got it. We pointed to the wrappers and gestured toward a nearby bin. He smiled. Bet David Davies and Dominic Raab wished the Brexit negotiations were that easy - mind, at that point the referendum had not even taken place. Suppose it showed that you don't need a bureaucracy to enhance international cooperation.

Having ascertained that we were not litterers, we were now his friends. I was happy to try to chat too, now that I knew he was not after our cheese. We did have some grapes, but he did not seem to fancy those. He pointed to himself and announced slowly what I assumed to be his name. I responded by pointing to myself and stating my name. I'll point out here, that Mark, very wisely, was keeping a slow and seamless stream of tasty morsels going from hand to mouth.

Our friend looked surprised. Pointed to himself again and re-peat-ed ve-ry slow-ly his previous statement. Ah! By George! It was not his name. He had told me his age. Well, I could have actually managed to reply "twenty-one" in German, but I don't think he would have believed me.

"English nichts", or something like it. I got that. "Russich!" He gestured - blimey he'd have been good on Give Us A Clue, even resembled Lionel Blair in the coiffure department. "Schule." Got that. He'd learned Russian at school. Of course, he would have done. I didn't, so that was no help.

He looked out across the paddock, looked at us, looked down at the ground and announced with a sigh, "Russich nichts gut". It was heart-felt. He looked at us again and shrugged his shoulders. He said good-bye and turned to enter the garden gate. I called good-bye, but he did not look back. He disappeared. I imagine that he had been taught at school that he was one of a generation who would atone for the sins of their fathers by creating a fair and equal society that would reject fascism and Nazism in the name of international brotherhood. You could sense that, in fact, most of his life - the prime of his life - had been spent under yet another authoritarian regime with its favourites and lies. And today he

253

had met an international comrade whose first reaction had been to fear that he was after a tomato.

****

One of my favourite cycling books is "The Race Against the Stasi" by Herbie Sykes. Meshing interviews and documents, the author tells the story of the Peace Race - the Eastern Blocs equivalent of the Tour de France - through the eyes of Peter Weidemann. Alongside this runs a love story and the rapid disillusionment of Weidemann and his East German contemporaries. A great read, so I won't give any more away. But in its light, "Russich nichts gut" spoke a lifetime of disappointment and distaste.

Of course, we rode on. We whose nation has not known modern conquest or authoritarian rule. Protecting democracy, sovereignty and cooperation with others - however, imperfect they may be - ... all come down eventually to the ability to cycle happily along the Elbe, go for a walk, be on friendly terms with those you meet, have a career, family - should one wish - and to have a say about how you'd like your world to be.

Fortunately, such hefty mental luggage was soon ditched as the outskirts of Dresden approached.

The cycleway ran by the river, next to a railway line, it passed football pitches and sunbathers. It hid in the shade of bridges and rail embankments until it gave an eyeful of the dome of the Frauenkirche above wharves, busy with tourist boats and a cluster of historic buildings. Only, of course, most are not very old at all - not completely.

We'd booked rooms at the Youth Hostel, a magnificently modern building with cellars that could have housed a hundred bikes or more. We quickly got ourselves ready to head out into the town. There was a real sense of anticipation.

As this isn't a tourist guide, there'll be no detailed sight-seeing tour; as it is not a history of the heavy bombing raids, there'll be no in depth analysis of the air raids that almost destroyed the city in a far from unique conflagration. Yet, you cannot visit Dresden without considering both. It is the very historic restored architecture that makes the scale of the bombing of Dresden more shocking, although there were cities that were bombed more and suffered heavier casualties.

The Bank of England was relocated to the Potteries during the Second World War, setting up shop in the Trentham Ballroom in the grounds of the largely demolished Trentham House and Gardens. The House had been abandoned and largely destroyed by the Fourth Duke of Sutherland. The great lake became polluted and the local councils turned down the opportunity to take on the estate free of charge. At the time of the outbreak of the Second World War Trentham was outside city limits to all intents and purposes, but Stoke-on-Trent was far from a safe place when it came to bombing. Michelin and Dunlop, steel works and coal mines were likely targets. There were raids, not on the scale of London, Liverpool and some other cities, but just as destructive to individuals.

Underground, as we have seen, miners were not guaranteed a safe return to the surface. Sneyd Pit and Mossfield disasters saw major loss of life, but there were frequent serious injuries and deaths inflicted day to day. Coal was vital to the British economy at all times. Wartime demands made it even more so. It had always come at a cost.

Industrial relations between miners and mine-owners were rarely smooth. Wages improved during the Second World

War, receiving a boost of two shillings and sixpence per shift for adult underground workers as a result of the Greene Committee's recommendations in 1942. Even so, it was possible to earn more in the munitions factories, though there may be longer shifts. One can imagine hardened miners finding their daughters bringing in more money than they were, we can see the young men - those not in the forces - taking a more attractive option. Though few miners were active communists, the vast majority were staunch trade unionists who looked to the Labour movement politically and were internationalist, at least as far as other miners were concerned.

When Barnett Stross sought the help of the North Staffordshire Miners Federation, he was probing a thick seam of concern, generosity and common experience.

The Lidice Shall Live campaign was launched at the Victoria Hall, Hanley, in September 1942. The fund was opened by the Lord Mayor of Stoke-on-Trent with £100 and £1250 from the North Staffordshire Miners' Federation. The latter was, according to The Sentinel newspaper, the result of a self-imposed levy. At that time there were around 23,000 people employed in the collieries of North Staffordshire, including surface workers, clerks and management, as well as underground workers. Underground workers accounted for some 17,000 of those. Records of numbers were not collected during the early years of the war, so these figures are estimates. By the end of the war the City had raised some £32,000.

Of course miners across the UK supported the campaign too, whilst those of Cwmgiedd, near Ystradgynlais in the Swansea Valley, stood in for the people of Lidice in the film The Silent Village. Directed by Humphrey Jennings, the film was part of the Why We Fight series of films made by the Crown Film Unit. There is no doubt that the people of Stoke-on-Trent would have understood this as well as any others. Yet always at the back of the minds of many, especially those on the left of politics, was what the world would be like once the victory over fascism had been won.

Reconstruction and a new hope for the future demanded that Lidice should live again - even if it was to be left under the authoritarian yoke of the Soviet Union. The latter was, of course, something that some people did know about at that time, but preferred to ignore the prospect, whilst others were genuinely ignorant. Why think ill of Uncle Joe Stalin? He was on our side, even the right-wing papers and politicians said so. Comrade workers in the USSR were exactly that. Comrades, however oppressive their government was.

The Silent Valley, tells the story of Lidice and ends by stating that far from being obliterated the name of the community has been immortalised. Certainly, the name Lidice was immortalised in Czech history, but memories faded in the UK, even in Stoke-on-Trent where the campaign to bring the village back to life began.

The British population rightly remember the Blitz and D-Day and Dunkirk and the Battle of Britain. They remember sacrifices on the home front and eventual victory, even as the slightly diminished ally of the USA and the USSR. They remember the Holocaust. Many even know of the bombing of Dresden.

Was Dresden a sensible target? Was the bombing an atrocity in itself? How many people were incinerated in the firestorm? Was it a war crime? Did the raid gain much advantage for the allies? The discussion goes on. Historians have held conferences about it, produced an array of literature on the

259

subject - from the sensational and partisan to the carefully argued and balanced.

One thing is certain, the last of Dresden's Jews were due for transportation the morning after the raid. They were saved, if they survived the flames.

Though the bombing of Dresden did not result in the highest loss of life in an air raid on Germany, it is felt by many Germans, not just those few in the neo-Nazi ranks, to be wrongly understood or even ignored. Indeed some, and not only Germans, claim that the bombing was a war crime. I have read that, in the view of some legal historians, there is no doubt that the bombing of Dresden was a war crime. In 1944 there was no international law against bombing of civilians. All sides did it. Ask Rotterdam, London, Hamburg and Warsaw.

No one knows how many people died on February 13th and 14th 1944, when two major raids hit the city within hours of one another. Figures between 25,000 and 40,000 are generally accepted, but 75,000 is not impossible. The 500,000 to be found on some websites is tosh. Why does no-one know? A mixture of partisan use of the event and ignorance. The extreme right neo-Nazis project Dresden as an example of allied hypocrisy and criminality; the post war communists portrayed it as an example of western imperialism and savagery. Ignorance? Well, who could count? Who even knew how many people were in the city on that night? Any of informed guesses would amount, I'd hope, to more than anyone would like to countenance.

On a personal note, my young brother's mother-in-law, Elsa, was an eleven year old living in the north Bavarian countryside, roughly half way between Munich and Nuremberg. Her parents received a letter from an uncle and aunt, civilians in the army pay corps. The letter was dated February 12th. They had reached Dresden and hoped they could come to their relative's home in Kipfenberg. They never arrived and no more was ever heard of them.

Coventry - where around 560 people were killed (the number is not clear as some people assumed dead had left the city and, sadly, some of those seriously injured joined the list of those who died later) - is twinned with Dresden. Coventry too, was both a city with industries and ancient architecture. Coventry, remember, was a medieval city when Birmingham was barely a market town.

261

Our afternoon and evening in the city certainly gave us no notion that the city had once been the scene of a conflagration that destroyed almost all of what we saw.

Dresden is not alone in having rebuilt its landmarks after war, but the complexity of magnificent architecture grouped so tightly makes it extra special. In contrast the Dutch authorities paid little attention to the past when rebuilding Rotterdam. Seeing the opportunity to do away with some of the problems of industrialisation and population growth, they did not let sentiment for medieval architecture and regal grandeur stand in the way of a bright modern future. By 1950, Rotterdam was well on its way to being the enterprising new city it is today; its glassy building literally reflecting its commercial prowess as one of the great ports of the world. In the city centre, but a few buildings remain from the pre-war era - mind you, only a few were suitable to be salvaged. Even so, the Dutch did not rebuild the old, they look optimistically to future prosperity.

In Dresden's Military Museum there are exhibits from air raids on Dresden and Rotterdam.

****

Walking into the centre of Dresden from the hostel, one first notices wide-open roads, tram-lines and tenement blocks. Then, just across an interchange from some Soviet style blocks, is the approach to the Zwinger and one is in the realm of golden domes, finials, formal fountains and all the rest of it. Three hundred years of history, on the face of it, in a few yards; a journey from the brutal to the baroque, simply by crossing the road, after the tram rattled by.

Graffiti covered the hoardings and ripped plastic sheeting behind which the flats were partially obscured. It seemed that some locals felt that these buildings would make fine homes for folk on lower incomes, were they returned to habitable condition. Guessing that this was really about the gentrification of the heart of the city as money came in from the West, it was almost as if there was a past that Dresden wanted to preserve and a past it could not forget but does not shout loudly about. Hardly makes it unique though.

What does make Dresden unique is the complexity of the exuberant buildings at its heart. So, we strolled and admired and became a bit confused about which architectural magnificence was which and spent time rectifying our ignorance. The view from the pinnacle of the Frauenkirche is my best memory. Lording it over the river, one could look back and see the way ahead. Oh yes, the inside is spectacularly decorated with wonderful murals, but the work of God, or nature, sticks in my mind more than the works of humankind - except for that magnificently stark contrast between baroque glory and post-war tenements.

In the main square was a conference cycle. Ever seen one? Seven seats, sometimes more or less, arranged in a circle so riders face each other, each with a set of pedals to drive the contraption. One, hopefully expert, individual steers, and, if expert enough, causes the whole crew to scream with a series of sharp turns and sudden halts. Stability comes from the weight and the numerous wheels upon which it rolls. I wondered if they did town tours on it. However, the owner didn't seem to be about. I hoped that if we gawped for a while the driver might show up, but nothing happened. So we wandered into a restaurant where I seem to recall eating a very large salad. Mind you, my memory might not be all it was, so the aberration can easily be explained as pure fantasy.

Chapter Fifteen

Our last day in Germany began with a long, idle breakfast amongst the numerous groups of youths from around the world who were staying at the hostel during their trip to Dresden; to learn, admire, meet, perform, fall in love, who knows.

Down by the riverside the tour boats were boarding. The last of the morning's cycle-commuters arrived along the riverside path which we took out of town toward the Czech Republic. Did they feel the same tinge of envy that I feel when on the way to work and I see someone who is clearly going to have a good day out? Who knows? Some people really just do use cycling as a means of transport by which they can get the better of the motor traffic and arrive at work at a predictable time. None the worse for that.

Our day would not be especially long and almost all would be on riverside cycle track. Exiting the urban was almost immediate. Dresden is a small city, though it has extensive suburbs. Those along the river were neat and tidy in a very German way.

Small settlements were interspersed with some very grand houses in extensive gardens. Merchants and entrepreneurs from Dresden's past, members of the Saxon aristocracy wanting to live close to the court, Soviet era officials living above their supposed political principles, new wealth from the West? With the forested banks of the deepening valley to the rear, they were caught in the morning sun, as they had awoken to each new era in the turbulent times they had seen. Whoever lived there, whenever, was certainly on the sunny side of the valley and probably history. "Russich" may have been "nichts gut", but in the years immediately after 1945 there were probably those who thought Stalinism was just the ticket. Maybe it was better than Hitlerism. Followers of that cult had probably preceded the communist well-to-do; clever ones may have slipped nicely from one to the other and on to the next as regimes changed. On the other hand, they could have been hot-beds of sedition.

The great Elbe has cut its way through the mountains creating a magnificently narrow gorge from which the hilltops of the Sächsische Schweiz ("Saxon Switzerland") are hidden. Deep down by the river one cuts through the Ore Mountains along with the main road and railway. Much is a Nature Park, protected by legislation, hikers and cyclists have a merry time of it. Their jaunts are assisted by the presence of numerous ferries and riverside settlements with more than their fair share of bars.

The theme is continued across the border in the Czech "Bohemian Switzerland National Park". There are not quite as many settlements, things are rather less strictly-ordered and the beer is cheaper. Neither the Saxon nor Bohemian Switzerland's are very much like the alpine peaks of the real thing. But romantics and promoters of tourism have never let reality get in the way of comparison or publicity. Nor was it just the Saxons and the Bohemians who sought to draw wealthy people into the area with scenery and promises of health giving waters. They wanted less-wealthy folk to mine the ore.

However unlike the mountains and gorges of Switzerland it might be, it is a very beautiful ride along a twisting river with rarely more than a few metres between the riverbank and the valley side, with the cycle track squeezed between. Tremendous stuff and a credit to the governments who decided to put a cycle route along the Elbe.

Anticipation began to mount as we left the environs of Dresden. Stopping to chat to a young lady who was pedalling slowly in our direction, she told us that we would have a lovely ride all the way to Děčín. She was just taking a leisurely ride to visit a relative, but would not think of travelling any other way on such a fine morning.

Quite right too.

No need for SatNav or map or thought, just turn the pedals and follow the signs, past the last of Dresden's tail of riverside suburbs, Pirna. Diversion necessary. The sign told us that we must cross the river at the next ferry as there was major maintenance work on the route and the cycleway was closed to all traffic.

Obedient as ever we followed the instruction. A couple of Euros took us to the other bank, where, a short step from the jetty stood an enticing bar. We opted for fortifying black beer and watched the ferry cross several times while we sipped away - well it was not quite even lunchtime. Every trip filled with hikers, cyclists and people just wanting to cross the river to one of the bars: turned out there were four more just around the corner.

As we left we thought that a sign suggested we take the next ferry across the river to get back on track. We misunderstood. The sign told us that we must take the next ferry. Our ignorance, combined with a lengthy queue running back from the next jetty, led us on a track into the woods. Decent enough at first, it quickly became a dirt trail. Lifting the bikes over tree roots should have given us a clue that this was not a cycle route. Maybe we thought it might be for mountain bikes. Possibly we had seen UK cycle routes that were even less-likely. We stuck to our guns and pushed on.

Mark, who in my opinion watches too many films, seemed to be convinced that we were going to be murdered by locals in some bizarre man-hunt game or become slaves to woodland weirdoes, possibly elves.

Deeper into the forest and over a spur, more carrying and pushing. Down into a dip and up another spur.

"This is not a cycle route," said a couple of hikers.

Too bloody right. Even we had worked it out by then, though having confirmation from people who could actually understand the signs was helpful, if not especially appreciated with a loaded touring bike over one shoulder.

We reached a peculiar looking house. Just beyond it, we heard voices. Cackling laughter, even. So, there we were. Was this it? Were we really to be lost in the woods and never seen again, in best Brothers Grimm fashion?

Well, you can guess the answer. We pushed our bikes stealthily past the laughing party, whose members were enjoying a beer or two as they looked out over the river from a stoney balcony-cum-viewpoint. By the looks of it they'd been mountain-biking. More than we had managed for a while. At least they were real people with no interest in enslaving us.

Asphalt, lovely asphalt. What a blessing it is and how happy we were to get rolling at more than walking pace. Two hundred yards later we halted. There was a jetty, at the end of it a ferry. We crossed to the better bank and turned left, following the sign for the Elbe Radweg.

The sign was really unnecessary. This was not a small Pyrenean stream! Yes, we could tell the Elbe from the Ars.

270

Well worth wading through fourteen chapters for that. (Note; L'Ars is also known as L'Arse. It is a small river in the French Pyrenees.)

We passed Bad Schandau station. The town centre is on the east bank of the Elbe, the station on the west. A ferry connects the two. This time we stuck to the cycle track by the side of the railway.

I'd made a mental note that Bad Schandau was the last town on the Elbe in Germany. It's a major centre in the Nature Park. Restoration projects in the first decade of the twenty-first century have returned the town to something like its pre-war glory. A spa town with botanical gardens and river front of hotels, it has suffered severe flooding at times. Dating back long before the waters were discovered, it is now, once again, a tourist town. I would have liked to take a closer look, but our walk in the woods had set us back.

Here the gorge seems to be narrow enough to make it a tight fit for a bike. We went on down the track, the railway line and the hills to the right, the river and the hills to the left. A few kilometres on and a prominently pink coloured building appeared. The skies had clouded over. Pink paint stood out

271

in the murk. Getting closer, great pillars or rock could be made out across the river, contrasting starkly with house, hotel, whatever it was. Between those columns the Kamenice river flows into the Labe. The village was Hrensko, that side of the river was now the Czech Republic. The Elbe was on that side, the Labe.

Hrensko was originally a trading community, but now acts as a gateway to the natural wonders of the area and feeds the tourists. We could see little of it on that dull afternoon. Be nice to visit sometime, I thought. Take a walk in the hills. Strange thing that, in the hills, yet Hrensko is the lowest point above sea level in the Czech Republic.

****

It was across the river, at old Hrensko, that Anna Kohlíčková and her mother-in-law from Lidice had reached their homeland in 1945, three years after they had been incarcerated in Nazi concentration camps.

****

On our bank, we were still by the Elbe, in Germany. As Hrensko disappeared behind us we reached some iron poles bearing the arms of and the name Republika Čechoslovenská, the Republic of Czechoslovakia. I must admit, that I was not expecting this. May seem odd, but having cycled half-way across Europe and done lots of research, I was expecting to arrive in the Czech Republic, with no Slovenska added on, or Czechia, as it had recently been rebranded.

Given the time span, I'd not expected Czechia at the border, but I had imagined that they'd have moved on from Czechoslovakia. Happy enough about not entering Czechia - the name has not caught on in the country - I liked the Republic element. A statement of intent, introduced when the Habsburg Empire fell to pieces at the end of the Great War; democratic principles, a declaration of values. Independence and democracy may have been put on hold from 1938 to 1989, but they held on to them. Czech society was decapitated after the Battle of the White Mountain in the middle of the seventeenth century. The national story has been built by the working and middle-classes, rather than the great aristocrats.

Slovakia and the Czech Republic split amicably in 1993. United from 1919 to 1938 and from 1945 to 1993, there were considerable differences in social, economic and historical backgrounds. Some we met regretted the Velvet Divorce, most accepted that it made sense and whilst a shame, there was no hostility.

One Slovak, with whom we stayed for a night, told us that the Czechs were always talking and did nothing and that the Slovaks were the opposite. Not that she felt any dislike for the Czechs - indeed she lived in Prague and worked in the environmental department of a major extractive industry. The Slovaks were just different. "There are fewer of us, a lot fewer, and we don't want to be dominated by the Czechs."

One Moravian Czech told me, "The Slovak's have a different story. Some of them welcomed the Nazis because they didn't like Czechoslovakia. Not all. Many hated the Nazis. A lot of Slovaks fought with the British. So be careful about thinking it is simple." I'd mentioned that many Czechs had escaped the Nazi invasions to fight again.

I wondered how long it would be before we had a Republic of Bohemia and a Republic of Moravia? There was once a

274

Moravian Empire. Oh, yes. History moves rapidly round here. There seems little doubt that the Czech Republic has strength and part of that is the story of Lidice.

When you get into Central Europe you find that history is full of twists, turns, angles and perspectives. There's a lot of it too. Study may make one better informed and listening and looking will make one wiser, but if it is definitive answers one wants, then search on.

Since returning to the UK, I have pondered why the border posts have not been kept up to date. Must be that they have just not got round to it - maybe the Slovak lady was right about the Czechs. On the other hand, all the Czech people I spoke to expressed, if the opportunity arose, pride in their nation. A proud, young country might be expected to declare its identity as such with vigour. Maybe two posts on a cycle track don't top the list of priorities, but as a rebranding exercise they'd be easy to replace. Or were they deliberately left as a symbol of the past?

Whilst I imagine that markers like this were common at one time, the only others vaguely resembling them, that I've seen, were on the border of Belgium and the Grand Duchy of

Luxembourg. Almost like old-fashioned long artillery pieces turned on-end, muzzle in the ground, they stood lined-up across the fields and were ignored by everyone - possibly since the day they were put there. On the other hand, we know that borders were patrolled by guards and ordinary folk should have taken note.

Back on the German-Czech border, we spotted a sign stating that the track ahead was closed. I would not claim to understand Czech very well even by comparison to German, but it was clear from the symbols on the signs. Work was being undertaken. An arrow pointed to the river bank and a jetty by which a ferry was moored.

We looked across at the hills, the woods, glanced at the map. We recalled our bike and hike through the delightful Saxon Switzerland. Despite the prospect of further rambling in the delightful Bohemian Switzerland, we declined the offer and planned to throw ourselves on the mercy of the Czech cycle-route maintenance force.

After a kilometre or so, we came across them, cutting back undergrowth and sweeping the smooth asphalt surface.

Spotting us coming, they waved us through and we exchanged smiles and words; clearly amicable words.

Vindicated, the clouds began to part and we emerged on a road near a railway station and a bridge over the river - narrower here - for our first night in the Czech Republic, at Děčín.

I'd like to visit Děčín for a longer period. It is something of a tourist centre. Castle overlooking river, synagogue, hiking and cycling country, river trips, attractive market square. And in many ways, its history serves as an exemplar of Central European History.

The town was not too busy; there were people out shopping, but not too many. Our hotel took pride of place in the main square. The Ceské Koruna was welcoming a number of guests. I waited behind two Germans and two Italians. I noted that the receptionist spoke fluent German. Well, not surprising really, many tourists along the Labe are from Germany. Conveniently, the Italian couple switched into German when it came to their turn.

I attempted Czech. As an independent tourer with no particular skill in, or knowledge of, languages, I generally try to get a few basic phrases off by heart and then wing it as far as possible. Trouble was that most of the journey had been in Germany and as German had marginally improved, Czech had been driven from my mind. Blogging and rehydrating had taken up most of each evening, so there'd been few opportunities to revise. In any case, until one hears a language spoken by someone fluent it is impossible to grasp the rhythm of the words and, in my opinion, that is half way to making oneself understood.

The receptionist came to my rescue. She spoke fluent English too.

Incredibly cheap, the room was comfortable. Bikes were stowed, along with a number of others, in a sort of second lobby defended by stout wooden doors. The hotel declared its bike friendliness with a sign proclaiming membership of a national scheme. Like so many countries, the Czech tourist trade is recognising that cyclists generate business.

Taking a brief stroll to survey the town centre architecture and coincidentally check out which bar to go to for dinner, there was a happy buzz about Děčín. We selected a bar on the road that ran down to the main bridge. We ordered two half-litres of Staropramen - a common enough beer in the UK, although that in Děčín was actually brewed in Prague and had a much clearer, stronger smack of flavour.

We took a table which overlooked the main drag. There was no window, so we had a balcony like view. Smokers on the next table and buses chugging up and down the hill caused us to question the wisdom of our choice. The first brace of beers disappeared nicely, so we ordered more.

Mark produced his phone and tried out Google translate. I continued to try to drag a few words of Czech up and make them into a coherent sentence likely to get a beer or two, or accidentally, three or four should fortune favour me.

The waitress-cum-barmaid praised both our efforts with smiles. We were clearly accurate, as we got a beer each. She explained that Staropramen was brewed in Prague, but that there were more local breweries. However, she did not rate these as highly, so the bar did not sell them. When I say she explained, don't misunderstand. We communicated in a mixture of sign language mixed with a few words in Czechlish. Wonderful thing language.

Apart from being jolly, sympathetic and having a taste for heavy metal on the sound system, the waitress also had a display of interesting tattoos. Of course, we only got to see those on her arms and legs - she was wearing shorts.

We ordered food. This was the second time I'd tried to order food in Czech. My first attempt had been in Leicester. I'd got a round of applause from the mix of Czech, Slovak and Polish expats in attendance on that occasion. Maybe I said something profound or humorous by mistake. Don't think ordering a plate of pork and dumplings could easily become, "A Czech, a Slovak and a Ruthenian walked into a Polish bar…" The Děčín audience were harder to please and merely looked at us, bewildered. We weren't even German, that was obvious.

Like most people these days, all sorts of food are available in the Czech Republic. I didn't see a curry house. I like to eat traditional local dishes anyway. Restaurant and bar menus seemed to offer a selection of these. The thing that struck me most was the array of dumplings. I'd half expected this. They run from those that approximate to German Klossen, to what looks like, and has a similar texture to thick, steamed slices of bread. Most translations simply state that these are dumplings. If you, like me, don't have your Observer's Book of Dumplings to hand, then you'll learn by experience. If I had one recommendation for the Czech tourist authority, it would be to produce a short guide to dumplings and suchlike - preferably an illustrated one. Maybe, scratch and sniff.

Svíčková turned out to be much what I expected from the German translation on the menu. Roast beef in thick puree-like sauce, hearty slices of bread-like dumpling and a dollop of fresh cream. Very tasty and satisfying with a clean, crisp beer. Later in our trip, it came as a surprise, when talking to younger Czechs - yes, we spoke to youths - that many said this was their favourite food and directed us to the bars that served the best.

****

The two step translation from Czech to English via German would have been a one step process a hundred years ago - in most circumstances. The vast majority of the population of Děčín in 1916 were German, or at least, German speakers.

281

As with many Central European towns and cities, Germans dominated.

Central European history is far from straight-forward. The situation is not helped by the complexities of the past, nor does the tendency of each nation in each past era to view the past through contemporary values and aims. This happens everywhere of course, but in Central and Eastern Europe, where Emperors ruled and national boundaries and ethnicity vie with one another, it is even harder to see through.

Děčín or, in German, Tetschen, is first recorded in the ninth century, but became important in the tenth and eleventh when the Dukes of Bohemia constructed fortresses there. Initially, on the left bank, then high on the current castle site, when floods - a common occurrence - wrecked the original. It was at the invitation of the thirteenth century King Ottarkar of Bohemia, that German settlers flooded into the area. In the next seven centuries the town grew in importance, along with Bodenbach, Czech Podmulky, on the left bank. Bridges were built, railways came, boat-building and industry flourished. Until 1945 the town's population was mostly German.

****

The last day of our trip from Burslem to Lidice dawned, dull and wet. This provided an excuse to take even more time than usual over breakfast. Saveloy-like white sausages were my savoury, followed by a mixture of bread, cheese and salami, fruit and yoghurt. How do I usually manage when at home, with a bowl of cornflakes?

Most of the guests spoke German, but there was another British cyclist who was on his way to Bad Schandau that day. He asked about the route as he was travelling without map or GPS and hoped direction signs were adequate. We were happy to say that the surface was good and that he would have no trouble on the short trip. He planned to stay in the hotel as long as he could so the worst of the rain would pass. We did not have that luxury, as we needed to be in Lidice by about five o'clock.

The rush? Well, we'd already mucked up any chance of a welcome ceremony. This was really more of a matter of miscommunication, than us being slow. Even so, we were booked to stay in the hostel which forms part of the Art Gallery. There's no separate reception, so a good night's sleep depended on getting there before the gallery staff headed home. Alan and Cheryl, who know the area well, had

283

told me that the nearest Hotel was in Kladno. This they said, was a fascinating experience in retro-Soviet era architecture and, on their first visit, service. Now it was just the architecture that looked back.

Dark clouds lay across the valley, blotting out the hills and delivering a steady flow of rain. It was the sort of day when you just knew that, however well one's loins were girded, moisture would accumulate. Why? Because some types of rain just seem to penetrate, and because, with that lot on, on a mild summer day, you are just going to sweat.

We donned overshoes. Never disregard these; in my opinion the misery of wet feet is far greater than wet legs. Even so, with waterproof leggings and jackets we pedalled down the hill towards the river. A sign took us onto a side road and down to a quay. Some damp tourists were pondering a boat trip as we rumbled past. Above us was the rock on which stood the castle, but there was no sign of it. A riverside promenade decorated with flowerbeds took us into an area of light industry and out of town. Excellent surfaces on the cycle track.

Děčín, definitely worth a sunny day visit!

Although it sits in the hills in a deep gorge, Děčín is one of the lowest points in the Czech Republic. This made the initial riding quite weird. Generally, when you climb through a desolate plateau or a summit in the UK, where distant views are reached, but on the Labe this doesn't happen. One emerges from what looks like UK lowland.

It wasn't a dark and stormy morning, but occasional car lights shone brightly. An old railway track ran close to the path, occasionally sliding away, only to return a little further on. No trains passed us, but across the river, on the main line, Deutsche Bahn trains from, and to, Germany were mixed with long lines of goods wagons pulled by diesels that probably roared, but could not be heard across the river. Colour contrast was added by the blue of the České Drahy livery.

The day needed all the colour it could get.

Having said that, there were high points and lows. Ústí nad Labem is a large town on the left bank of the river. There is only a small settlement on the right bank where the cycle route lies. Across the river the town ascends the valley side. It may have streets of gold - it certainly is an important industrial town - but it has suffered. Razed during the Hussite wars, it was burned down in the sixteenth century and sacked in the seventeenth. In the nineteenth century it rose once more as an industrial town, building ships, processing chemicals, making textiles. Like Děčín, its populations was predominantly German. It became a centre of agitation during the Sudetenland crisis of 1938 and was once more wrecked by allied bombing in 1945.

"Sudetenland" is an interesting concept - if you like this sort of thing. We use it to describe the border land of Bohemia and Germany, usually in conjunction with the term "German". The "Sudeten Germans" and their alleged mistreatment were the spark that led to the Munich Agreement. Yet, the term was only coined in the early twentieth century, the late nineteenth at the earliest, and did not come into common use until after the peace treaties that followed the Great War. It is not a term that Czechs at the time would recognise. In other words, when we speak of the "Sudetentland" we are using the language of wronged German nationalism, not that of Czech nationalism. Not that nationalism of any kind had anything to do with the growth of large German communities in the Czech lands hundreds of years before.

Maybe it was the rain, but I picture Ústí's sprawl across the river as a contrast of rust-red industrial complexes with silver-grey chimneys emitting vapours that dissolved immediately into the clouds. Amidst, or above the rust-rim of the river bank, emerged dull-shaded blocks of flats. Don't get me wrong, this is home to many people and where would we all be were it not for the products of industry? It may not be a thing of beauty but it looked busy.

In the 1990s it hit the international headlines when the mayor proposed to build a wall dividing one side of a street from the other. On one side was a Roma community, on the other lived mainly Czechs. Built and then dismantled, the story hidden somewhere in the curtain of drizzle sweeping the across the river. I am told that the town does have modern, open spaces, but they were not visible from this distance.

Maybe I'll cycle past on a sunnier day. I bet they had their fair share of bars. Maybe some sold Březňák. One of the high points was a shipping-container-type box, with long grass growing around it. Painted on the side was a picture of a bald gentleman with a neatly cut, though long, beard, holding a tankard of foaming beer to his lips. Nearby was a jetty. I guessed that on sunny weekends a ferry carried folk back

287

and forth from the town to the greener side of the river. While waiting, they could pass the time with a refreshing half litre of beer from a temporary beer-shack.

I have, for several years, seen the gentleman on the Moretti beer bottle labels as a role model for later life. Now he had a rival. I think the stylish hat of Moretti Man and the neat moustache outdo the full-set and balding pate of Březňák, though, in fairness, the Czech beer outdoes the Italian, in my opinion.

Litomerice is a different kettle of fish to Ústi. Or, at least looked to be. We were starting to think about getting to the end, to Lidice. We did not see the centre of Litomerice, which is, I am told, thought to be pretty. With notable exceptions, towns along the Elbe stand back from it, with their centres on hillsides above. We did not see the best of Litomerice, but by the level of the water in the river, reticence to living too close was understandable.

We'd passed huge sluice gates and ship-locks to let river traffic through. Even so, despite the best efforts of man, flooding can be ferocious. In 2002, the Elbe rose to ten metres above its usual level and five runaway barges had to be blown-up to prevent the destruction of bridges.

Fortunately it had stopped raining.

****

We were still in what had once been the heavily Germanized area - handed over to the Third Reich by the British and French at the Munich Conference of 1938. Not a "by your leave" was asked of the pugnacious Czechoslovak government which had mobilised its army and air force.

Germans tended to dominate in the towns along the Bohemian borders (and also in some others), although the rural areas were primarily Czech. This had not been a matter of invasion. Town dwellers from what we now call Germany, were often invited to bring their entrepreneurial drive and experience to help central European nobles and monarchs of all races, to make the most of their real estate - the towns and markets they had established. In some areas they were also brought in to replace rural populations devastated by war and invasion from the East.

In the middle-ages, Germany existed politically, only in the sense of the Holy Roman Empire of the German People. This Empire included a number of areas largely populated by people who were clearly not German too - Bohemia for example. The Emperor was elected - at least from 1356 until dissolution in 1806 - by a group of Electors (seven to start with, nine by the Empire's end). Amongst these was the King of Bohemia (not always a Bohemian). There does not seem to be any real sense in which Bohemia can be described as German other than its inclusion in the Holy Roman Empire. It came under the rule of Austria in 1526.

On the dissolution of the Holy Roman Empire, Bohemia, Moravia and Slovakia (chunks of Slovakia were in Hungary) fell under the sway of the Habsburg Empire. Initially this was officially the Austrian Empire, but a few years later it became the Austro-Hungarian Empire.

The Habsburg dynasty had acquired its lands by marriage and inheritance for the most part and the Empire was renowned for its ethnic diversity. Before 1806, parts of it had been in the Holy Roman Empire and others had not. Large chunks of Poland had been added to the Habsburg domain as that Kingdom was dismembered by Prussia, Russia and

Austria between 1779 and 1795, for example. Moreover, there were considerable Habsburg lands in Italy. By the start of the twentieth century, it was generally regarded as a ramshackle mess and quickly became a burden to its German allies. Yes, German. Germany had been united under Prussian rule in 1870. Austria, though German in language and culture, had been deliberately and forcefully excluded.

So, in 1914, the Czech's were under the control of a German-speaking Austrian Empire, whose official language was German, that was not part of Germany and whose Emperor had once had a say in electing despite not being German; whilst some Czech towns had, for centuries, been largely populated by Germans who had never lived in Germany. During the collapse of the Habsburg Empire in 1918, Czechoslovakia was formed as part of the peace process. This was largely down to USA President Woodrow Wilson's doctrine of national self-determination and the exploits of the returning Czech legion which had fought its way home from Siberia. However, there were sizable ethnic minorities; Germans, Hungarians, Poles and Ruthenians. The destruction of the Austrian-Hungarian Empire did not end the "problem of minorities"; it merely transferred it to a number of smaller states.

Of course, self-determination was not granted to the large German population of the border country. They had a clear preference to be included in Germany. Self-determination was a tidy idea for a messy geography. Clearly it was not possible to meet the aspirations of the Czechs and apply the same doctrine to the Germans. Equally, to give the border lands away would leave Czechoslovakia with a border that could not be defended. In addition, the Germans had lost the war and could, therefore, be ignored. Only, of course, in the long run, they could not.

Within the new Czechoslovakia there were those who were discontent. Many, though by no means all, Slovaks demanded that there should be a Slovak nation. A Prague based government did not fulfil their aspirations. Unsurprisingly (especially as there was a strong nationalist right-wing movement, the Hlinka Guard) the German invasion of Bohemia and Moravia, and some tricky Nazi diplomacy, signalled the formation of a Slovak Republic under the protection of the Nazis.

History is a pest.

It is easy to smile at this when one lives amongst a nation of people that has held its fundamental identity as a nation for centuries. In Western Europe we are not really used to grand fluctuations of borders. So, Bruce Bairnsfather, the famous Great War cartoonist, poked fun at Central and Eastern Europe in his cartoon, "One of Those Balkan Muddles". The cartoon shows an injured PoW grasping the barbed wire that imprisons him. The caption reads;

> *His Father was a Czech, but his mother was a Serb. He used to live in Bohemia, but his sympathies are all Italian. Fought for the Austrians in Galicia owing to his love of the Croats and Magyars. Suspected of being a Slovac (sic) or Ruthenian, he was sent to the Italian front, where he slipped on a banana skin in Goritzia and was captured.*

As with the best humour, this has an element of truth. Probably not complex enough. Equally, it displays the ignorance of many of us in the West regarding Central and Eastern Europe: there is no way that a Czech is from the

293

Balkans, neither is a Pole, a Slovak, a Ruthenian or a Magyar.

It is easy to laugh at the aspirations of ethnic and national groups in Central and Eastern Europe. It's been suggested that there is an element or racism in this. The Ruritania of Anthony Hope's novels may be quaint but no one can, surely, take such exotic entities seriously, can they?

Why can't some people just put up with alien Empires and why are they all mixed up and not confined to neat lines drawn on a map? History, let alone modern day politics would be much easier if they did and were, wouldn't it? Look at the consequences. War in Yugoslavia, the Ukraine split, modern politicians satisfying their own ends by manipulating age old rivalries that go back centuries.

The Velvet Revolution and the split between Czech and Slovak were without bloodshed. The solution to the German problem was not.

****

We rode on, skirting Litomerice. The river appeared to have widened and filled to the brim; I momentarily thought we had gone wrong and arrived at a lake. Quickly realising we were still on track, we headed on. Had there been time I'd like to have visited Terezin. Originally named Theresienstadt, it was purpose built by the Habsburg's to defend their Bohemian lands from enemies heading up the Elbe, especially the Prussians.

It consisted of two fortresses, the Great and Small. During the Second World War it became a concentration camp. A party of Jewish inmates were sent from there to Lidice, to clean up the slaughter. After the war, many Germans spent time here during the mass expulsion of all Germans from Czechoslovakia. Initially, President Beneš suggested that many Germans would be able to stay in the places where they had lived for centuries, but, understandably, he eventually opted for the more extreme course of kicking the whole lot out. Uprooted from their homes, sometimes abused by former neighbours, sometimes waved a sad farewell, a whole new procession of refugees headed for a Fatherland that they had never seen. Conditions in the Small Fortress were not good; death continued to stalk there, just with victims from a different graft of the tree of humankind.

For now a visit was out of the question.

A sign pointed down a cart track with a surface resembling primeval broth - not that I have ever seen the latter. We followed dutifully. An angler got up from his stool and rushed towards us, gesticulating and speaking. He'd no angling knife for gutting his prey, so panic did not really set in. In any case he was smiling and looking worried. He pointed across a field to a road and swept an arm round as he gazed down our way ahead.

I wish I'd understood even half the words he spoke, but suspect it was along the lines of "Why come down here? Look at it, you jolly foolish fellows! There is a substantial quantity of slime and muck, by George! I say, you chaps should go back and follow the road around. Just the other side of the hedge over there. Gosh!"

Sadly, all we could do was say, thank you - in Czech - and pedal on, back wheels slipping with each attempt to push forward. He probably despaired, but went back to his fishing stool. What is Czech for, "Bloody Foreigners?"

In the distance we spotted a couple of cyclists coming towards us. The track might have been a cycle route before the rain; by the looks of it heavy agricultural vehicles had been uprooting a crop and taking half the earth with it, leaving a morass of spindly stalks and puddles.

"It is like this for a couple of kilometres," said the cyclist, "And then ok." We pressed on, failing to understand that anything would be "ok" after the quagmire. Slough of Despond would be going too far, but it was a depressing mile and a half or so along a section of route that would disgrace any cycle route. We should have noted that the powerfully built German cyclist who spoke to us was some 400 metres ahead of a female companion hauling her bike through the muck. She may have been swearing, or contemplating divorce to help pass the time.

On the outskirts of Roudnice nad Labem we came across a rather perplexed looking lady cyclist sitting in a bus shelter. Bike was turned upside down, wheel removed, tyre on the ground. We'd discussed Buddhism a bit that morning and trekking along the mud slide had convinced us we needed to do something about our Karma. Having pulled up a few yards on, we turned back. We decided that we would rather be late in Lidice than disregard a fellow cyclist in distress. Fortunately, she spoke some English. Clever folk these Central Europeans. Had she only known Russian we'd have been stuck.

We gestured toward the bike. She did not have to tell us it was a puncture. So we offered to help. We did not have a spare tube of the necessary size, but we had a repair kit. Where was the tube? "It was all OK," she said. We needed to do nothing. Her friend had gone to buy a new tube. "We have had a lot of problems. So, we cannot make it work anymore. So we will buy a new one."

They were heading to Prague and would follow the riverside trail to the confluence with the Vltava. For us, it would be across the bridge and into town, and farewell to the Labe-Elbe, to a river that unites the German and Slav lands via a narrow twisting gorge; a channel of commerce and fearsome torrent linking "neighbours, friends and enemies".

Roudnice nad Labem was drying out slowly as the spell of heavy rain reduced itself to a drizzle and, whilst we ate pizza outside a café, to nothing. The sun began to throw light onto the cobbles that covered the market square. Well, less a square and more an open area sloping gently toward the road down to the river, surrounded on three sides by buildings and gardens.

A steady trundle of vehicles went down the hill and grumbled up it. Shoppers and workers looking for a bite to eat seemed little bothered by the traffic. Ambling about, chatting and wandering across the road carelessly was the order of the day.

This is neither a tourist gem nor an industrial complex. A neat, tidy provincial town where one can watch real life go by. We did for a while. This was the first time on the whole journey we had eaten in a restaurant at lunchtime - the Blauwe Douwe in Schoonhoven did not count, it was too late in the day and we only had a snack. It was also one of the few occasions on which I had not gone for the traditional option.

In the UK it is rare to find a restaurant or pub where one can get steamed-for-hours steak and kidney pudding, spotted dick, liver and onions, fruit crumble with a proper crumble topping rather than a light-weight mix of nuts and oatmeal. This is a good thing for cyclists - and if you do not believe me try cycling along the back lanes of the Marches after a bellybuster of suet pudding. On the other hand, it does seem to me that we Brits are less attached, at least on a day to day basis, to our native "delicacies" than are the natives of the Czech Republic. As one young trendily bearded chap told us later on when we were in Brno, "Head up that street for a mile and you will come to a bar on the left where they serve the best Svíčková. It is my favourite and theirs is the best. I eat there often, you will like it, but it is not a tourist bar."

I wondered if a taste for chicken tikka masala and naan breads would come as their nation-state as democracy grew older. Curry and cynicism hand in hand. Well, some say that, at base, politics is a matter of "knife and fork". In terms of nation building, there's much to be said for food. Grub helps define our national identity, be it haggis, bratwurst, roast beef or Svíčková. In truth, many dishes cross borders - goulash is common in the Czech Republic and Slovakia as well as more famously in Hungary. The Czech diaspora often hold tightly to Czech traditions; I follow a Czech Cookbook Facebook page - based in the good ol' USA.

Anyway, our light lunch done, we were on the final stretch to Lidice.

Our route did not look especially interesting in terms of fascinating guidebook destinations: that does not matter to me. Like many touring cyclists, you can plan in some great monuments, but you stumble upon little things as you go. It is all about seeing what is there. So, as we went along, we did.

This was very much the fields and pastures bit of Bohemia. Gently rolling land with the occasional deeper valley and a prominent hill or two dotted about. Tractors and the occasional speeding driver were all we came across.

As we headed away from the river, the tourist prosperity seemed to reduce, much as it had done in Germany. Most cyclists would have continued on the Labe, turning alongside the Vltava to end their trip in Prague. Not us. Many people like the reassurance of being on a signed route in the certain knowledge that settlements along the way will be ready for them and there'll be people who speak your language, or something like it.

There is little to fear getting off the beaten track. People are not unfriendly or unhelpful on the whole. Possibly the least original thing to say about travel by bicycle is that it seems to bring the best out of the people one comes across. That was not always the case in the early days of cycling, but in the modern age it seems that travelling by bicycle proclaims a certain gentleness, a lack of threat, a plain, easy-going attitude, a lack of arrogance and overbearing wealth. It brings a welcome change.

There are places in the world where you need to keep your wits about you and your guts will tell you when you need to pedal on more rapidly, but, at least for me, these have been few and far between.

To be honest we were not that far from the tourist corridor or that mighty wen of tourism, the twenty-four hour a day, three hundred and sixty-five days a year mecca that is Prague. Yet the feel was very different. Quiet with patches of rural poverty.

For much of the first part of our journey from Roudnice nad Labem our route ran close to the winding railway line - typical of many of the rural lines - through Kleneč, Vražkov, Straškov-Vodochody and other villages that may never have seen cyclists from Stoke-on-Trent before.

In one, a small group of swarthy children in tee-shirts and shorts rolled around the street on motley barn-find bikes. Scottish kid's used to call them "junkers". Concocted of bits and pieces added onto a possibly sound bike frame, held together by rust, grease and the occasional bolt, a "junker" is an excellent machine, so long as you don't value your limbs too highly.

I've ridden into villages before and kids ambling about on bikes have come to ride at my side, looking at your gear and then shyly asking where you come from. Of course, they don't get much info because I can generally understand absolutely nothing that they say. Yet, if you stop, they'll have chat and a closer look and many are pleased to see someone from the other side of Europe.

These children kept their distance - no problem with that - and anxious looking parents came to the door and called them away. All fair enough, but there was something sad in their dark eyes. This is a big call, and maybe utterly unjustified, but I wonder if they were immigrants from further east in Europe, maybe even Roma or Sinti, and were suspicious of visitors.

Later on, several of the Czech's we met were concerned about migration and its effects. They were not mad racists. No, they were worried about the cost on benefits budgets and downward pressure on wages in lower paid jobs. Whilst that combination has always struck me as a bit ironic, they were exactly the same concerns that many in Britain were voicing during the Brexit debate. Whilst that ignored the fact that not all migration came from Eastern Europe, it was a big factor in North Staffordshire, where Stoke-on-Trent polled one of the biggest votes for leaving the EU.

Of course, there has been a Czech and Polish community in North Staffordshire for many years. In many mining areas Poles from Silesia's coalfields worked in British pits. As the Beast of Bolsover, Denis Skinner said, "They were paid the same, they had the same rules, and they were in the same Union". In other words, there are other reasons for downward pressure on wages. Barnett Stross was a Pole, a Jew, a GP - mind you, we are generally pleased to have GPs from other lands.

Velvary is a large village with a narrow bridge across a slow stream. Traffic was building up through the main street. Maybe a few people were leaving work a little earlier than usual. We followed the cars that rumbled over the setts that surfaced the crossroads in the village centre. The Church and houses stood like a disused film set awaiting a lick of paint to prepare it for the next production.

A quick crossing of a main road, busy with all kinds of motor vehicles agitated by the Friday afternoon desire to get home from work or get the last job done, led to quieter lanes. Time was drawing on. For us a few more bucolic whitewashed villages took us to Buštěhrad.

This was the larger village where the Lidice children had attended the SOKOL gym; where miners begged returning Lidice men not to go into the smoke. This was where the five miners had handed over their bikes; this was the village where people witnessed wagon loads of animals, as Lidice was plundered.

This was nearly the end of the journey. After all that mileage, a journey, however long, must end. Lidice was our destination. The end of the road. It is only now, as I write this, that the irony of this strikes me. What has become a byword for destruction and the start of myriad tales of death and suffering, was, for us, the end of a bike ride. A long bike ride, but just a bike ride nonetheless.

There's a steep little climb out of Buštěhrad, on setts again. Quickly across the main road, into the main avenue of Lidice, gently to pull up outside the Galerie Lidická. The end.

Every ride comes to an end. Only this one had not, not really. We had decided to take up an invitation to cycle across Bohemia and into Moravia. More importantly, we wanted beds for the next two nights in the hostel attached to the Gallery. The bikes were begging for a really good clean - even more urgent when the kind lady who showed us into the hostel said we could keep our bikes in our room for safety. This did not look like a high-risk-of-theft area, but why take any chance?

She brought buckets and rags and the bikes soon scrubbed up nicely, so we chained them up to dry whilst we went for showers and a change of clothes. It was tempting to rush to the far end of the village where the memorial and museum stand above the site of the old village. Of course, the museum would be closed and we had arranged to go there first thing next morning to pass on Mark's and Harry's creations to the museum director.

So, brushed up and ready to eat we dropped into the bar, café, restaurant, that was attached to the Gallery along with a row of shops from which, we decided, we would buy food for breakfast next morning.

It was a sunny early evening and the restaurant was pretty full, though we found a table for two and the waitress-barmaid began the usual attempt to understand our interpretation of the menu. Fortunately, like many younger Czechs, she spoke a good deal of English and even taught us some correct pronunciation, without breaking into a laugh.

As ever, beer arrived first. We drank a toast to our trip. This was soon followed by starters, which required more beer to help wash it down. Likewise the main course needed half a litre of cool golden Czech beer radiant with the glow of the summer evening sun. We drank no beer during the dessert. So we had another as we relaxed, replete.

The jollity had been enhanced by the arrival of a chap who set up a keyboard and amp, added a microphone and began to sing familiar tunes in Czech. He appeared to be a wanna-be mix of Roy Orbison and some other country singer I have no idea about. Definitely not just Roy Orbison.

We tried to get into it, but despite having another beer as an aid. It did not help. By great contrast some of the locals, of a certain age and with smaller glasses of beer, applauded loudly. Some began to dance, closely, as couples. Encouraged Roy rose to new heights of crooning. All soared on a spiral of happiness.

The barmaids-cum-waitresses did not look so enthusiastic. We asked them whether there was a local or national spirit that we should drink. "Becherovka", they said. "Becherovka", we dutifully repeated. "Becherovka", they said. "Becherovka", we tried again. Scintillating stuff for a Friday night. "Dvé, prosím", I said - that is your actual Czech and must have sounded something like it - we got the drinks.

Two more Becherovkas each and we decided to pay the bill. We looked at the total in shock. Eight beers, six Becherovkas, two three course meals. How many thousand crowns. Rather a lot, but put it into Sterling and it came to less than the price of eight beers in the UK - and a bag of pork scratchings, for me. We left a hearty tip and, as we left, noticed that good old Roy-a-like had packed up and headed for home.

There's a strange link between Becherovka and England. The Becher family who developed the liqueur in Karlovy Vary, at that time named Karlsbad, got the idea for the particular herb mixture from an English doctor who frequently visited their shop when accompanying his rich patients to the spa town. Initially, the concoction was called "English Bitters", becoming popular as a cure for stomach ailments and as a restorative for the soul. Indicative of the German influence in Bohemia, Beckerovka was renamed Karlsbader Becherbitter.

I can vouch for its efficacy. Next morning I and, I think, Mark felt tip-top.

Chapter Sixteen

Lidice woke up before us. It was a morning in the midst of summer. Through the open window came the sound of children playing. Looking out of the window a cat lay on a low roof, soaking up the sunshine. At the shop, people were buying bread and milk and all those day to day things that are best fresh. A couple of people got on the bus to Kladno that swept into the stop just outside the Gallery.

We ate quickly and wandered off to the Museum where we handed over the precious works of art by Mark and Harry Davies. Works that symbolised suffering and militant joy. Photos and greetings taken and given, we were told that the Director of the Museum must rush away to officiate at a wedding.

We entered the museum.

We looked around separately. I generally enjoy museums. I tend to approach them with an idea of what lies behind them. Most have a purpose, to tell a story and leave an impression. There are exceptions, I am sure. The Lidice museum tells a story. It tells the story of a typical Bohemian village, not so unlike many European villages, its utter destruction and the miserable fate of its inhabitants at the hands of a despicable regime that wiped out all that was preciously every day. With many museums one can question the message behind the exhibits, but not here. How could the story of Lidice be told in any other terms? Mind you, it had been for several years.

"Exhibit" seems a peculiarly inappropriate description of the artefacts and displays. They show all that is left of so many lives, so many lives of folk like the rest of us; people who wanted to see their families prosper amongst all of life's travails, to celebrate at the pub and hear the band play. The older may remember how they once rode their bikes through the fields and courted, as the younger one's pedalled off on bicycles handed down by that generation, but with the same thing in mind.

Although Lidice is a very important event in the Czech national narrative, the overwhelming emotion I left with was not one of national pride, but of relief. Fascinating though it was, informative, beautifully presented, heart-wrenching, stepping out into the sunshine was an antidote to so much sadness. Perhaps one realises how lucky one is to be able to do something so simple.

311

Even then, to say that one is "lucky" might suggest that the people of Lidice were "unlucky", despite the fact that they were deliberately murdered or imprisoned by a malign force which they could do nothing to resist. It should not be by luck that one feels the breeze touch one's skin as one cycles down the road.

One of the Nazi perpetrators stated that the men went to their deaths with dignity and that, despite seeing their neighbours shot before them, there was no "unmanly behaviour". No, the unmanly behaviour was to be found in the ranks of those who had power to enact their Fuhrer's will.

God, what a mix of emotions and thoughts. I suppose that engaging with the past when presented so rawly should evoke confusing thoughts, rational and emotional. I needed to go and look at the Lidice fire engine.

I can remember going to veteran vehicle rallies with my father and uncle, where machines like this took their place amongst the vintage cars and the steam traction engines and the horse-drawn machinery. All polished brass and shiny paintwork. The Lidice engine sits behind a huge pane of glass. It would have been nice to get closer, closer to those happy times when Mr Hanf and the fire-fighting club had so many hours of fun.

How long we were in the museum, I do not know, but there were a number of people sitting in the courtyard outside sipping coffee, licking ice-lollies, chatting and reading newspapers, when we came out. Rather incongruously, above and behind them were murals showing the interpretation placed on Lidice during the Soviet era. Workers and soldiers uniting to slay the fascist beast and replace it with a new world of freedom and unity. Well, we all know what that consisted of for the people who had been willing to stand up for democracy in 1938. Hitlerism was replaced by Stalinism. Not much of a swap.

Of course, the murals show only the heroic Red Army, the heroic workers and heroic hope for the future. During the Soviet era Lidice became - after the immediate post war years - part of the Communist Party's propaganda. Most Czechs became sceptical about the way the events were presented; rather a symbol of oppression than stirring memory for a liberated people. Communist Party officials and their guests turned up each year mouthing words that had no sincerity and bore little resemblance to reality.

313

I walked down the steps and into the valley where the old village had stood. There are a number of memorials; the cross that marks the men's mass grave, a memorial to the women, the breath-taking monument to the child victims of war. There stands the pear tree, grafts of which have now been sent all over the world. It was all that was left standing when the village was destroyed.

As first time visitors we were both open to all the emotions places like this can throw at you. I doubt that familiarity reduces the impact much, but the ease with which some people moved about suggested that they came here more frequently. Two children were riding their mountain bikes along the track, some adults were wheeling theirs having, by the look of the basket strapped to the rack, cycled there for a picnic. They had a toddler sitting in a child seat. Dogs were being walked, on lead, by the pond. Rugs were spread in the shade of trees and people spread themselves out to enjoy the day. I thought, "You should not be doing that. Riding bikes, walking dogs, preparing picnics, sunbathing. Look over there; the children of 1942 Lidice stand in bronze because they were gassed, over there the men lie buried because they were murdered on a summer's day."

Mark and I followed separate, but parallel courses up to the rose garden, the largest in the world; this was one of Barnett Stross's big ideas. Roses from all over the world, colours and scents uniting people in an annual festival of blooms. Imagine the air of a balmy summer evening filled with the deep perfume of thousands and thousands of roses on thousands of bushes?

We were probably a bit early for the best. Bending to sniff the scent I suddenly realised that care was needed. Away to my left was a bride in white and groom in grey and an assembled group of friends and relatives. There, too, was the Director of the Museum (this was, it turned out, the second wedding of the day).

A photographer was battling the glare of the sun to capture the happy couple with a background of roses; then parents of the bride... the groom... bridesmaids... siblings... cousins... friends... and I would be in all of them if I were not careful.

I doubted that they wanted me in their memories of their special day. Nor did I wish to be included. How bizarre, I thought. How could anyone, why would anyone want to marry on the site of one of Europe's many wartime atrocities, a place of death and immortal memory?

Only then did it strike me. Lidice lived because of the boys riding their bikes past the memorials, the children sucking ice-lollies in front of the Soviet murals, because dogs exercised amidst the monuments, because the cat idled on the sunlit roof and the children shouted excitedly in the sunshine of a June morning. That was Lidice living; the toddler riding in his bicycle seat to have a picnic with his parents; the time-old celebration of a marriage with generations of relatives and friends smiling, hoping and wishing-well.

Were it just another memorial to a wartime atrocity, it would not be the same. The Lidice Shall Live campaign would have failed.

****

Mind you, not everyone, in those post war years, wanted to see Lidice rebuilt. Stross had grand plans for a village, gallery, rose garden and mining education and training institute; the Soviets wanted to show that Soviet Communism had been victorious over fascism and was the new hope of the World. The Czech government wanted a national symbol. Many of the former residents thought more than twice about the rebuilding and relocation. Everything they held dear in old Lidice was gone. Where were their children? Well a few had been found, but the rest were lost, forever. A new Lidice might well mean nothing to them.

For me and Mark, the next bit of living was to go back to that jolly bar. The barmaid recognised us and quickly served us two lovely, frost crisp, amber beers. We ordered some snacks. A mixture of things including a sort of crushed, creamed pork scratching with more accentuated consonants than I could bother counting in its name. Delicious, unless one is an artery. Dripping?

****

The Lidice Shall Live campaign had its origins in Stoke-on-Trent, in an amalgam of Dr Barnett Stross and the North Staffordshire Miners' Federation; though it should be noted that in July 1942 it was suggested at a national miner's conference in Blackpool, that money should be raised to rebuild the village. It spread rapidly, soon Lidice Shall Live committees were to be found in many cities and all mining areas. Particularly popular amongst miners, other workers put their weight behind it too. Equally, left wing academics, such as Professor JBS Haldane - a mapper of genetics amongst other things - were involved.

It seems that North Staffordshire contributed some £32,000 in total, with, at least £16,000 coming from miners, although the total given could be considerably larger. Miners pay received a boost during the Second World War, but was hardly generous and it was still over ten shillings a week below the rate for 1920. Average pay was higher than in the potteries, where average wages had also declined since 1920. Lower averages could be explained in part by the huge range of jobs in the pottery industry and the number of female employees. Mining was for men and boys.

It has been said that miners gave a day's pay each week. To give up a day's pay would be a huge sacrifice; to do it each week would have placed an unimaginable strain on most mining families' budgets. It has also been said that some miner's contributed a week's pay over the life of the campaign. More research is needed. Numbers, press reports and other sources can be ambiguous and do not seem to add up. A job for the future.

Normal mining data was not collected during the war, so it is hard to get detailed figures. A reasonable estimate suggest that there were around 17,000 underground workers in North Staffordshire's mines. Adults earned somewhere in the region of £4 3s a week. At best, this gives around fourteen shillings (about 70p) a day. They weren't all over twenty-one, of course. Boys from fourteen to twenty years of age formed a considerable part of the workforce. They earned less. For example, after June 1942 a fourteen year old working underground would earn around £1 12s (£1.60) a week. Pay rose with age. Some surface workers were paid less, others more. There were some 6,500 of them, men and boys.

It is clear that the miners and other workers in the area generously gave what they could. Miners from across the country, did the same. Some, naturally, gave more than others. That does not demean the effort or lessen its generosity. Rather, it puts it in the perspective of low pay, hard, dangerous work, looking after your own family and wartime hardships; in fact, it makes it even more remarkable. Maybe it was because of their dangerous daily work that miners shone a light of hope.

Miners, for example in County Durham - where the annual Miner's Gala, the "Big Meeting" still fills Durham City - passed resolutions and raised funds. Money came into the fund from other sources too, and pretty quickly. In July 1943, some nine months after the official launch, Barnett Stross wrote to Professor Haldane about the plan for a "Safety in Mining" Institute. In the letter, he explains that plans for the rebuilding of the village were in their infancy - apart from the obvious need to remove the occupying Nazis - but that funds available were already approaching the "first hundred thousand pounds" and that the campaign will be conducted in Nottingham and Derby in August, and in Manchester in October.

After the war, the rebuilding eventually went ahead. Modern houses with modern facilities in a setting, a little like a mini garden city, were built on a new hill-side site. The latter was very much at the insistence of the surviving pre-war residents. The old site, in their view, should not be built on. There would be a gallery, museum, memorials and a rose garden, but no mining safety research centre.

Post war events in the village were heavily influenced by the new direction in which Czech life was directed by governments either petrified of, or in hoc to, the Soviet Union. In 1946 the Communist Party won power in a general election and turned Czechoslovakia into a one-party state in 1948.

The village was rebuilt just as the Communist takeover was completed. People began to move in shortly before Christmas 1949.

Willing to accept the assistance of the "workers" of the western nations, the new Communist government no longer extend the same gratitude to those who had fought alongside the British to defeat Nazism. There was much debate over whether Horák and Stříbrný should be allocated houses - remember housing was under state control. The notion for the new-built Lidice was that houses would be allocated to all the widows and for any child who had returned as a complete orphan, but not for the men who had gone to Britain to fight.

Some former residents felt that they should be made welcome. Indeed, at a meeting in Kladno, at which the decision was made, Minister of the Interior, Václav Nosek, stated that he thought they should be included. Anna Kohličková recalled him saying that as he had been in Britain during the war too, he knew what they had been through. He came from a mining background and was a thoroughgoing Communist. He oversaw the development of Communist security agencies and was instrumental in crushing pro-democracy demonstrations during the 1948 coup. His wife had died in Auschwitz and his son had died on a Death March in 1945.

Another thorough going Party apparatchik Ladislav Kopřiva - later to be head of State Security - turned to practicalities, stating, in effect, that two more houses meant less money to spend on the rest of the others. Whether this debate was a setup, the majority of women at the meeting supported the exclusion of the two men. This was far from unanimous, but the decision was made.

Stříbrný and Horák were in the meeting, but listened in silence. They already knew that in the eyes of the new government they were no longer patriots who had gone into exile to fight against the Nazis. They were now tainted with the tar of imperialism, capitalism and bourgeois liberalism. How things change.

There were also stronger emotions influencing the way the survivors thought. Two survivors confronted the men, blaming them for the destruction of the village and the murder of their children. Irrational maybe, but understandable. Horák returned to the UK. He died in an aviation accident a few years later. His descendants still live in England. Stříbrný stayed in Czechoslovakia with declining fortunes and died in Písek, very much forgotten.

Horák's sister, of course, was offered a house in the village, but because of the hostility, did not return there for many years.

The planned church and priest's house were, needless to say, dropped from the plans too.

The Lidice Shall Live campaign also suffered from controversy after 1945. Set up as an apolitical organisation, there were claims that it had become an instrument of the left-wing, and that Stross was behind this. It was even suggested that Stross was a Czech spy, but information about Labour Party policies which he was supposed to have leaked was available in party literature.

****

As we visited the gallery in the late afternoon, the frantic continent of change that was post-war Europe, was kept to the fore. The gallery was created largely because Stross saw art as a unifying force amongst humans. He was also a collector in his own right. Artists from all around the world were invited to contribute works. There is much in store and the public collection is changed.

On our visit the focus seemed to be very much on works examining guilt and redemption. Yet, perhaps the most revealing work is displayed in the upper gallery. There is the work of young people from around the world who have participated in the International Children's Fine Art Competition. This is administered largely by Alan and Cheryl Gerrard at Theartbay, Fenton, Stoke-on-Trent. Visit the gallery or look at the website to discover what a wonderful world we live in, or just how frightening growing up can be.

Naturally, much depends on the preferences of art teachers. There are, however, some truly shocking images to shake any complacency about how well we have done in "saving future generations from the scourge of war", as we promised in the UN charter.

324

After such a long and thoughtful day, we spent some time reading, before heading into the bar - again - and pursuing the usual discussion about beer and grub. You'll be spared the detail. Once again, there was a large party on the far side of the restaurant. Glasses clinking and chatter bubbling away. We sat in the small bar where several locals were smoking heavily to comfort themselves during one of the European Championship football matches. The Czech's were having a poor tournament. Lidice was living.

Chapter Seventeen

Next morning, an early start for a long day, saw us out and on our way to Prague before anyone in Lidice seemed to be in the land of the living. Our aim was to break the back of the onward journey, leaving half a day's ride to reach the Moravian town of Třebíč.

Shortly after Mark and I were interviewed by Jiri Hosek for Czech National Radio, I'd received an email from a guy by the name of Milan Kčmář. He had cycled from near his home in Trebíč to London a few years before. Why? Well, a few kilometres over the hills to the south of the town is a village by the name of Dolní Vilémovice. This was the birthplace of a Czech hero, a martyr even, by the name of Jan Kubiš. It was Kubiš and his Slovak partner, Josef Gabčík, who had assassinated Heydrich in May 1942.

Milan had been part of a group who wanted to preserve the old Kubiš house as a museum; to keep alive the memory of Jan and his family, and the world in which he was born. Needless to say, the Kubiš family felt the full force of Nazi revenge.

To raise awareness - and money - for the project, Milan set off on his bike, eventually reaching the building in the Uxbridge Road, London, where the mission was planned.

Very kindly, he suggested that we continue our journey to visit Dolní Vilémovice and said, even more kindly, that he would act as our host - despite arriving home from a holiday in Mallorca in the early hours of the morning on which we were scheduled to arrive.

Rolling along the silent streets of Lidice we passed the neat houses, descended to the stream and curled back around the far side of the shallow valley to leave with a view of the monuments and memorials where, eighty years before, an unremarkable, ordinary, village would have been preparing for a Sabbath day of rest.

Our plan was simple - get into the outskirts of Prague, pick up a numbered cycle route and follow it until we hit open country and then to head across country to Kutná Hora before heading south through Čáslav, to spend the night at Havlíčkuv Brod. Easy? Hundred miles on a hot day, with some rolling country and some long, though not steep, climbs.

327

A few villages, each getting larger, soon became the Prague suburbs. A mighty long downhill, for much of which we were followed by a bus driven by a very patient driver, brought us under a railway bridge and onto an empty main road by the banks of the Vltava. Decent cycle tracks took us toward the city centre, but we turned off before then, into the inner-city suburb of Karlín. I knew the name from the Good Soldier Švejk and His Adventures in the Great War. Having been imprisoned as a malingerer Švejk is taken to the wonderful Army Chaplain, Otto Katz, in Karlín. Not much use for finding cycle routes.

Heading away from the river, things went pretty well for a while, though we occasionally missed a sign and ended up under a major road bridge with little idea of what and where we were going. Various maps saved to the mobile helped.

Despite electronic aids and following the signs, one cycle route suddenly headed up a lengthy flight of mud-covered wooden steps. Reaching the top, we decided we'd had enough of such shenanigans and would stick to the road.

Eventually, we even took to a main road, National Route 2, no less. Almost empty of traffic, it gave the most direct route

328

to Kutná Hora. This could have been because it was a Sunday. The road skirts most towns as it rolls over a stretch of undulating farmland and forest. Skirting towns means no shops. A hot day, with water running low and little sign of food. Pressing on, rather than diverting, we swung up a hill into Zásmusky, one of the few settlements of any size on the road. A shop. A shop with food and drink. Mark went and did the honours whilst I sought a sliver of shade.

A little further on, we sought to fill water bottles at a petrol station. Generally, petrol stations have a public tap from the main. This one was no exception. Whilst we filled up we chatted with a local cyclist who had been buying a chocolate bar. In a broken conversation he seemed to be telling us that this was a great area for road cycling. It was, I think, his home area. He gestured that it was a long climb to Havlíčkuv Brod and we had to go through Kutná Hora and Časlav first to avoid the worst of the hills. Milan had already advised us of this.

Kutná Hora has been added to the list of places to go back to. A charming historic town centre grew on the back of mineral mining. Such was the prosperity that silver brought that Kutná Hora rivalled Prague for wealth in the later part of the middle-ages. It is now a UNESCO World Heritage Site. Current prosperity appeared to be created by people eating ice-cream. I'd quite like to have contributed, but not being as quick as we once were, we decided to push forward.

There was a cycle route - on road, I thought - that linked Kutná Hora and Časlav. The road did not quite live up to the customary expectations one has of a road, for example, after a decent distance as a country lane, the surface slowly changed into a rough track. Eventually, it returned to something approximating to a traditional country lane, then to smooth asphalt.

During the trip we had learned a new word in Czech. "Brod"; we deduced it meant a shallow gully with water crossed by a cycle path, or maybe, just take care. We had seen it before, on signs where a cycle path crossed small open channels of water. On the way to the smooth asphalt, Mark saw the sign; I saw the sign; Brod. I stopped and used a footbridge; this was more than a gully. Mark, fearless as ever, went straight for it. Whether it was the slime or a patch of loose stone, Mark went for a burton.

We, especially Mark, learned that Brod was the Czech word for "moderately deep ford" as well as gully. Thanks, Mark, for expanding our vocabulary. A group of Czech children playing nearby heard a lot of interesting English words that were unlikely to be found in their text books, too. Maybe they asked their teacher about them when they got to school the next morning.

Mark removing algae and weed, opined that I was less than suitably sympathetic being, quite clearly, the cowardly sort who stood slacking on the footbridge whilst nobler descendants of the heroes of the Charge of the Light Brigade hurtled bravely to their doom. He was probably correct, but at least I was dry.

Language lessons done for the time being, the sunshine lasted long enough to dry Mark out. I'd like to say the humidity caused me to envy his dip. It didn't. However, by the time we reached the main road junction in Časlav, the sky was turning deep black. The town's building - glowing in the rays of sun that resisted the advance of darkness - shone out as the last beacons of light.

We decided to take the main road, to avoid the increasing number of climbs and descents that became a feature of more minor roads as we entered the Bohemian-Moravian Highlands. Added to this it was a more direct route and was, frankly, a little busier than a Sunday afternoon road should be.

The road climbed and climbed and went on climbing, always gently, but always upward. Kilometre after kilometre of steady pedalling, eventually interspersed by short steeper sections. In opposition to this rise, the cloud continued to settle lower and lower whilst darkening and ever darkening. Lights on, cars headlights shining at about five o'clock on a June afternoon, but it could have been midnight - it bought fond memories of England.

Crackles of lightning spread across the distant sky, creating a halo of light on the hilltop horizons. Still it remained dry and we pushed onward and upward. A few spots of rain, a blast of wind, closer and closer came the lightning. We kept our cadence and hoped we might get to Havlíčküv Brod and our hotel, nice and dry.

Around seven o'clock, we began to descend and into the town we swept - looking much less knackered than we actually were. The sun returned as we searched for the hotel, which turned out to be down an unpromising little back street. Finding it so rapidly was thanks to a young gentleman, who on being asked if "Mluvíš anglicky" not only had the ability to understand what we asked, but smartly spotted that we were not native speakers. Clearly a fellow of great erudition, he replied, "Yes, I do, can I help you?"

He gave directions which were correct both geographically and grammatically.

The hotel appeared to be locked. There was no sign of life, no bar, no restaurant full of locals tucking in to a family dinner. However, knocking on the door brought the attention of a lady, who showed us to comfortable rooms and told us to put our bikes in a large empty hall for safety.

A few minutes later, scrubbed up and hungry we stepped back out into Havlíčkuv Brod and headed for the main square. The sun shone gently on the river and lit the buildings warmly. Ahead we could see the old houses that surrounded the cobbled square. There we expected to find food and drink.

Well, we weren't disappointed, but we took some time to wander round and admire the town before we filled our faces. Havlićkūv Brod is not a huge city, but the square is that of a significant town and could have hosted a very, very big market. That evening a handful of cars, white-globed street-lights and fountains and statues were the only inhabitants. Experience of the Czech Republic lasting for a whopping three days and nights seemed to suggest that bars were always well patronised. Maybe Sunday was a day of rest on the water-wagon.

There were a few other diners in the restaurant as we entered. Not before time did we decide to refuel. Sunday seemed to be early closing day, but the waiter showed us to a table. The decor was grand in a building dating back to the sixteenth century, at least, and maybe well before. Massively sturdy stone arches combined with baroque decoration. This will be pricey, we thought.

Of course, it was not expensive by British standards. The beers available were all unfamiliar, so we enquired the waiter. He explained the nature of the different offerings, pointing out that some were special summer brews, whilst others were

334

available all year round; all were brewed by local brewers, some to age old recipes.

Mark seemed to be getting into the pork diet at last. OK, he was not quite at the artery-clogging stage yet, but he was definitely softening by small degrees. He declared that he was going to try a pork based dish. I was left to maintain our healthy eating stance for once, and, needless to say, failed miserably. We ate and drank well. We even went for a liqueur.

By the time we had finished, the waiters were sitting at a table chatting and all but two other diners had gone home. We left a decent tip.

A long day on the bike, a hearty feed and stepping out into a lamp-lit market square surrounded by charming buildings - there is indeed much more to cycling than riding a bike. We took a few photos and wandered slowly back to the hotel.

Chapter Eighteen

Although we appeared to be the only guests, a great spread was laid out for breakfast. So we ate and ate. This was less due to hunger than the weather. Outside the rain was heavy and persistent.

Eventually we could neither eat more nor overstay our welcome. We girded ourselves in waterproofs and overshoes and decided that we would follow that none-too-busy main road. Why take the winding country route when the view would be zero and we needed to get to Milan later that day?

Well, for starters, the none-too-busy main road had become a constant stream of traffic - on later examination it linked the north to a main east-west motorway. Our lights flared across the wet tarmac in the pouring rain and the motor vehicles kept their distance well.

Quite suddenly, a few miles out, we became the fastest things on the road. A queue of vehicles, miles and miles long, caused us to filter on the right, alternating between cruising and teetering between the lorries and the verge. Mark rolled more quickly along, but I eventually caught up. We nearly diverted to a village named Stoky, just to see how much like good old Stoke it was. Traffic appeared to be trying its luck too, so we kept on the main drag and eventually arrived to a mixture of a road traffic incident and road works.

A burned out lorry stood on the grass. It could have been there just a few minutes, though it looked well-rooted and could just as easily have been sitting there for months. We'd already filtered past a tailback suitable for the M6 on a Friday evening, so we raced past the traffic lights that controlled the roadworks - turned out to be no more than resurfacing - keeping pace with the stream of lorries with little effort.

Of course, back on the open road, as it slithered uphill toward the low ceiling of rainclouds, the stream of lorries and cars wanted to overtake us. They did so, slowly, without the hoot of a horn and, though the carriageway was far from wide, without threatening our well-being.

Despite the careful drivers - I don't think I speak only for myself - I was heartily fed up with trudging along the same old main road. Yes, the traffic lightened up as we passed the motorway junction and the bulk of the vehicles headed off to Brno or Vienna or Prague. Yes, we had broken most of the day's journey, but we had seen little - unless you count a variety of HGVs and sodden verges. Wordsworth used to get quite excited by dank undergrowth, but I don't.

Negotiating our way through a light industrial area - a little confusing until we saw a bus heading for the town centre and followed it - we reached the river that passes through the centre of Jihlava; the River Jihlava. Much of the rest of our route would follow this. The maps showed that the cycle route was incomplete, but there were options.

The rain continued, swelling the river with the boisterous waters of highland streams. The route skirted valley-sides covered in deep pine forests, wiggling its way in a corridor between the trees and the river. With the railway line running alongside, we looked forward to following the river, almost all the way to Třebíč. We were mistaken, but not until after lunch.

When this route is completed as a well-surfaced cycle path the ride from Jihlava to Luka nad Jihlavou will be a magnificent outing for cyclists of all abilities. Not least among the factors contributing to this is the charming open square of Luka, set in the hills, with bars and cafés catering for outdoorsy folk - even very wet cyclists.

We were so wet that we felt embarrassed to go into a café. We peeled off our overshoes and waterproofs outside and locked the bikes up. Venturing slowly in, the barman-waiter, who turned out to be the owner, batted not an eye-lid at the pair of sodden middle-aged men who crept in. He showed us to a table and asked if we wanted a drink. We began with a hot coffee, which I took with sugar - something I tend to do only when wet or cold, or both.

A bowl of soup and a big glass of beer soon followed. Beans cooked with large chunks of smoked sausage. Just the stuff for a wet day, even in what was meant to be summer. The next day, we would be looking back on the relative cool with envy, but, as true Britishers abroad, the weather was never quite right. No more right than it ever was at home.

The barman-owner spoke pretty good English, so we were able to have a good chat. He had spent a few months in England, setting up business in Luka, with his wife, shortly after returning to his home country. He knew of Lidice and, indeed, had been to Stoke-on-Trent. They did not, he said, get many English visitors. Apart from Czechs and Slovaks, most customers - especially those passing through on bikes - were German.

He brought out a liqueur bottle and asked if we would like to try some. I looked at Mark and we silently agreed to have a go. You have to take the opportunity when it arises. We stuck to one though. This was not Beckerovka. The rest of the day has washed away memory of its name.

The rain had stopped when we left and the temperature had risen a little. It was now pleasantly warm, or maybe that liqueur was taking effect. Constructing an ad hoc drying platform on a bike rack, using bungees and Velcro is a common enough affair for cycle tourists, but sometimes it is quicker to dry stuff by wearing it. So, jacket stayed on; gloves and waterproofs were lashed to the rack, to be turned at rest stops. Overshoes stayed on. Surface water gets your feet just, if not more, wet than rain.

Heading out on a mixture of rough cycle track and road, we climbed up one side of the valley. We passed by a railway station identifiable as such, only by a vague glimpse of rail through the clumps of grass. Did trains ever come this way? Well they did, because, next day, we caught one that had come along this line. There was also a small house decorated with colourful gnomes, proving that pottiness is not confined to the UK.

We then descended to the river and clambered breathlessly up the far side of the valley. We ran back down to the river and decided we were getting fed up with this vertical zig-zagging up and down the steep hills - even if there were nice-if-hazy views from the top of each. One descent was idiotically steep with a rapid change of surface from asphalt to forest mud-heap. There was a shrine at the top, to pray for one's brakes or give thanks that the climb was over - depending on which direction one was travelling in. Actually, crosses and shrines often marked the entrance or exit from a village.

We could have done with St. Christopher, or the patron saint of maps, navigators and GPS devices. We could have addressed prayers to Saint Brendan, the Navigator, who is, believe it or not the patron saint of navigators, sailors and elderly travellers. "Two out of three ain't bad," as Meatloaf sang. Having said that we could have stuck with St. Arnold of Soissons, the patron saint of brewers. Actually there are other patron saints of brewers; Augustine of Hippo and Nicholas of Myra, to name two. Guess it was an attractive billet. Is there a cycling saint? Of course there is; Our Lady of Ghisallo, is patron saint of local travellers and has been adopted by the Roman Catholic Church as that of cyclists.

341

Well, we needed something. With wild swings back and forth across the valley - blinking steep in places - we reached a point where a remarkably placed sign proposed, depending on where one stood, three possibilities. One was across the river, one was into a field and another was up a track into the forest.

Later, we were told that, although the cycle network was developing rapidly, where it was incomplete or waiting for development, there was a tendency just to stick a sign on a tree and hope for the best. Actually, the Cykloatlas gave pretty good guidance - good surface right through to passable only in dry weather or suitable for a mountain bike are indicated in a variety of colours and hatchings. The trouble is it takes a while to work out how these relate to what is on the ground.

We first took to the field and retraced our steps a few minutes later. We looked across the river, but decided that the route could not go that way and was clearly heading for another big swing through the trees. So, we followed the stoney track, which was the left fork. This soon brought us into someone's garden.

342

The owner emerged. He may have told us to get off his land, though his manner was much friendlier. He recognised that we clearly did not understand and quickly decided, quite correctly, that we did not know which way to go. Yes, we were English; did he know the way for bicycles? He took the map and showed us, but stated that was a way for walkers, a hiking route. Even so, he said, climb and go straight on until we come to a road.

"Would this take us to Třebíč," we asked. Alright, actually, just "Třebíč" which an inflection. To the road, turn left, then turn right and turn right again. Well, if that was not what he meant it was a damn good translation because it was spot on.

We waved goodbye. He returned our gesture. A few moments later we were on a narrow, overgrown track stumbling up steps made of tree roots amidst rock and mud. Hauling laden bikes whilst trying not to turn a backward somersault down the hill could have earned us some money on You've Been Framed, had there been a spare hand for a camera.

When things levelled out onto a hedge-lined farm track, the going got a little better and some cycling was possible. Had we been ambling along during a drought with the love of one's life (other than one's bicycle), it would have been the ideal spot for a perfume advert. Fragrant summer flowers filled the afternoon with a swathes of scent as the warm air began to hum with buzzing insects. Potentially a sweet place, but not for cyclists in knee length grass, wet grass that even ensured the overshoes failed.

A low gear and a bit of fish-tailing, powered by a desire to escape, carried us through. Emerging joyfully on a well-surfaced lane, we turned left, as instructed. We commenced to climb, but gently. To our right was a valley of ripening wheat with patches of rich green pasture against a backdrop of coniferous forest.

The first left turn looked like a decent road. Later on, closely looking at the map, it seems that we should have been able to emerge there on a section of route designated as "unpaved but passable". So, where had we missed the other end?

The valley had become shallower by the time we reached the right turn our kind guide had suggested we take. It took us from some nice asphalt onto a loosely gritted surface. It looked like British surface dressing without having so much of a surface to dress. It ran down to a farm in the valley bottom. We hoped it swept up the opposite side.

The view was perfect. Dark clouds had returned. The whitewashed farmhouse walls, the red-tiled roof and the range of barns and outbuildings stood amongst a small group of hedged pastures bounded by forest. This was how I had imagined the countryside of the Bohemian Moravian Highlands to be. The Highlands sweep round to the western end of the Carpathian Mountains.

We raced down the road as the grit covering disappeared and braked sharply to wiggle through the pastures by the farm, trying to keep momentum for the climb through the forest by the little Leštinsky Brook. Enchanting. I love this kind of cycling. New roads, pine-scented fresh air to breathe, a steady incline, a stream running by.

At the end of the forest, the climb carried on, suddenly steepening in Červená Lhota. We kept climbing more or less to skirt Čihalin and reach the road somewhere around 580 metres above sea level. No, we had not climbed that far, we'd started well above sea level, this is, after all the middle of the continent. Yet the descent seems to go on for ever, or all the way to Třebíč.

We had successfully located road number 351, which appeared to be the equivalent to a UK B road, i.e. decent surface, wide enough for two vehicles, but not too busy. We could let rip most of the way. So we did. We ignored the cycle route when it left the road at Račerovice.

It was a great freewheel. Třebíč arrived rapidly. We rode into town through the area known as Zámostí - literally "over the bridge". On this day there was no chance of going over the bridge as it was being rebuilt. This was a touch problematic as we had arranged to meet Milan there. We had visions of him being on the other side waiting for us. I looked for someone to wave to. Not knowing what he looked like, I decided against it.

Of course, we quickly met up as Milan cycled around over another bridge and arrived about five minutes later. A tall young man on a hybrid bike. We were easy to spot and he rolled in with a jolly "Steve, Mark?" and a big smile.

Třebíč is a relatively small town, a regional centre with a population of some 37,000. However, it has two UNESCO World Heritage Sites. We'd landed right in the middle of one. "Over the bridge" was so named because of its fourteenth century inhabitants, who were not allowed to live in the main town. This Old Jewish Quarter is a muddle of streets and alleys, with two synagogues. It is well-documented and was once home to around 1500 people. However, the number of them identifying themselves as Jewish had declined to about 300 by the 1930s. There are now none, as far as I am aware, of Jewish origin, though a handful returned after the Second World War.

The second site is the Basilica of St. Procopius, on a hill above the Old Jewish Quarter. Both will serve as reasons to go back to Třebíč. The best reason though, will be to drag Milan out for a dinner to thank him for his hospitality. He'd also arranged a couple visits for us, neither of which included UNESCO, but focussed on more recent history and looked to the future.

First, though, it was time to head off to Milan's flat in a community of high-rise tenement blocks on the southern side of the town. We followed him along some urban streets through the pretty riverside town, briefly onto a main road and then onto well-made cycle paths climbing through woodland. As we went Milan pointed the way to Alternátor, the centre for alternative technology where he works.

Milan's flat was in a brightly painted block. I imagine that this was a Soviet era housing scheme. If it was, it actually looked pretty good. OK, it had been renovated, but the buildings were spaced out, evenly in regimented lines. There were trees and spaces to chat and play.

Bikes were locked up in the basement cellar and we walked up the stairs. Milan showed us around the flat. Then, very generously, he offered to take all our dirty washing round to his parents. They had a washing machine - he hadn't - and they, more than generously, had offered their services to launder sweat-soaked filthy cycling gear belonging to two people they knew nothing of, from a country far away.

Milan popped off and we took showers and sorted our gear out for the next morning. We'd offered to take Milan out for dinner and a few beers, but he'd only got back from a holiday in Mallorca that morning, arriving home around dawn, so wasn't up for it.

Milan's Mum - God bless her - had made a great pile of traditional Moravian snacks and dainties. Swapping the washing for them, Milan returned balancing them skilfully. How generous people have been when I've been cycling away from home. Travel by bicycle or on foot - friendly, egalitarian even. There is no edge, no threat, no show of wealth or status. Hope it was worth repeating.

So, beers and tasties were lined up on the table and we got down to talking about... well, fortunately Milan, like many young Czechs, speaks excellent English. So, the conversation naturally began with the purpose of our visit and our ride so far. What was the Czech cycle network like? How did it compare to the UK? To Germany? What was our opinion?

Then we got round to Milan's 2012 bike trip to London. He told the story of how the Kubiš house had been bought. Sadly, it was in a pretty dilapidated state and restoration and conversion into a museum needed to be paid for.

A group of local supporters, of which Milan was one, had assembled, led by the village mayor, Jitka Boučková. There was strong community support, but awareness and money

349

was crucial. So, Milan offered his skills in public relations and press and communications work, then deciding to ride his bike from Dolní Vilémovice, with its memorial to Jan Kubiš and his family, to London.

"I made a list of places that I really wanted to visit on the way," he said. "I think you came a straighter way."

Eventually, donations from ordinary Czechs, as well as support from the Ministry of Defence and other organisations, were added to the proceeds of concerts, talks and tours, and the money was raised.

I asked about Kubiš. "You will see plenty tomorrow, but he is a hero in the Czech Republic, even today, because, as you know, he killed Heydrich. For us this is very important, but more than that, he came from a normal home in a little village."

"So, what about Gabčík," I asked. "Does he have the same status in Slovakia?"

"Not really," he replied, "It is getting better, but there were some things that make it harder."

He went on to explain that, at the time, there was a much stronger right-wing movement in Slovakia. "There were some fascists in Slovakia and many there said that they were not treated fairly in Czechoslovakia; some saw the Germans as liberators, at first. Also, Gabčík spelt his name Josef, like a Czech, not Jozef like a Slovak. So, it has been a long time for him to be seen as a hero there." There is a memorial to Gabčik near his birthplace in Zilinia, Slovakia.

We then got onto cinema. Milan had a great liking for films. The magic of the silver screen was celebrated everywhere. Czech films have a reputation for being pithy and creative and stand at the forefront of modern European cinema. Fortunately for Milan, Mark was a bit of an expert. I listened and learned.

I could join in more when the conversation turned briefly to actresses of the golden era of Hollywood. Milan had posters aplenty to discuss. Fortunately for me, my father had taken great interest in the subject. He was always a strength in a Trivial Pursuit team and one could only admire his long memory for the names of 1940s and 1950s stars and starlets.

351

Naturally things progressed to Brexit and politics. In Milan's view it was a necessary evil. "I think we would think the same as many on the UK, but we are too small an economy to leave. But then, we do not know what Russia is going to do, so it is good to be in a bigger group."

Perspectives vary. The UK referendum had not yet taken place. Polls suggested it was a close thing. The EU flag was prominently displayed in Prague, much more frequently to be seen than in areas like Stoke-on-Trent, which benefitted from a lot of EU investment.

We talked about all sorts of topics. Perspectives may differ, but common themes persist. Cost of living? "I saved up to buy this flat. It was not too expensive, but I would like a house. My parents have a flat, but they also have a little cottage in the country. In the Soviet days people could not travel much and almost none could leave the country. My Father built a little hut and a garden and he still loves going there."

"Cars here are expensive," Milan said. "There is another reason for riding a bike."

We remarked that beer was very cheap. Milan smiled.

Chapter Nineteen

The morning was already hot when we cycled across a small industrial-cum-retail area and into the countryside. Slathered in sun-screen, we soon began to sweat. The temperature was due to rise rapidly into the thirties.

A quick dip down and across a valley of ripening wheat resulted in the inevitable ascent, much longer, into woodland and upward. Long-legged Milan levered the pedals round. Even with around a thousand miles in our legs, we lagged. The forested summit offered some solace from the scorching sun. We drank. At this point I, and possibly Mark, began to reconsider our plans. Neither said anything, however, we both thought that things were getting too hot.

Milan pointed out the gently rolling lands that lay in front of us. Although moderately undulating farmland and forest, its gentleness defied its height above sea level. Milan had explained, as we stood on the small balcony of his flat the previous evening, that there were few winters when he had been unable to put on his cross-country skis and head out in the direction we would travel the next day.

The descent came as a pleasant relief, though the air was hardly cooling. A turn down an unpromising unsigned road, brought us rapidly into the home village of a Czech hero; Dolní Vilémovice. Dolní translates into English, roughly, as "bottom" or "nether" and both were appropriate. The speed of our arrival suited "bottom" and the size and isolation suited "nether". It must have, in many ways, been an idyllic place to grow up, but maybe a little small for a man of action, such as Jan Kubiš.

We took our bikes into a small yard; a cool, shaded haven. As we entered Jitka Boučková came to greet us and show us around. With an obvious, but not pompous, sense of pride she explained about the Kubiš family and how the house had been bought and restored. Even better, she unveiled drinks and cakes, as well.

Disciplined as ever, we decided to examine the displays first, commencing with a short video presentation about Kubiš and Operation Anthropoid.

This is not a huge museum, but necessity being the mother of invention and due to imaginative selection, it is quite fascinating. There's a bike that the young Jan Kubiš and, doubtless, others of his family may have ridden around the area - to work, to visit friends or to go courting. Then there is the intended assassination weapon used by Gabčík, or, at least, one like it.

Then there are the family photos, and, perhaps my favourite exhibits, gloves and handkerchief's belonging to Kubiš and his girlfriends. I am told by those who know about such things that if young Jan was half as dashingly handsome as he is portrayed by the bust that stands outside the house, he would have been quite a catch. Not just in Dolní Vilémovice and its neighbours, either. That bicycle may well have covered a good few miles.

Some of the gloves and handkerchiefs were made for Jan by his sisters with particular girls in mind. They weren't made for a hero; they were made for a brother, much-loved, but a brother all the same.

****

Born in 1913 - the birthplace museum opened one hundred years later - Jan Kubiš would have been just over five years of age when Czechoslovakia was founded. Life in rural

Moravia gave way to military service around the country in 1935. Mobilised in 1938 to resist the threat of German invasion during the Sudetenland Crisis, the pusillanimous actions of the British and French, well-intentioned though they were, put off the fight. Czechoslovakia was sold down the river at the Munich Conference. Demobilised, he was discharged and went to work in a brickworks.

The Czechoslovak military was effectively disbanded when the Nazis took over the rest of Bohemia and Moravia, at the same time establishing a puppet government in Slovakia. At this point Kubiš headed for Poland, so did many others, including, of course, Horák and Stříbrný, from Lidice.

German victories on all fronts eventually drove them to Britain, to form a Czechoslovak military force, along with the Czechoslovak government, in exile. There he trained and trained and trained, passing through a variety of army schools, preparing himself for special duties behind enemy lines.

When Operation Anthropoid - the assassination of Heydrich - was planned, Kubiš volunteered, but was not selected. However, he got his chance when Karel Svoboda was injured in training. Off the subs bench, he turned the game. He and Gabčík, inflicted sufficient injury on Heydrich, which led to his death. The cause of Heydrich's death was officially sepsis. It is rumoured that medical complacency also played a part.

Kubiš was buried in a mass grave after his death in the siege of Prague's Cathedral of Saints Cyril and Methodius. Some people would like to see his body exhumed and given a suitable hero's tomb. Whether that is practical or desirable is a matter of debate.

Pretty sentimental family gifts or the monumental sarcophagus of a national hero? Which is more appropriate to the memory of a young man born in the Austro-Hungarian Empire, brought up in a rural backwater of a democratic republic, dying to show that the leading Nazis could not expect to be safe from the consequences of their actions, during some of the darkest days in Czechoslovakia's short history?

We took photos with Jitka and Milan and the bust of Jan Kubiš, in the sweltering sunshine at the front of the house. Some other visitors arrived as we tucked into our cakes. Czechs do seem to do cakes very well - and often.

357

When we left, Milan took us a little further on to see the village memorial which predates the museum. It is not just to Jan, but to the rest of his family, as well. The Nazis rarely missed an opportunity to terrorise; the Kubiš family was destroyed at Mauthausen Camp.

The mercury had climbed much quicker than us as we headed back over the hill to Třebíč. Milan's parents met us at his flat with freshly laundered and ironed clothing. Mark was embarrassed by my padded underwear. He suggested that Milan's mother and father would assume it was some sort of continence product and nothing to do with cycling. They, needless to say, did not bat an eyelid. We thanked them profusely. Dirty gear in these temperatures would have been intolerable for both ourselves and anyone within several metres.

Collecting our bags, we rolled down the cycle paths to Alternátor, Milan's official place of employment. Sited in the Borovina area of the town, it takes up part of the site originally developed for shoe manufacture. Baťa created a major industrial complex, including housing for workers that makes up the older part of Borovina.

A centre for alternative technology, especially electricity, is an appropriate inheritor of some of Baťa's site. The shoemaker was not only a worldwide success with innovative, quality footwear at affordable prices, but also a pioneer in manufacturing and employment conditions.

Milan took us on a tour. Fascinating ways to show how energy was, and is, generated and used, and how it might be done better and more cleanly. We even got a ride in an electric car, frighteningly silent from a cycling perspective. Yet, we are now looking forward to driverless ones.

Parties of school children were being shown round, but we got a private show in the fabulous theatre. Digital views of the sky and our little planet. Real time global displays flashed before one's eyes. Blimey, it is frightening to think of the scale of environmental issues when you step outside your own little sphere. A top spot to visit.

So, we had been to a town in Moravia with two UNESCO World Heritage Sites and explored neither.

As we sat down for a drink and Milan checked details for an article he was writing for a cycle touring magazine, we decided that things were simply getting too hot to handle. With the forecast for even hotter days, we decided to take the train back to Prague. Riding over the Bohemian-Moravian Highlands did not seem attractive. A visit to Tábor, one of the major historical towns of the Czech Republic, would have to wait until another trip. It had been the fortress of the Hussite People of the Chalice – they, and it, plays a huge part in the Czech national narrative – although, as with every nation's national narrative, things turn out not to be quite as straightforward as they seem.

Chapter Twenty

Milan cycled with us to ensure we arrived in plenty of time at the little station at Borovina. This was very helpful as, although it was easy enough to find if given good directions, it was disguised as a neglected outhouse on a rough platform beside an overgrown set of rusty rails. A single sign designated it as Třebič Borovina.

There was some fairly unpleasant graffiti which required limited Czech to understand. Symbols provide something of an international language, especially swastikas and hammers and sickles. Given the amount of stuff daubed on the small brick building that had neither a timetable nor an obvious door, the station must be quite lively at times. Only Social and Christian Democrats, Greens and Independents seemed not to drop by for a spot of artwork.

Milan pointed out the direction the train would come from - this was a single track line and not all trains stopped here. Not that there were that many, but they tended to be prompt. Given that there was no timetable, I wondered how he knew, but he said he had checked.

There was no tumble weed blowing about and Borovina was certainly not a ghost town, but its station could have been abandoned. Even so, before long a rumbling diesel train rattled to a halt with an arthritic grinding of brakes.

This was our first introduction to České Dráhy, the Czech national railway company. We helped pass the bikes up the steep steps to the bicycle compartment in the designated coach. The guard looked on approvingly. Milan waved farewell. A crescendo of the type that only a diesel engine or Motorhead at full pelt could provide, a lurch forward and we were off.

Next came the expected test: buying tickets to Brno from a Czech train guard at a backwoods station. Keeping things simple seemed to be the key. No need for sentences, they'd know we were foreigners without the embarrassment of trying to be accurate. Be effective and have a go. The translation app would be useless given the power of a mobile phone speaker opposed to the rattle and roll of the small train hurtling downward into Třebíč proper.

"Dvě..." I pointed at Mark and myself, and was encouraged by a smile of recognition.

Now I did not bother with "ticket" - incidentally, it is "jízdenky".

"Brno…" There was no point pointing as it was a good hour or so away still. There was another smile. Czechia, do as the Czechs do.

A bike ticket is required for any journey too. So, I indicated the bikes, but the guard had clearly picked up that they were ours when she watched us heave them on. She was ahead of us.

Needless to say we did not understand the amount she asked for. I find numbers notoriously difficult, but it seemed to be quite a small amount. She handed us the tickets. Rather like in the UK there were plenty of them. One for each of us. One for each bike and a receipt of the amount paid. Each showed every element of the transaction in detail, in a depth that a pedant could only dream of. Great reading for a long journey.

I handed over a few crowns and got some change back. Very good value, seriously.

At Třebíč a number of people got on, many looked like students, either from school or college, but there was plenty of space. Even so, with the babble of chatter and the rumble of the engine as it pulled out of the station, it was pretty difficult to hear my mobile ring. It was BBC Radio Stoke after an interview about riding to Lidice from Burslem.

Fortunately, it was not live. Lots of repetitions and say-it-agains, but the gist was shared through a combination of volume and sharply punctuated enunciation; the sort of rather rude approach usually reserved for speaking English abroad in the vague hope that it will be understood. Please, no comments that English is not spoken in the Potteries. It is, but I am a fan of dialects and like the fact that I can walk into some pubs in any of the six towns and barely understand a word until kind locals realise that they are speaking to someone from the Home Counties.

Interview over, one could look out over the countryside. The good old loco was getting more and more impressive. Once it had blown out the cobwebs, it cruised thunderously on forested hillsides and held the careering carriages back as we descended through pastures. The region seems to be quite sparsely populated, with only occasional villages appearing on either side of the line. The train halted at Vladislav and Studenec, though the latter station was a tidy walk from the village whose name it bore. Then a much larger settlement, Náměšť nad Oslavou came along.

The scenery really was very pretty. The line climbed and descended far more that the average British railway. It curved and cavorted more too. This was an entertaining ride.

Suburban stations on the approach to Brno prepared us to get the bikes off and cart them down the steps.

Taking a look at the excellent Cykloserver maps, I think a mix of train and bike would be a great way to explore the Czech Republic. There really is a very good network, although some journeys can be long and not quite as logical as they may appear. All trains, including cross-border, carry bikes; the trains are cheap and seem reliable. Do not forget your bike ticket, you will be asked for it. If you can buy your ticket before getting on the train then you should do so, bike ticket included. The guard on our train was very friendly and we had to buy the ticket on the train, but others stated that any cyclist with no bike ticket for their journey should expect no mercy. Bike tickets, like seat reservations, refer to specific trains. If you miss the one you are booked on you need to buy another.

From a British perspective, this is not too much of an added expense.

In best cycling tradition - though it could have been when in Czech do as the Czechs - we exited the station and stumbled into the first bar. It looked like rush hour. Trams rang warning bells, buses swept in and out of the bays outside the railway station and pedestrians marched purposefully back and forth.

We paused to sort out accommodation for the night. Mark called a nearby hostel and promptly got us a room. We did not rush. The shade was pleasant, despite the heavy city centre air; the beer was suitably cool and the company cosmopolitan.

When we set off across Brno's heart, it was beating festively. Brno is a fine city, make no mistake, but compared to Prague it lacks the mass of tourists and the hurly-burly of finding a way through a packed town centre. Rather, people were coming and going, wandering as opposed to following an itinerary from one sight to the next.

In the great square a jazz band played at a street corner bar. We climbed across a cobbled area and headed for the side streets. Check in at the hostel was in a café next to a rather grand arch. Passing through the arch, having stowed the bikes in a cellar, we climbed sets of stairs to the right of a door that appeared to lead into a large hall. It felt like the place was once a very grand house indeed, but that was just a guess.

Our room was on the upper gallery of the very top floor. We opened all the windows, we sought a draft of air, but it was sweltering in the attic. A few contortions brought a view of rooftops through one of the windows, but there was no breeze.

On the way up we'd passed through a couple of lockable doors. With a couple of keys, I popped down to reception to check which door we should lock. Turned out there were people in the room next to ours, so it was a good job we did not lock the door at the top of the stairs.

The visit to reception had an interesting side-line. Whilst I was talking to the guy in the café who appeared to be running the show, a taxi pulled up outside and a young lady dressed in a leather skirt, a crop top and high-heels got out. She took a suitcase out of the boot and walked through the archway into the hall. A moment later, another lady of similar age - this time wearing a crisp white blouse, mini-skirt and knee boots - followed her in, pulling a suitcase behind her. Almost immediately, another young lady, and another brought their suitcases in and disappeared into the dark.

I'll confess to considering what kind of things went on in the hall beneath our room. Would it keep us awake all night? I say, healthy mind, healthy body! Careful not to acquire these foreign ways! Back in the room, cleaned up after the day's activity, we headed off to find dinner. Back in reception, the young guy in charge directed us to a bar a little way out of town, in one of the inner suburbs. "It is my favourite, the Svičkova is the best. Have you had that? It really is special."

So off we went. His instructions were spot on, though our interpretation was less perfect. Even so, there eventually appeared a broad building with a large, decked, shaded outdoor area. Not so much a beer garden as a beer deck, but full to the brim with people eating, drinking and chatting. We found a table in the half-deserted, but joyfully cool, interior.

The waiter popped over with menus and to get our order for beer. He must have heard us speaking English and immediately said, "No English. Czech, please." Now this could have caused a few difficulties, except that the beer menu was clear and we could easily order. "Dalešice, prosím," I said. Mark followed suit.

The beer arrived. We did our best to pronounce "Děkuji". The waiter looked less than impressed, but optimistically returned in the hope that we could do better when it came to food. "Morávská Plata," brought a smile to his face. "Very good," he said. I was too chuffed with pride at this recognition to remember what Mark ordered or to realise that even if the waiter had only a little English, it was, at least as good as my Czech, and he did not have a script to read from.

I'd guessed that what I had ordered was some kind of platter of traditional Moravian dishes. I'd gleaned from the German translation that there was sauerkraut, red cabbage, some kind of sausage, a roast something and some other things, too. Made sense, "Morávská plata" must mean Moravian platter. Wrong, it seems, but even so, it was jolly hearty. I love sauerkraut and the sausages were splendid; one with a slightly smoky flavour, the other with a touch of paprika, maybe. The roast something turned out to be duck. There were other morsels, too.

Perfect. I tucked in bravely.

No dessert being necessary or feasible for my belly to cope with, we ordered another beer and mulled over the plan for the next day.

Then came a moment of truth. We wanted no more beer and dinner was done. The waiter circled the table and loomed over us with a pleasant, friendly smile.

I muttered to myself, "Conto, bill, recknung… oh… err…"

The waiter gestured encouragement.

I continued to dither, or, rather, think. "Ah! Yes! Uchet prosím!"

"High five!" The waiter squealed with pleasure, in very good English, at the same time as waving his right hand.

We paid and left a tip.

Strolling back through town, Mark dropped in to a supermarket to get another bottle of beer or two. Brno was relaxing into café culture. The jazz band still played. Big open spaces in the square easily swallowed the mix of tourists, doyennes and students on a hot midweek summer evening. Prague has the glorious buildings and the ocean of tourists; Brno chilled in the heatwave.

The mystery of the scantily clad young ladies with suitcases entering the dark hall by the archway under the hostel was solved without fuss or concern for our moral welfare. Loud music banged away inside, but the stream of teenage girls with pom-poms and batons, dressed in carnival costumes, told that there was some kind of dancing contest. Even if this was the wrong impression, the threat of any such thing was more than enough to send me racing up the stairs and off to the land of blog, whilst Mark read and drank his evening beer.

Chapter Twenty-One

The next morning dawned as oppressively hot as the day before had been. The roof-tops were already burning in the sun when I stuck my head out of the window and looked around. Another train day was a good plan.

We took a bite of breakfast in the café-cum-reception. We were not the only cyclists there. Turned out that our next door neighbours were taking on the heat, but were only going some twenty or thirty miles that day.

"We are going from Vienna to Gdansk, but not today," one of them said, as he pulled a large trailer up behind his bike, which was propped against the hostel wall.

The gentleman's wife carried some panniers around the corner and joined in. "Yes, we do not go very far each day, but we take a long holiday each summer. Last year we cycled into France from Linz."

She left, only to reappear a few moments later, ushered onto the street by a floppy-eared dog, which jumped into the trailer with the obvious intention of doing as little leg-work as possible until the weather cooled down.

I felt a bit ashamed, about our cycling lethargy. At least we'd have a chance to take a good look around Prague. So, as the dog was towed off in the general direction to the Baltic Sea, we pedalled the few hundred metres to Brno railway station, where we were issued, in return for a miserly fee, with tickets to travel to Prague, two tickets showing our seat reservation, two bicycle tickets for the next train and a couple more, the purpose of which was unclear.

Somehow we managed to miss the next train to Prague. I think we were a bit confused by the noisy building works, which may have led us to miss the announcement. I returned to the ticket office - the booking clerk spoke very helpful English - and obtained two more bike tickets for the next train to Prague.

To be honest, one gets exactly the same number of tickets in the UK when travelling on a train where a bike must be pre-booked, but the level of detail on the paper tickets issue by Ćeské Dráhy was spectacular. Each one a novel, or at least a short poem. Of course, I hadn't got the first idea what most of it meant.

Fortunately, the booking clerk had circled our bike space reservation numbers. Yes, wonder of wonders, express trains can carry a large number of bikes, each one allocated its own spot. Our train was going to be one of the Railjet services that seems to provide the cross border runs. As a seasoned train/cycle traveller, I observed where the cycle spaces were located.

Getting closer to a loudspeaker to avoid another trip to see my friend the booking clerk, it turned out the announcements were in English as well as Czech. The next train at platform one was the "Railjet train of the Company České Dráhy to Budapest calling at Bratislava (or somewhere such as that)". The cycle storage was clearly marked in the rear carriage.

I have had enough frantic rushes down platforms to get to the right place to hang my bicycle to be obsessive enough to look at bicycle markings on train doors in depth. So, when the train was announced, I'd head down to the end of the platform. That plan was scuppered when the "Railjet train of the Company České Dráhy to Vienna" pulled in to Brno with cycle places split neatly into pairs in at least four locations spread along the length of the train.

The good news was that the timetable was sensible enough to avoid the kind of tension caused by yelling railway staff encouraging you to get a move on as the train needs to go within a minute of it arriving. So when the "Railjet train of the company Česke Dráhy to Prague calling at Česká Třebová" - I think - "and Pardubice" drew up at the platform, we took a relaxed stroll through the crowd and had our machines neatly stored in the allocated place before it moved off. Mark actually ignored his bike ticket in the sort of rebellious act one expects from one of artistic temperament.

The guard spoke English to us when he checked out tickets, including those for the bicycles. Either he did not spot Mark's deliberately defiant act or he did not care. He wished us a safe journey. The train gathered speed smoothly, the air-conditioning worked equally well. Mark read and I stared out of the window. It was a perfect rail journey.

In Prague, we booked beds in a hostel as we sat outside a bar in the new town. Whilst doing so, someone on a Segway sent my bike tumbling. Segway's are great fun, but in the crowd they seemed a bit of a risk to the life and limb of everyone else - and, even worse, to my bike.

Cycling in Prague city centre was an interesting experience. I plotted a route, using a map, through the town centre; Mark, using the SatNav, came up with another route skirting the centre. We set off on Mark's version, but a sudden change of traffic lights and an impatient lorry driver left me standing as Mark headed over a bridge and out of sight. I followed, but was sent down a slip road by a car that cut in front of me at just the wrong moment. I gave up the chase and followed my own route.

Despite my way being shorter, Mark reached the hostel first. Cycling through much of the old town was impossible. Narrow streets and alleys full of tour parties anxious not to lose their guide, ambling couples and everyone seeming to be going in a different direction to everyone else. The Charles Bridge was a tsunami of tourists.

Still, by the time I got to the hostel - right in the heart of the tourist trail up to the Castle area - Mark had booked us in and sorted out deposits and found the steps down to the cellar where the bikes could be safely stored.

There is a huge amount to see in Prague and a vast number of people wanting to see it. Cycling-wise, we did none the next day until we picked the bikes up in the late afternoon to go off to our warmshowers host.

There were lots of cyclists in the city, but we walked, took in the sites and got tired of the milling crowds. Prague could take a long, long time to explore. The heat was intense, so we sought the shade, deciding against the queue to enter the Cathedral of Saints Cyril and Methodius, where Kubiš and his colleagues had met their deaths.

Escaping the tourist crowds, on both of our full days in Prague, we found a nice little park that was more popular with local families and groups of students wanting to enjoy the hot weather and warm evenings, by indulging in things such as low level tight-rope walking. We even found our own bench from which to watch the world go by. Better still, hidden away over a little bridge was a little bar with a shady beer garden.

In the evening of the second day, we cycled out of the heart of the city. Mark had arranged for us to be hosted by a warmshowers host in Pankrác, a suburb towards the south of Prague. The SatNav took us pretty much straight there along some undulating city roads, with little traffic and a good few cyclists, and even the odd tram.

Bicycle wheels and tram tracks do not always mix well, though most locals seem to show little fear of those slippery tyre-wide ruts. Mind, the scariest thing, and not a very frightening one at that, was when the rumble of a tram approaching from behind coincided with a narrowing of the road. It's surprising how fast a middle-aged chap can ratchet a half-loaded steel-tourer up a hill on a hot evening.

Our host, warned visitors that it was difficult to find her flat. The SatNav delivered us there directly and without hesitation.

She was preparing a tasty dinner, which we took turns to assist with, whilst the other took a much-needed shower. Over dinner we talked a lot about environmental issues and cycling. Our host worked for a large business where she acted as their environmental conscience. She also headed off on cycle tours when she got the chance.

Needless to say, the UK referendum which was taking place that day, cropped up eventually. Our host was a Slovak, a nation of a little over five million people that split peacefully with the Czech Republic in 1993. They remain close - relations are described as those of siblings (which is not necessarily a synonym for harmony) - and amicable.

I mentioned that we had spoken to some Czechs who had said that they thought it was a shame that Czechoslovakia had split into two. I'd read that some Slovaks had always felt that Czechoslovakia was too Czech centred and Slovakia was easily ignored by government. She did not cite this. She'd seen it as a positive thing. "I don't live in Prague because I don't like Czechs! No, we are just that bit different. Czechs are very philosophical and talk a lot; Slovak's just get on with doing things." No, she liked Prague and living in the Czech Republic.

As for the European Union? She found it hard to understand how many people in the UK wanted to leave. Not so much because she thought the EU was perfect, but because, in her view, it was generally a "good thing" and the alternatives were worse.

It was still stinking hot the next morning. Work began early, so we were out of the flat before seven. By that time, it was clear that the UK had voted to leave the EU. We sat under some trees next to an overgrown children's play area and planned a leisurely day which seemed to consist of a visit to buy packing tape, a quick tour of the Old Town and a long sit on the bench of our choice. We no longer planned to visit a bar; they just came along and we acted accordingly.

There comes a point in any cycle journey - with a few notable exceptions - where you have to face the fact that the end is nigh. Reluctantly, we rode away from Prague's grand core, initially into the inner suburb of Smíchov to turn west onto a long, long ascent. Away from the glories of one of Europe's favourite tourist cities, into the modern estates of flats and houses. Rather like any British city, groups of new modern buildings and light industry in neat little zones. Then, just like in Britain, an encircling motorway is crossed and the first countryside appears. Villages that may soon be swallowed up are shown on signposts. Including our destination.

My throat was itching for a good swallow of Bohemia's best beer - which one that was I do not know, but it would surely be exceptionally good and well worth the chase. Eventually we pulled up at the end of a newly made road, with modern houses in the plots along either side. The SatNav was unaware of this addition, but two figures waving from the pavement at the end of the cul-de-sac, confirmed we had reached our destination.

It might seem strange that a ride across Europe to celebrate the historic links between North Staffordshire and the Czech nation reaches its end in a modern cul-de-sac. But it did. Let us all hope that is not an allegory.

The family were about to have their relaxing late afternoon interrupted. They'd actually only just returned from a cycle tour in New Zealand. In fact, both parents were exceptionally well-travelled and had no intention of letting small children and baby put a halt to globe-trotting. They must have made a fine sight with bikes laden with luggage, child seats and child trailer. Where do some folk get their energy from?

And then two tramps from the UK send you a request to come and stay a night just before they head home. Well, what do you do? "Bugger off" or its equivalent must be somewhere in the Czech lexicon, but not here.

I felt guilty for all the things we had added to the request to stay. They had already mailed us to say that they would sort us out some bike boxes for packing our machines ready for the flight. Then they declared, much to our admiration and gratitude, that there'd be no need for a taxi as we could load the bike into their estate car and they'd drive us to the airport first thing in the morning.

Little daughter sped up and down the drive and into the back garden on a balance bike. Screeching to a halt just in time to avoid imprinting her image in the garage door, or crashing through the fence, or disappearing into the undergrowth. She petrified me, but her parents showed admiring confidence in her ability. And they were right.

We soon got down to the business of stripping down the bikes and packing them for the journey home. Mark's Stoater has S&S couplings, but he had not practised much when it came to the split. He went for a box half the length of that needed by my old Supergalaxy. So, off came the racks and the wheels and the pedals and all the rest. In went fork inserts – our hosts had, once more, provided - many thanks – bubble-wrap padded round the chain set, cranks and rear mech; grimy chain wound up and secured in a plastic bag - one of my own; bars twisted and dropped, tyres partially deflated; panniers emptied and packed around the disassembled bike-carcass in the box.

Throughout the process speeding daughter continued to demonstrate her prowess á vélo by rocketing within a fraction of an inch of my legs. Her skill was admirable, but I kept spanner and Allen key safely out of range. Now the main work was done, she abandoned her balance bike and rushed over as I began to apply the parcel tape in my usual cack-handed fashion. This usually results in much greater expenditure of tape than necessary. It seems to twist if I cut it, contort itself along its length if I attempt to break it with my fingers, get stuck in my teeth if I bite it.

Fortunately, daughter was keen to help with the tape and smoothed it down beautifully as I stretched it out. All that was left outside the box was my camera, travel documents and a change of clothes.

Right first time. Mark was still engaged in squeezing bike bits into the box, but he had not had any help. In any case, disc brakes and modern stuff takes a bit more care than I need to lavish on my Supergalaxy; even so, I owe it more than it owes me, after all these years and so many miles.

We'd been working in the shade. Our hosts had been pottering around the garden and mixed cooing over the baby with preparing dinner. As a warmshowers host, you decide what you want to offer in terms of food and services, such as doing laundry. I usually offer to cook them something followed by a wander down to the Royal Exchange to try out the offerings of Burslem's Titanic Brewery.

We ate heartily. Some unfiltered beer in a two-litre plastic bottle was produced to accompany it. Baby fed, too - no, not even in the Czech Republic do babies have beer along with their puréed veg. Another beer bottle of equal size appeared. Between mouthfuls, we chatted about our travels, their travels and so on.

Dessert arrived and was accompanied by another large pop-bottle of beer.

Our hosts had bought this plot of land for their self-build project, which was just about finished, with only minor additions to be made. They both worked, but built things around the family. He often worked form home, running an online cycle store selling gear they had been impressed with during their extensive tours. I like to think we were doing him a favour by using two old bike boxes that he'd otherwise have had to take to a recycling centre. Our good turn for the day.

384

After dessert, as we spoke more about their travels, some nibbles appeared. These required another bottle or two of lip-smacking, cold, unfiltered beer to wash them down. Then came beer on its own.

This delightful brew came from a small brewery in a nearby village. Our hosts did not say which one, maybe as he felt too much knowledge might result in dearth of supply, but more probably because they recognised that we'd have had no chance of pronouncing it even if we could remember it in the morning.

Yes, you just popped down to the brewery and bought as much as you wanted in plastic pop-bottles. You then went back with them. Repeat. They were quite definitely of the opinion that the Czech Republic's most renowned brewers, makers of beer I really like, were not a patch on the more authentic small brewers. The former were internationally owned and could not brew solely for the local palate; local brewers maintained traditions which mass production belittled; why should anyone want to filter beer when you could have it like this?

Milan had told us about a Czech village with a brewery but no bar. The brewery had developed what was believed to be the world's first beer dispensing vending machine. Needless to say, it also became something of a tourist attraction, though not on the same scale as the Charles Bridge - though you could say it was just as useful, in its own way.

As you can imagine, recollection of the conversation as the evening progressed is vague in proportion to the hour, bottle even. In spite of this, I had no hang-over in the morning. That, in my view, is a clear demonstration of the quality of the beer and the benefits of a few days healthy exercise.

****

As we were driven to the airport, the mercury was already up into the low thirties. If you have never flown with a bike you will not understand just how grateful we were that they had been so kind to sort out boxes and to drive us to the terminal. No need to prepare the bike for flying in the midst of a busy terminal, no need to search for a box, if that is what the airline requires. No arguments with the baggage check in staff about the difference between what their colleagues had told you when you asked about packing the bike and what they are insisting on.

Cyclists' flying experiences could fill quite an anthology. Amongst my contributions would be:

1. Having to allow an airport official to roll my rear wheel through chemicals before flying to Italy during a UK outbreak of foot and mouth. As a result the quick-release skewer came loose, punctured the cardboard bike box and disappeared somewhere into the aircraft's hold. "Asse posteriore" - that is it in Italian. I feared embarrassment when asking at the airport, in my first tremulous words of Italian, about it: almost all Italian airport staff associated with security seem to carry guns. Unfortunately, or fortunately, the airline also lost my panniers, so we had a day free to pop into Rome and find a bike shop. There I was able to point at the relevant part as well as speak. Phew.

2. Arriving at an Airport by bike and prepping it to the airline's standard. No box, just turn the handle-bars, partially deflate tyres, remove pedals and bubble-wrap the drive train. I had not got beyond the first when a security guard distracted me - he was obviously

concerned about the terrorist potential of bicycle tubes. Whatever his worries, I accidentally gave the expander bolt on the headset an extra twist and it plummeted down the steering tube. A bout of muttered oaths followed and the security man became interested in how I was going to get it out. Fuss and fiddle. Eventually, I got my tent out - much to the security guards dismay - and used one of the poles to poke the expander back up the tube. At that point the guard left, obviously content that I was not setting up home on the airport concourse.

3. Charming French baggage handlers who carried our bikes into the baggage area and - I guess it was the Lycra - spotted us waiting at the carousel, and delivered them personally. Even better, they just smiled and turned away without hanging about for a tip - though they'd have got one. I have known Spanish handlers to do the same at a smaller, regional airport.

4. There'd be more; I still wonder exactly what it was those security guards thought I could be concealing when wearing just a short-sleeved cycling jersey, Lycra shorts and socks - I'd taken my shoes off because of their metal cleats. I could have understood it if they'd searched my similarly clad girlfriend. Chacun à son goût.

On the whole, on balance, I get as clucky as an old hen fussing about her chicks when my bike is in the care of an airline. Getting the bikes back at Stansted came as a relief. We decided not to unpack them until we got home. Susan had promised to pick us up in the van when we got to Stone.

And that was the very happy, but rather reserved end of our quest. Alfred Wainwright pointed out, at the end of his venerable guide to walking the Pennine Way, that at the end no one else would really appreciate your sense of achievement; certainly, no one would understand your journey or why you had done it. The erudite and intelligent audience for this book, will obviously be an exception, being possessed of superior taste and intellect to the rest of the population.

Personally, I think of a bike ride - even a long one - as a joy. Every turn of the pedal won't be a pleasure, but overall I am suspicious of overstating the "gruelling" elements and describing any lengthy ride as a massive challenge. Challenges are individual. Had someone asked me if I could ride a thousand miles in twelve days, I'd have said yes. So could a lot of others.

Truth is, it is wonderful to return to one's loved ones in the family home. To catch up on news. To see the dog bouncing about in welcome. Lidice lives for those very reasons. It was daily, mundane pleasure that filled the village before June 10th 1942; a feeling denied to those who returned in 1945.

I have generally planned cycle tours with the aim of getting off the beaten track, climbing some passes and taking in great scenery. This trip had been different. Getting there was the be-all, really, so the route ran across very flat land for much of the time. There were fabulous scenic sections; the Elbe, the Weser, the rolling country of the Teutoburg Forest, even the rainy uplands of Bohemia-Moravia. Grand cities too; Prague and Dresden, of course, but also Münster, Halle and Brno. Smaller towns - Goslar, Quedlinburg, Detmold, Einbeck, Warendorf - in Germany, and Trebíč, Havličkuv Brod, Kutná Hora in the Czech Republic. Yet, the serendipity of the former East of Germany - of half derelict villages in Saxony Anhalt, unannounced remnants of the Nazi past and of the richness of its medieval heritage fascinated us.

Of course, much of Europe has suffered tragedy, one way or another, but any cycle journey - a truism confirmed time and time again - brings the traveller into contact with so many

390

individuals with stories and reflections and experiences. A bit of broken German or Czech or some very good English, can take one into a world, in this case a Europe, where perspectives are very different from that of an island in the West.

It may be hard, at least at the time of writing, but forget the European Union. Across Europe there is a common past, though we may look at it from different points of the compass and through national eyes. As we pedalled through Germany, and that is where we did most of the mileage, one reaches a point where one feels Central Europe has been reached. A point where borders have shifted and nations risen, disappeared and fragmented. It crept up on me.

There's no reason why a cycle tour should be continual laughter and light, though there was plenty of both. We'd stumbled across the site of mass murder, spent a night in a city once swept by a firestorm and celebrated reaching a village that exists today, which was once wiped from the map along with all its men, most of its children and a lot of its women.

Yet, that same village had been built after a campaign had begun by a community that understood that it was up to them to aid their fellows and stand against vile oppression. Their example went around the world, let alone across Europe; much further than a simple bike ride from Burslem to Lidice.

Postscript

At the time of going to press things have developed.

Progress on rebuilding links between Stoke-on-Trent and North Staffordshire has set on apace. Rather wonderfully, the Lidice Resident's Association has sent grafts from the pear tree that survived June 10th 1942 to communities that played a leading part in preserving the name of Lidice in 1942. One small pear tree is now growing in the heart of Hanley, a few yards from the Victoria Halls where the Lidice Shall Live Campaign was launched.

I attended the planting ceremony. Speeches were made as the Messenger of Hope began to sink its roots into the soil of Stoke-on Trent. The Lord Mayor spoke, as did Alan Gerrard. A representative of the National Union of Miners said that we should remember what happened when fascism flourished and be on our guard.

Alan and Cheryl Gerrard have continued their duties as unofficial Ambassadors for North Staffs to the Czech Republic – as well as campaigning in other spheres and running a successful business. On the 100th anniversary of the founding of the Czech Republic in October 2018, they attended the unveiling of a ceramic collage by Stoke-on-Trent artist Alan Hardaker at Lidice. Accompanied by their official counterpart, the Ambassador for the UK, this was an important gift, but also seems to show that the wider implications of restoring strong bonds are being recognised.

In the meantime, land has been obtained to create a rose garden in Stoke-on-Trent; a mirror in minor of Lidice's. There is also to be a statue of Sir Barnett Stross, a real role model for today. The whereabouts has not been disclosed, but maybe this is a sign that the city and its surrounds will begin to feel greater pride and see tangible benefits from international friendships.

In County Durham, the Durham Miner's Association has been recalling its involvement in rebuilding Lidice. The story is to be the subject of a new drama.

I've made no progress in locating the detailed records of the Lidice Live Campaign – mind you, there have been a lot of distractions.

Let us hope for even more in the field of friendship across borders, and all the good things that can bring.

SD October 2018

Credits and Acknowledgements

There is a wealth of literature on the Lidice atrocity and Operation Anthropoid and its aftermath. There is rather less extensive work on the Lidice Shall Live campaign.

For Lidice, the atrocity, and the experience of its people, I have, in particular, used two books by Eduard Stehlík, *Lidice: The Story of a Czech Village* and *Memories of Lidice.* Both translated into English by Petr Kurfürst. Stehlík's research included hours of interviews, from which I have quoted at various points in my book. Both of his books are highly recommended, not least for their extensive collection of photographs and numerous personal stories. I have relied heavily on this for detail of life in Old Lidice and the experience of the Lidice women in particular. Of course, a visit to the Lidice memorial and museum provides a lot of detail, too.

A number of other works have provided additional material, but these are too numerous to mention.

From the Stoke-on-Trent/North Staffordshire perspective, there is rather less literature. Two notable books are Russell

Phillips' *A Ray of Light: Reinhard Heydrich, Lidice, and the North Staffordshire Miners* and *Roses from Ashes* by Fred Hughes. The first brings together many elements of the story, whilst the second is especially powerful in relation to the work of Barnett Stross, including his many other interests and activities.

The extract from Will Lawther's Presidential Address comes from the online archives of the National Union of Mineworkers. There's a great deal of material available online regarding the Lidice Shall Live campaign, especially the British Newspaper Archive and other collections of documents. However, it is, as far as I am aware, in 2018, yet to be put into a full history – even if all the relevant documents could be found.

There's a strong Czech community in the USA. Amongst it is Charlotte Brendel, who has collected details of how Lidice has been commemorated around the world in *Lidice: Remembered Around the World.*

SD November 2018

About the Author

A Bike Across the Sea sees author Steve Dyster back on familiar territory after his excursion into fiction in *The Navigator*. His bicycle has taken him across all of the UK and much of Europe, with many trips published as magazine articles. Graduating from Sheffield University, where he studied history, occasionally, he taught the subject in high schools for many years. Fortunately for him and the pupils who had to put up with him, learning about the past is also a hobby. A geriatric Dad, he has a son, a fabulous wife (who is more than happy for him to go on cycling trips, honest she really is) and two rescue dogs. He is co-editor of www.sevendaycyclist.com. As a former teacher with withdrawal symptoms, he is available for talks about his books but promises not to go on after the bell has rung.

www.stevedyster.com